READING THE CHILD IN CHILDREN'S LITERATURE

'David Rudd addresses points central to the study of children's literature. The ideas are provocative, intelligently managed and well developed.' – **Carole Scott**, *San Diego State University, USA*

'An exciting catalyst for innovation within Children's Literature studies.' – **Liz Thiel**, *University of Roehampton, UK*

David Rudd takes a lively and controversial look at the critical representation of the child in children's literature, arguing for a more open and eclectic approach: one that celebrates the diverse power, appeal and possibilities of children's literature.

Drawing on psychoanalytically informed perspectives, Rudd shows how theory can be both exciting and liberating. He offers fresh and stimulating close readings of key texts, ranging from established classics – such as *Alice in Wonderland, Peter Pan* and *Winnie-the-Pooh* – to more modern works, including novels (*Peter Pan in Scarlet, Holes* and *The Children's Book*) and picture books (*Zoo, The Missing Piece* and *Where the Wild Things Are*).

Sophisticated yet highly approachable, this is essential reading for anyone with an interest in the study of children's literature.

David Rudd is Professor of Children's Literature at the University of Bolton, UK.

Other works by David Rudd

Enid Blyton and the Mystery of Children's Literature
A Communication Studies Approach to Children's Literature
The Routledge Companion to Children's Literature (editor)

Reading the Child in Children's Literature

An Heretical Approach

David Rudd

First published 2013 by
PALGRAVE MACMILLAN

Palgrave Macmillan in the UK is an imprint of Macmillan Publishers Limited, registered in England, company number 785998, of Houndmills, Basingstoke, Hampshire RG21 6XS.

Palgrave Macmillan in the US is a division of St Martin's Press LLC, 175 Fifth Avenue, New York, NY 10010.

Palgrave Macmillan is the global academic imprint of the above companies and has companies and representatives throughout the world.

Palgrave® and Macmillan® are registered trademarks in the United States, the United Kingdom, Europe and other countries

ISBN 978–1–137–32235–7   hardback
ISBN 978–1–137–32234–0   paperback

This book is printed on paper suitable for recycling and made from fully managed and sustained forest sources. Logging, pulping and manufacturing processes are expected to conform to the environmental regulations of the country of origin.

A catalogue record for this book is available from the British Library.

A catalog record for this book is available from the Library of Congress.

Contents

List of Figures

Acknowledgements

My thanks first to Sonya Barker at Palgrave Macmillan for helping this volume come so speedily to fruition and for being so attentive throughout (and Felicity Noble, too!). My thanks also to colleagues at the University of Bolton, from cleaners to professors, for their friendship and support (and a special 'shout' to Tara Brabazon, who eased my workload – and was an inspiration); likewise, to all my students (BA, MA, PhD) for making me think that little bit harder. The two online discussion lists, Child_Lit, hosted by Michael Joseph at Rutgers (USA) and children-lit-erature-uk, are also always out there, with a collective brain the size of a planet – thanks to them (and to Cari Keebaugh for the Bettelheim). My *Children's Literature in Education* editorial pals also deserve a shout (Geoff, Victoria, Vanessa, Cathy, Annette). Particular thanks, too, to Cathy Butler, Vanessa Joosen, Rod McGillis and Anthony Pavlik for reading drafts of different chapters and for their helpful feedback.

Much of Chapter 1 first appeared (in slightly different form) in *Children's Literature Association Quarterly* 35(3); my thanks to Johns Hopkins University Press, the publisher and copyright holder for granting me permission to reproduce this. Also, some of the material in Chapter 3 was first published in 2008, in an article in *The Story and the Self: Children's Literature: Some Psychoanalytical Perspectives* (University of Hertfordshire Press), drawn from a conference run by the late Jenny Plastow (who is much missed!). My thanks to the University of Hertfordshire Press for permission to reproduce this material. I'm also grateful to the University of Roehampton for inviting me to be a keynote speaker at their National Centre for Research in Children's Literature (NCRCL) Conference 'Children's Literature and the Inner World' (12 May 2012), where some of Chapter 6 first had an 'outing'. Finally, the illustrations taken from *Zoo* by Anthony Browne, published by Julia Macrae Books, are used with the permission of The Random House Group Limited and Macmillan USA (and I'm especially grateful to Anthony Browne himself for his kind comments about my 'perceptive analysis').

And now to family matters. Sheena: without you, nothing – as you know! Duncan: a special thanks for the Borromean Knot. It'll be with me always! Sophie: keep that missing piece circulating! And lastly, as Erin got the previous dedication, this one must be for Felix: stay happy!

DAVID RUDD

Every effort has been made to trace all copyright-holders, but if any have been inadvertently overlooked the publishers will be pleased to make the necessary arrangement at the first opportunity.

Note on the Text

Terms which (on their first use) are **emboldened** are included in the Glossary at the end of the book.

Introduction: An Energetics of Children's Literature

> All theorizing is flight. We must be ruled by the situation itself and this is unutterably particular. Indeed it is something to which we can never get close enough, however hard we may try as it were to crawl under the net.
> (Iris Murdoch, *Under the Net*, p. 91)

Let me begin by commending the incredible range of scholarship that is currently being undertaken in children's literature studies. It is making strides as never before, perhaps especially in work on earlier, formerly neglected periods (eighteenth-century studies have been particularly productive, e.g. O'Malley, 2003, 2012; Grenby, 2011; Horne, 2011), but also in work that ensures that children's literature is seen in the wider context of children's studies (in cinema, toys, new media, pastimes, subcultures, ethnographic studies, etc.). But while celebrating this, I also have a sense of something missing. Namely, that we sometimes seem to be trying too hard, that we have become too ponderous in our deliberations about children's books (we murder to dissect), such that we lose the actual excitement of reading. To borrow from Peter Brooks (himself borrowing from Jacques Derrida), I would suggest that there is too much 'mechanics' and not enough 'energetics' in much of our analysis (Brooks, 1984: 47).[1] Thus our increasingly sophisticated vocabulary for discussing key issues around texts for children is sometimes in danger of itself becoming a straightjacket. In Foucauldian terms, that which escapes our grids of classification is often neglected. But this is not in any way to suggest that we need a more finely graded mesh; in fact, the opposite. I am arguing for more openness, more edginess. Neither is this a call for a return to some illusory realm labelled 'post-theory'.

In some ways, I connect this latter attempt with the state of higher education in the 2000s. After a burst of energy in literary and cultural criticism between the 1970s and 1990s – the excitement of opening (indeed, 'exploding') the canon, bringing to English Studies an awareness of children's texts (amongst many other, formerly neglected areas), coupled with the work of new, often more innovative, universities and their associated curricula – most of us have had to retrench in these more straitened times. But it does not seem coincidental, for instance, that the death of theory (following the demise of the author a generation before) should have come at a time when Higher Education was itself becoming increasingly locked into materialistic concerns about its economic contribution, with research being required to show its 'impact', or 'footprint', at which assessors gaze with an imperiousness that surely exceeds that of Robinson Crusoe. Generally, a more utilitarian approach to the teaching and use of English has prevailed (from the National Curriculum in the UK compulsory sector, up to a growing uniformity in courses at Higher Education level), often at the expense of new ideas, of the delight and fun of seeing them explored in and through texts. The fact that what was formerly regarded as the heart of ideas in any university, the Philosophy Department, and which now seems an endangered species, is indicative of this; just so, perhaps, is feminism's morphing into post-feminism, which one might link not simply to the 'pinkification' of the Labour Party in the UK in the 1990s, but also to those endless aisles of 'girly' products that swamp toy and clothing stores.

However, before this soapbox becomes malignant, let me say that there are also more positive developments. High theory of the 1980s did have its downside, as its hieratic name suggests. Though there were more, innovatory, theoretical grids in those days, many readings took no prisoners, stripping-down texts, grinding them up and reconfiguring them, never to be quite the same again. Even the word 'deconstruction', originally having a quite specific meaning in Derrida's usage, gradually came to designate a more nebulous and de(con)structive process: of disassembling the text as thoroughly as Humpty-Dumpty ever was. Moreover, there was also a sense that, at the end of such analyses, the disassembled texts uncovered nothing more than a number of sociological facets ('middle-class', 'colonialist', 'gender imbalanced', 'racially stereotyped'), under which they were filed for further reference, often being assigned a score on a scale of political correctness, too. Again, I don't wish to traduce excellent and essential work undertaken in many areas, but when it comes to asking whether Babar, as a colonialist's pawn, should be burnt, I begin to worry, and seek out my non-flammable copy of Ray Bradbury's *Fahrenheit 451*.[2]

Theory had originally become more explicit in literary and cultural studies as a way of articulating the interests of particular oppressed groups as a result of the Civil Rights Movement in the USA (and similar movements elsewhere, often associated with the young). Marxism was thus extensively used to theorise issues of class, of colonialism and, often, of gender oppression; psychoanalytical thought likewise found favour; and out of these general sociological and psychological approaches came more specific theorisations around feminism, racism, postcolonialism, queer studies, ecocriticism and so forth. However, in some cases these theoretical discourses not only divested themselves of authors, but of their clientele as well, seeming to float above them all with a will of their own (with their own free-floating signifiers, to boot): they became constructions without visible signifieds. The young daredevil theorist, formerly declaring, 'Look Mum, no hands', now began to return more empty-handed: 'Look Mum, no teef'. The loss of any sense of the real, of any social relevance (not merely utilitarian, of course), eventually took its toll, and accusations of theory being irrelevant, dry and boring (let alone sometimes difficult and jargon-ridden) grew – reaching their own theorisations in what could only be called post-theory.

Again, I don't want to lose sight of the excellent work that came out of this period and a whole toolkit of useful concepts and approaches with which to discuss various aspects of children's literature texts, let alone of the debates around the problematic figure of the child. But I fear that the excitement of those earlier days has gone, and there is a certain predictability in much that appears in our journals as yet another feminist, postcolonial, ecocritical or 'fill-the-gap' reading is undertaken (and I am aware that I might have served this production line, too – but I'll avoid harping back to the effects of Research Assessment Exercises on scholarship).

However, though I hold my hand up as sometimes guilty, I always like to think that I have tried to be light on the 'mechanics' and celebrate the 'energetics' of texts. I am attracted by Gilles Deleuze's notion of theory, wherein it is seen not as detached from ordinary human activity, but as immersed in it, in what Deleuze and Guattari (2004: 9) describe as tracing new 'lines of flight', that is, releasing new possibilities for experiencing texts (as the epigraph from Murdoch avers). As Clare Colebrook (2002: 151) puts it, 'the challenge of "Deleuzism" is not to repeat what Deleuze *said* but to look at literature as productive of new ways of saying and seeing'. In what Deleuze and Guattari term a 'rhizomatic' way of thinking, notions of hierarchy (critics rule!) are abandoned. This is a model that seems more in keeping with the egalitarian ethos that the Internet and the new social media have inaugurated, where open-ended dialogue is the norm, as the increasingly prevalent Australian interrogative (uptalk) might suggest. Final readings, the sense of an ending, are ever more things of the past. Rather than murdering to dissect, then, we hope, more fruitfully, to reconnect!

It might seem that what Deleuze and others suggest is itself anti-theoretical, to 'go with the flow' (whether it be into a Bravely Pink New World, or whatever) rather than question it. But this misses the point, which is to recognise that all texts offer possibilities for developing new 'flights' of thought. Moreover, this does, indeed, apply to *all* texts, including our prized theoretical ones. These are not holy writ, or instruction manuals; rather, they are there to help us release new ways of viewing the world and its cultural products. So, as I have always maintained, to think that one is ignoring theory is, in fact, usually to be enslaved by it, by the very thought patterns handed down to one as 'Just So Stories', as 'common sense'. One cannot read any text without certain theoretical notions being invoked (of gendered beings of a certain age, ethnicity, nationality, etc.), just as no fiction writer can escape his or her socio-historical coordinates.

The word 'theory', which I have dealt with in more detail elsewhere (Rudd, 2011) could therefore do with greater clarification. Raymond Williams (1983: 316) gives its etymology in the Greek *theoros*, meaning 'spectator', which itself has its roots in *thea* (the same root as 'theatre'), meaning 'sight'. It subsequently moved to imply not just 'looking' but 'contemplating or speculating' (Wolfreys et al., 2006: 347). So, all creative writers give us works that involve shaping or crafting the world from a particular perspective. Sometimes, of course, we are offered far more than one perspective (Melvin Burgess's *Junk* (1996), for instance, involves ten voices). But even the lone, supposedly omniscient narrator is awash with theoretical presuppositions. And, moving across to the audience's side, we as readers are required to fill in the many gaps that even the most fastidious narrator leaves (how characters look, their locale, their motivation, their possible futures, and so on).

It is this perception of theory – as a way of framing life, existence, meaning (something that all creative works do) – that I want to pick up on, for it involves matters that no one can be indifferent about. Moreover, theory becomes a two-way street with this approach: not only do certain theoretical lenses (feminist, Marxist, psychoanalytical) illuminate primary texts in particular ways, but the texts themselves help to inform our ways of thinking. As we know, Freud drew on myth and fairy tale extensively – most famously, of course, in 'the one about Oedipus', drawn from Sophocles' Theban plays. Turning to children's literature, works like Lewis Carroll's *Alice* have proved a playground for philosophers, mathematicians, logicians, chess players and, of course, psychoanalysts – let alone countless other creative writers and, let us not forget, children. More recently, one might single out Philip Pullman's *His Dark Materials*

University Centre Library
The Hub at Blackburn College

Customer ID: ******19

Title: Reading the child in children's literature :
an heretical approach
ID: BB58252
Due: Mon, 04 Jun 2018

Total items: 1
30/04/2018 19:34

Please retain this receipt for your records
Contact Tel. 01254 292165

with its theological and cosmological speculations. In my earlier piece on 'Theory', I concluded my thoughts by suggesting a definition by which I stand: 'theory helps us see how a particular constellation of linkages throws into relief particular elements of a text, and how productive this can be for our understanding of society, its people and artefacts' (Rudd, 2011: 219).

We should be clear what is being claimed here, then: that there can never be an end to theory in literature (or, more generally, in Cultural Studies, let alone Life), because both theory and literature are involved in charting, in their different ways, what it means to be part of society, from whatever perspective. Thus works of fantasy, horror, romance or utopia, whether traditional or avant-garde – none can escape this fate: all will refract the concerns of a particular time and place. At a later period, of course, we might attempt to recreate how we think contemporary readers would have made sense of these texts (a task that New Historicism sets itself) but we will also be approaching these texts from our own, current viewpoint. Indeed, the very fact that certain texts have an appeal to us at any particular time is often itself informative.

In terms of theory, the focus on 'text' was one of the main shifts to occur in the wake of structuralism, and it proved liberating. It allowed us to set 'classic' and 'popular' texts alongside one another; to intermix fiction with non-fiction; and, moreover, to include films, paintings, pictures, plays, operas, musicals, architecture, furniture, landscapes, clothing, food, toys and, indeed, new social media. It is the way that a culture uses these various items to create meaning that is crucial; thus, armed with our tools of textual analysis, we could start to explore patterns of signification and then to ask why 'texts' were 'read' in the way they were (classics vs ephemera), often challenging traditional value judgements.

More recently, a number of theoretical developments have taken a similar line, such as that known as 'new aestheticism' (Joughin and Malpas, 2003), which offers a far more open approach to texts. Like the nineteenth-century aesthetic movement that inspired it, new aestheticism emerged as an attempt to escape the confines of academic political correctness and social utilitarianism. As the editors put it:

> In the rush to diagnose art's contamination by politics and culture, theoretical analysis has tended always to posit a prior order that grounds or determines a work's aesthetic impact, whether this is history, ideology or theories of subjectivity.... Theoretical criticism is in continual danger here of throwing out the aesthetic baby with the humanist bathwater. (Ibid.: 1)

In contrast, they argue for

> the equi-primordiality of the aesthetic – that, although it is without doubt tied up with the political, historical, ideological, etc., thinking it is as other than determined by them, and therefore reducible to them, opens a space for an artistic or literary specificity that can radically transform its critical potential and position with regard to contemporary culture. (Ibid.: 3)

Isobel Armstrong, in an earlier work, *The Radical Aesthetic* (2000), speaks of this approach as one that 'escapes from the master/slave model of reading which is the dominant model in our culture' and is, thereby, not only more open and democratic, but perhaps more conducive to fields like children's literature, seeking to redefine the aesthetic in more playful terms, as breaking down categories, empowering and enabling us:

> The aesthetic energizes us by demanding not judgement but a desire of explication, an ever more adequate understanding of its possibilities, a repeated pursuit of the meanings informing it. Such arousal of intellectual and emotional desire, which persuades us not to judge or to consume, constitutes the importance of the aesthetic.... (Ibid.: 168)

That word 'energises' again. If anything could be seen to stand for my project in this book, Armstrong's statement captures it: an 'arousal of intellectual and emotional desire' in relation to various texts and to widen their provenance beyond restrictive notions not only of gender and class, but even of those categorisations 'child' and 'adult'. (I have always been fascinated at the seemingly more open attitude of our Victorian forebears to reading novels, with many of them discussing works that we now more firmly categorise as children's, hence things to be 'put away', to avoid 'infantilisation'.) There would seem to be potential in trying to 'see how the text thinks', as Armstrong puts it; to respond as 'the text calls out its need to "enter into a relationship with someone"' (ibid.: 101–2). The fact that Armstrong also draws on critical thinkers who have themselves been closely involved with children – such as John Dewey, Lev Vygotsky and D. W. Winnicott – itself seems positive (and perhaps less relevant, but the fact that Armstrong was sister to the recently deceased children's fantasy writer, Diana Wynne Jones, has always seemed noteworthy to me).

   Like Armstrong's book, then, this work is also theoretically eclectic, seeking to animate both primary and secondary texts as it progresses. A psychoanalytic undertow, however, is ever present (as, indeed, it is in Armstrong's work). To my mind, this is because the psychoanalytic has always been an approach on the margins, always heretical, never quite respectable and, therefore, it has more room in which to manoeuvre. It also seems pertinent in that it treats people in much the same way as books: we ourselves are texts, as Freud realised, and often quite enigmatic ones. In fact, as Lacan puts it, '[c]ommenting on a text is like doing an analysis' (quoted in Fink, 2004: 63). And, in order to read us, Freud drew extensively on literature to demonstrate the possible ways we operate. Though psychoanalysis has undoubtedly been responsible for producing more than its fair share of rather crude, reductionist readings, in ethos it advocates an open-ended, dialogical process; theoretically, it shuns the closed book in favour of the open text. It should always make us wary of the 'master's discourse' as Lacan termed it, of the person presumed to know.

When discussing children's books this is an area particularly fraught with difficulty, and one that Jacqueline Rose confronted in her ground-breaking work, *The Case of Peter Pan*, discussed in Chapter 1. There is the undoubted presumption that we, as adults, can know and speak on behalf of this 'simpler' being; that we can 'read the child', as my title expresses it. This belief derives partly from our claim that we too were once children, but also from the fact that we have developmental theories, to which psychoanalysis itself has contributed. Thus we might claim to be able to spot the attractions of stories like 'Hansel and Gretel' or *Where the Wild Things Are* because of their oral appeal (though we'd also have to account in similar terms for decidedly adult works like Rabelais's *Gargantua and Pantagruel* or Joanne Harris's *Chocolat*).

But the claims to understand the child run deeper still with the development of the notion that humans have an 'interiority', which Carolyn Steedman traces back to the late eighteenth century. Beginning with Goethe's figure of Mignon, the 'dislocated' child acrobat, Steedman charts adults' ongoing fascination with children out of place, children who became the object of spectacle, whether as actors, street children or other performers, such that notions of normal development were set alongside these 'abnormalities'. Steedman maps this focus on the child with the then voguish notions of cell theory (also explored by Goethe), eventuating in nineteenth-century physiologists tracing homologies between the child's unfolding being and conceptions of cellular development; that is, of the child arising out of a small, interior space:

> The metaphorical structures utilised by Freud involved the irreducible unit of physical organisation, the entity that was both a place, and a place where things happened: the topos of the cell. The cell, the smallest place within, promoted another set of analogies, for what the cell carried was the child turned within, an individual's childhood history laid down inside its

> body, a place inside that was indeed very small, but that carried with it the
> utter enormity of a *history*. (Steedman, 1995: 92)

This interior space also functioned as a realm that was seen to defy the normal coordinates of existence and chronology – that is, ageing and death – standing outside these, timeless and immortal (as Rose would characterise the impossible 'Peter Pan' child). As Steedman (ibid.: 96) puts it, 'the unconscious mind was conceptualised as the timeless repository for what was formerly the matter of time and history, that is, an actual childhood, an actual period of growth and its vicissitudes'.

The double-edge that the child has always possessed, as a being either innocent or evil, is played out in this scenario, where childhood is not only the source of all our later neuroses, but also the place which, once revisited, might be cleansed and renewed. The child and the unconscious, therefore, came to be ever more closely associated. By the early decades of the twentieth century this had become such a strong link that, as Adam Phillips (2000: 42) expresses it, the unconscious was being 'usurped by a new figure called the child'; hence, 'describing the child *was* to describe the unconscious. The child was, as it were, the unconscious *live*: you could see it in action. It had been found; in fact, you could virtually talk to it'.

This notion of the child as an unfettered and timeless id, arising out of Romantic conceptions of childhood, reaches its apotheosis in the almost parodic *Peter Pan* – 'I'm youth, I'm joy... I'm a little bird that has broken out of the egg' (Barrie, 1986: 187). But it also informs many later works of children's literature. For example, in Philippa Pearce's classic novel, *Tom's Midnight Garden*, the young protagonist, Tom, is quarantined in a Victorian house with his childless aunt and uncle. He has been sent away from his own family because his younger brother, Peter, whom Tom misses greatly, has measles. It seems to be Tom's loneliness and yearning for a playmate that bring the house alive, such that its owner, the elderly, widowed Hatty Bartholomew, regresses in her dreams to her own Victorian childhood, allowing Tom to enter her dreams and join her in the unconscious space of the home's walled garden, glimpsing what seems to Tom to be a lost golden age. And, in the process, the elderly Hatty is revivified, such that by the end she looks 'as if she were a little girl' (Pearce, 1970: 154).

Through the figure of the child, then, the unconscious, this 'timeless repository' (or Neverland), will be forever accessible: a place where a boy and his bear will always be playing (they are often male figures that inhabit this space, I grant). Before I get carried away by this rhetoric, though, let me return to my main point, which is to criticise the idea that the child is so easily 'read', 'written' or, indeed, 'paged'. This is Rose's point, too, although I also think that we need to consider very carefully why such an imaginary being is clung to so tenaciously – and to recognise how attractive we, also, find such a notion. This said, *Reading the Child* will mostly involve dismantling such binary oppositions as child/adult and innocence/experience. I am interested in relaxing our deployment of those jaws that bite and claws that snatch ('Damn braces: bless relaxes' as William Blake expresses it), suggesting that a more fruitful way of discussing children's literature is to push these artificial boundaries to their limits and, as Buzz Lightyear would contend, beyond.

In some ways, then, the essays in this book take an heretical approach to children's literature studies, using the word 'approach' in a fairly loose, non-formulaic way. They seek to maintain the 'energetics' of close reading, mentioned earlier. As for my main title, 'Reading the Child', this was originally to have been 'Texting the Child', but the rather misleading connotations of the latter made it inadvisable (as would be the alternative, 'Paging the Child'). 'Reading the Child', then, addresses the notion that we can, in some almost telepathic way, know what goes on inside the child's head (a notion bolstered by more recent, neuroscientifically informed approaches). Armed with this knowledge, a children's author is seen to write stories for children, 'filling them in' in some way, from the inside out, with notions of what it is to 'feel like a kid', to adapt Jerry Griswold's title (2006; see p. 34). Moreover, there is the related idea that we, too, as adults, can also come to know the child simply through reading children's books, effectively 'cutting out the middle man', the child her or himself. This is something that, as I suggest in Chapter 4, also happens when children's literature is treated as a genre.

Overview

Chapter 1 begins with a text from 1984, one that does not quite rival Orwell's dystopian commemoration of that year, but one that certainly caused many ructions and rifts within the field of children's literature studies. This was Rose's *The Case of Peter Pan, or The Impossibility of Children's Fiction*, the subtitle of which precipitated the outcry. My chapter grows out of an article appearing in *Children's Literature Association Quarterly* which looked at the impact of Rose's claim about this impossibility some 30 years on. Whereas we sometimes tend to lose sight of the aesthetic dimension of children's literature, reducing texts to their ideological coordinates, from Rose's position it could hardly be otherwise; that is, if children's literature is written and effectively controlled by adults, they will, in Rose's famous words, seek to bring that child outside the text 'within its grasp' (1984: 5). It is not just matters of gender and colour that are being subtly (or less subtly) encoded in these books, but the whole way that a child should inhabit the childhood that is being constructed – one that seeks to conceal the porosity of the symbolic order, offering instead the reassuring presence of the eternally young and innocent child. Thus 'writing' the child is also seen to involve 'righting' the child, setting it on the right path if not the actual path to righteousness. Broadly, though, the idea that this power differential thereby makes fiction for children impossible is rejected; for, it is argued, separating out children's fiction as peculiar in this way has already involved putting in place a category of being whose status is regarded as different from the rest of us: a special (if not Romantic) being. In contrast, I argue that, because language constructs positions for us all (the symbolic contract), we are, thereby, all potential contributors.

Mention of the **Symbolic** makes Rose's Lacanian thinking more evident; for despite his impact on her work, the French psychoanalyst seems conspicuous largely by his absence (though Rose admits that it was a remark by Lacan – about children's fiction – that sparked her interest: '*Est-ce qu'il peut exister une littérature pour enfants?*'[3] (quoted in Rudd and Pavlik, 2010: 227)). But, in the way that the child is not completely enslaved within the Symbolic, Rose does point towards Lacan's two other orders: most obviously, the **Imaginary** (with the child as an idealised being seemingly untroubled by language, sexuality, etc.), but also towards the third order, to something beyond; that is, to an insistent **Real** which causes the child to resist the Symbolic's 'grasp' and, we imagine, to savour that **semiotic**, somatic space where the young are 'for ever beaching their coracles' (Barrie, 1986: 19).

Of course, this is a line from *Peter Pan*, which is treated in depth in Chapter 2, but without in any way reading that work in a reductive, 'case study' manner. It is certainly there because Rose makes it such a test case, but this itself was because she realised the consummate power of the Peter Pan figure in capturing the essence of adult dreams of childhood: a being of the Imaginary. Chapter 2 therefore allows the further explication of Lacan's key notion that we all exist within these three overlapping orders, the Real, the Symbolic and the Imaginary (the **RSI**), which is how I have organised this book. These first two chapters, then, are more centrally concerned with the *Imaginary*, whereas the next two take us into more in-depth discussions of the *Symbolic*, and Chapter 5 deals specifically with the *Real*, before the whole *RSI* is brought together in Chapter 6. In French, these three spell out, in their pronunciation, heresy (air–ess-ee), which amused Lacan in the way that signification was forever ongoing, fluid and could never be fully mapped in any grid-like way.

In Chapter 3 the focus moves on from the Imaginary to the Symbolic, with an awareness that, although each of these registers of existence acts as though it defines reality, in effect, each is dependent on the others. In this chapter, then, the claims of the Symbolic to determine our existence are most strongly contended, such that, for some theorists (e.g. social constructionists), we are entirely defined in terms of our roles, as gendered beings with a certain ethnicity, colour, sexual orientation, religion, nationality, class, abled-ness, and so forth. As mentioned earlier in this Introduction, crucial though these socio-cultural dimensions are (indeed, they can mean life or death in some cases), they don't fully account for our existence because we are not merely symbolic function-aries. Chapter 3 thus takes issue with some critical positions that seem unnecessarily reductive in this way.

The critics mentioned here are not meant to be singled out as being exceptional in any negative sense; but I have drawn on them as indic-ative of a trend that I want to resist (even though I have no doubt also participated in it). For me, the critical apparatus that is brought to such analyses can end up losing sight of the primary text; it is like watching a work performed on an overly cluttered Victorian stage, where the proscenium arch, heavy drapes and orchestra pit effectively detract from the action. The result, as Armstrong (2000: 87) puts it, is often 'distance reading, not close reading'. An analysis of Milne's 'Pooh' books and Louis Sachar's *Holes* seeks both to demonstrate and rectify such short-sightedness.

Chapter 4 continues this tack of looking at how adult discourses can be seen to have such a controlling influence over children's literature. Of course, this was Rose's initial claim, hence her belief that the whole enter-prise was impossible, for the child can never properly flex that possessive apostrophe. Perry Nodelman (2010), who acknowledges his debt to Rose, still clings to the possibility of children's literature, but gives adults very much the controlling role, seeing a hidden adult figure lurking within its texts. From my perspective, as we are all beings located within the Symbolic, I do not see adults as having quite the colonising power that

Nodelman and some others grant, so I do not see his definition as determining the texts of children's literature in the way he depicts it.

Whereas these last two chapters are organised round the Symbolic, the next deals with issues relating to the Real; that is, it considers occasions where our symbolic universe is found wanting. In Lacanian terms, this can result in uncanny experiences. However, I shall argue that despite the uncanny's increasing deployment in discussions of children's literature, it is in effect a term often safely recuperated by the Symbolic, with the term's more disturbing connotations removed. There are, therefore, very few works of children's literature that confront the more troubling, uncontainable and unsymbolisable elements of the uncanny, but I suggest that Carroll's *Alice's Adventures in Wonderland* is one (again, partly responding to Nodelman's analysis).

As a result of my reading of *Alice*, where I suggest that we do this work a disservice by reading it as 'mere' fantasy – that is, as simply escapist, compensatory – Chapter 6 involves a closer look at the whole divide between fantasy and reality (or realism), arguing that we should rethink the difference between these modes of writing. Whereas the former chapters were organised according to their respective emphases on the Imaginary, Symbolic and the Real, Chapter 6 brings together all three registers in what Lacan termed the Borromean knot of the RSI. This knot is a topological figure, as is the more well-known Möbius Strip, which I deploy metaphorically in an examination of two celebrated picturebook texts – Maurice Sendak's *Where the Wild Things Are* (1963), arguably the most famous picturebook ever, and Anthony Browne's *Zoo* (1994) – with a third, Shel Silverstein's (1976) *The Missing Piece*, putting in a guest appearance, too.

Finally, in Chapter 7, I turn to a work that, though entitled *The Children's Book* (Byatt, 2010), is anything but. Indeed, it is a work that, I have discovered, many adults fail to finish. Does this mean that it isn't an adult's book, either? Somewhat ironically, it does contain some stories within it that, just like the Peter Pan chapters that were originally part of Barrie's adult novel, *The Little White Bird*, could easily be extracted and published for children, given some suitable illustrations (artists like David McKean and Shaun Tan come to mind). They would be dark tales, undoubtedly (as the children's novelist within Byatt's novel notes), but children *have* been here before. This chapter therefore forms a useful bookend to a work that starts out with Rose's claim about the impossibility of children's fiction; for, in her novel, Byatt half seems to test this claim, suggesting that the seductiveness of children's books can turn out to be quite dangerous. But Byatt also shows how problematic it is to make a divide between works for children and adults, given that we are all inhabitants of the Symbolic, let alone these two other orders that shape our existence.

For many people, the notion of framing this book in Lacanian terms, around his three different registers, will seem to be against the very openness I argued for earlier. But it needs to be emphasised that Lacan's three orders 'remain neutral on the question of truth .... The would-be truth-seeker will find that the Imaginary, the Symbolic and the Real are an unholy trinity whose members could as easily be called Fraud, Absence and Impossibility' (Bowie, 1991: 112). Hence Lacan's notions of 'heresy', mentioned above, and hence my adoption of this term in my subtitle, to suggest a more heterodox stance towards children's literature studies, arguing that one cannot live in the *Symbolic* alone, contrary to what the more sociologically inclined approaches to children's literature often suggest. There is always some residue, some deficiency in their codifications: something beyond that resists such tidy, lawful ordering (or awful laundering, even). This is the *Real*, felt indirectly, and always filtered through our fantasies, for it can be unnerving, horrific or, occasionally, blissful. On the other hand (there are three hands needed in this unholy model), we must recognise that we will always be captivated by idealised images of the child and all that has become associated with this figure (purity, innocence, wholeness, etc.) as it exists within the *Imaginary* – which is where, if you are all sitting comfortably, we shall begin.[4]

Part I

The Imaginary

1 Many Happy Returns: To Freud, Rose, the Child and its Literature

This chapter[1] looks back at Jacqueline Rose's seminal 1984 work, *The Case of Peter Pan, or The Impossibility of Children's Fiction*, with the hindsight of nearly 30 years, recognising how influential it has been, but also at how it has as frequently been ignored or, more simply, rendered innocuous, its radical, destabilising challenges repressed, much like the symptoms of an underlying trauma. Unfortunately, that rallying cry of her subtitle – 'the impossibility of children's fiction' – has often got in the way, being seen by some as a truth to be universally acknowledged or else, by others, as refutable simply by gesturing to the humanist child (e.g. Rustin, 1985; Hollindale, 1991, 1995;[2] Watson, 1992; Lesnik-Oberstein, 1994, 1998; Galbraith, 2001; Walsh, 2002; Chapleau, 2004). Though I go along with many of her insights, I will argue that her conclusion, that children's fiction is impossible, is untenable. Given that we are all creatures of language – that our very development proceeds in a 'fictional direction', as Lacan put it – then children's fiction must be as possible as any other. In fact, to single it out as distinct is, ironically, to hold on to a residual notion of the Romantic child: a being distinct from adults, standing outside society and language, rather than a being that is actively involved in negotiating meaning.

After examining Rose's case, and situating it within its cultural context – the state of theory in the 1980s – the chapter concludes by noting just how persistent the Romantic notion of the child is by looking at some more recent theoretical work on children's literature; work that has not only ignored Rose's more productive insights but often gives the impression that children's literature studies is concerned more with nostalgia and idealisation (the 'fictional direction', the Imaginary) than critical analysis. This leads into the second chapter, which looks more closely at the utopian appeal of this Romantic child in its most famous incarnation: Peter Pan.

Rose (1984), of course, bases her case on this text, for, as she puts it, this 'is the text for children which has made that claim most boldly' – the claim being that '*Peter Pan* ... speaks to and for children, addresses them as a group which is knowable and exists for the book, much as the book (so the claim runs) exists for them' (ibid.: 1). But, as she also says, '*Peter Pan* is that text which most clearly reveals it [the claim] as a fraud ... *Peter Pan* has never ... been a book for children at all' (ibid.: 1), and goes on to suggest, famously, 'the impossibility' of all children's fiction. Whilst I agree with much of her thinking – namely, that the child of children's fiction is a construct; that it is presented as innocent, pure and asexual, as a fetish allowing adults to disavow their own lack of completeness; that it is also seen as standing outside the general slipperiness of language and problems of identity; and, consequently, that it is impossible for any children's book to speak to and for children as a group – her next step, that children's fiction is thereby impossible, seems a non sequitur.

Let me start, however, by examining some of the evidence Rose draws on in order to substantiate her claim. She uses 'Peter Pan' for reasons given at the opening of this chapter, claiming that it 'has been almost unreservedly acclaimed as a children's classic for the greater part of this century' (ibid.: 4). However, although she repeatedly refers to this classic in italics, as though it were a single text, as 'the text for children' (quoted above) and as 'a children's book' (ibid.: 7), she also likes to keep its precise signification vague and often seems to refer to a whole body of texts, some of them not even by Barrie (for this reason, I have used the more common convention of quotation marks unless mentioning specific titles). This said, the title of Rose's monograph suggests that she is not generally alluding to the play as such (which, like most panto-mimes, is ostensibly addressed to the whole family), but the 'book for children' (ibid.: 1).[3] Yet this unsubstantiated statement has, in fact, often been challenged; for instance, John Rowe Townsend's standard history of children's literature, which Rose quotes elsewhere, explicitly states that the novel is 'not a very good book' (Townsend, 1976: 107), tellingly noting that 'the idea of a boy who never grows up' is probably not 'as appealing to children as it is to parents', and accusing Barrie of 'winking over the children's heads to the adults' (ibid.: 106). Thus the notion that Barrie's text 'most boldly' makes the claim that it 'speaks to and for children' – indeed, that it 'exists for them' – has itself been subject to contestation. Earlier criticism may not have followed Rose's poststruc-turalist line, but it has certainly not gone unrecognised 'that there might be a problem of writing, of address, and of language, in the history of

Peter Pan' (Rose, 1984: 6). Her declaration that the novel is 'virtually impossible to read' (ibid.), then, is not on the one hand especially new, but, on the other hand, it does draw the sting out of that initially bold claim of hers.

In fact, it is difficult from what Rose says in her book to be sure precisely why 'Peter Pan' is such an exemplary 'case', especially if we agree with her statement that it is actually 'one of the most fragmented and troubled works in the history of children's fiction' (ibid.: 11). How, then, can it be representative? Rose explains it this way: '*Peter Pan* is peculiar, and yet not peculiar, in so far as it recapitulates a whole history of children's fiction' (ibid.). Such a seeming contradiction might become clearer at a later point, where Rose likens Barrie's text to a Freudian symptom, 'which speaks what it intends, and exactly the opposite, at one and the same time' (ibid.: 38–9). 'Peter Pan' can therefore be seen to draw attention to the difficulty of taking up 'a position of identity in language', while also standing

> for its denial. The hesitancies of both language and sexuality which have appeared throughout its history cannot be separated from the very force of its image as purity itself, embodied by the eternal child. *Peter Pan* seems to have operated constantly on this edge, as if liable at any one moment to offer its disturbance to view but choosing instead to turn the other face of innocence. (Ibid.: 141)

While I would endorse the liminal nature of 'Peter Pan' (and we need to realise that Rose is here talking about Peter Pan as an almost archetypal figure, and not about a particular text), in no way does he appear to be the sole occupant of this no man's land (or Neverland, perhaps). Rose herself seems at certain points to recognise this. For example, she draws attention to other children's works that indulge in '[p]laying with language – in this sense of undercutting its transparency and ease', but argues that these have 'for the most part, been pushed to the outer limits of children's writing [*sic*]' (ibid.: 40). Here she names Edward Lear and Carroll as key 'nineteenth century exceptions'. While Lear might arguably fit this marginalisation – he is seen to be 'covered by the fact that he wrote poetry (specifically designated as nonsense)' (ibid.: 40) – it is certainly not true of Carroll, whose 'Alice' books are seen as central to modern children's fiction. Indeed, numerous histories see *Alice* as the landmark text; F. J. Harvey Darton (1982: 260), for one, states in his standard history that 'it was the coming to the surface, powerfully and permanently, the first un–apologetic appearance in print, for readers who sorely needed it, of liberty of thought in children's books', and, for Humphrey Carpenter (1985: xi, 68–9), *Alice* constitutes the origin of the 'golden age' of children's literature. Rose, though, suggests that 'Carroll's multiple use of the pun in *Alice* is generally recognised as something unique which tended to be related more to the eccentricity, or even madness, of the author' (Rose, 1984: 40–1), picking up on an earlier, unsupported remark of hers: 'it is argued, [by critics, that] Dodgson was a "schizophrenic"' (ibid.: 3).[4] Of course, it also needs emphasising that Rose carefully limits herself to children's *fiction*, avoiding discussion of children's literature per se. So, apart from removing individual authors that don't fit her scheme, Rose also sets aside 'the order of folklore, nursery rhyme and nonsense which', as she admits, she has 'barely touched' upon (ibid.: 139). This 'whole domain', she states, is 'normally placed in opposition to the canons of narrative fiction in the name of rhythm and play'. She continues:

> For as long as the first (rhythm and play) is seen as melody or archaic lore which stretches back in time, and the second (narrative fiction) as the forward progression of advancing literary form, then the challenge of the one to the other, the idea that one might actually erupt inside the other, forcing open the issue of what constitutes continuity in speech, is effectively denied. ... Classifying 'otherness' in language as infantile or child-like reduces it to a stage which we have outgrown, even if that stage is imbued with the value of something cherished as well as lost. (Ibid.)

As with her claim about 'Peter Pan' supposedly speaking to and for children, this 'classifying' seems to be Rose's own. The notion of language having both symbolic and semiotic aspects (to use Kristevan terms that seem to be tacitly invoked in Rose's statement), perhaps most famously explored in Dodgson/Carroll's *Alice*, is part of a tradition that has certainly not been relegated to the nursery; in fact, it is often seen as a tradition more suited to the sophisticated reader (examples such as Norman Lindsay's *The Magic Pudding* (1957), Astrid Lindgren's *Pippi Longstocking* (1957) and much of Dr. Seuss's *oeuvre*, come to mind). So the idea that 'this other side of language', which is 'an explicit challenge or threat to adult forms of speech, has largely been kept out of children's fiction' (Rose, 1984: 41), once again depends on Rose herself excluding it (and sticking closely to prose fiction). She agrees that her account 'does not claim to be a general history', yet she still wants it to be 'symptomatic and typical' (ibid.: 139), whereas to me it seems more partial and idiosyncratic, often tackling straw figures – a body of people, indeed, that sometimes appear as mythical as the pure and innocent child.

So, on the one hand we are presented with a grand narrative in which all children's fiction is seen to be singing the same tune (*'Peter Pan ... recapitulates a whole history of children's fiction'* (ibid.: 11)), namely that the child is celebrated as a point of origin and stability, concealing our more fractured and fragmented existence as linguistic beings; yet, on the other hand, we are carefully steered round any 'children's writing' or, indeed, any criticism that might complicate this picture.

Let me now move away from 'Peter Pan' itself in order to consider Rose's more general claim about why children's fiction is impossible, which, as I said earlier, seems to depend, ironically, on that problematic figure of the Romantic child. This, in turn, will lead on to a more viable view of children's fiction, which draws on Mikhail Bakhtin's work (and that of his colleague, Valentin Vološinov, 1973),[5] arguing that children's fiction is impossible only if seen in isolation from other literature, let alone being all of a piece.

Rose's opening claim, that '[c]hildren's fiction sets up the child as an outsider to its own process, and then aims, unashamedly, to take the child *in*' (Rose, 1984: 2), is explicit in stating her case. But in what sense, we might enquire, can the child have 'its own process'? Where, in other words, is the 'outside' of its textual representation? Where, precisely, is this child before it is taken in? This is where Rose seems to grant the child special status; and not only the child: books, too, are privileged. Yet surely, before any book starts its 'soliciting ... chase, or ... seduction' (ibid.) of the child, doesn't all language supposedly addressed *to* the child address it, specifically, *as* a child (linguistically constructed though such utterances are bound to be)? In fact, how is the book's attempt different from the initial 'interpellation' or 'hailing' of a subject of which Louis Althusser (1971) speaks (apart from the fact that children must initiate the former, unless the book is read to them)? In a shift from Rose's initial vocabulary (of 'soliciting' etc.), she later describes this difference as follows:

> All subjects – adults and children – have finally to take up a position of identity in language; they have to recognise themselves in the first-person pronoun and cohere themselves to the accepted register of words and signs. But it is the shift of that 'have to' from a necessity, which is shared by both adult and child, to something more like a command, which passes from one to the other, that seems to find one of its favourite territories in and around the writing of children's books. (Rose, 1984: 141)

It is of particular note that Rose, somewhat misleadingly, mentions adults here, in that the process of taking up a position of identity in language occurs in childhood – and, it should be emphasised, under the aegis of adults. In light of this, the distinction that Rose seeks to draw with the children's book ('which passes from one to the other') seems invalid, for both processes (learning to speak, handling books) involve similar adult–child interactions. So, returning to my earlier point, it could be said that the child, as child, is 'solicited' from the outset (if not before its birth, in fact); books simply continue this process in a more formal manner. On such a basis, one could legitimately claim that children's fiction is impossible only in the way that the child itself is; that is, as 'an outsider to its own process', subjected by an alien language. And in this sense, we *all* are – as, indeed, Lacan's theory has it: moving from an initial 'misrecognition' of ourselves in a mirror image to the later, empty significations of the symbolic order. But equally, there is nowhere else to be (short of psychosis). Yet Rose, for some reason, makes the child a special being, particularly so when it comes to fictional works which, in an ironic echo of Jean-Jacques Rousseau, she sees as singularly failing to reach children properly.

There are, however, other ways of conceiving children's fiction which are less insular and discrete than this stereotypical depiction by Rose: 'Children's fiction sets up a world in which the adult comes first (author, maker, giver) and the child comes after (reader, product, receiver), but where neither of them enter [*sic*] the space in between' (ibid.: 1–2). A Bakhtinian reading of the process, for example, would point to 'the space in between' as precisely where things happen (in what he terms 'the border zone'), instead of conceiving isolated authors (adults) in 'command', with passive readers (children) in danger of 'seduction', and insular texts waiting to trap readers with their baited 'image of the child' (ibid.: 2). Bakhtin's model is far more interactive, with words as the common currency, permitting – indeed, being unable to prohibit – border dialogue. As Vološinov (1973: 86) expresses it, '[a] word is a bridge thrown between myself and another. If one end of the bridge depends on me, then the other depends on my addressee'. One cannot, in other words, predict who will use that bridge or for what purposes; adults simply do not have this control. But, from first taking 'verbal shape' as a person, one is eligible to respond, regardless of whether it is to another person, to a fiction, a rhyme, a drama, or whatever. More precisely, Bakhtin's dialogism argues that: (i) we, from our own particular historical and social location, are forever in dialogue with the texts we encounter (e.g. as a child, female, middle-class, Northerner, fan of science fiction, or whatever); and (ii) these different discursive affiliations interact with a text that is itself made up of different discursive elements; to use the Russians' terminology, albeit in translation, a text has 'multiaccentuality' (Vološinov) or 'heteroglossia' (Bakhtin), such that a work is always dynamic, always subject to struggles over its signification (what I have elsewhere termed 'discursive threads': Rudd, 2000: 13–18). In this model, children's fiction is always and forever possible, though its effectivity can never be fully gauged.[6]

Let me now return to Rose's argument, armed with this Bakhtinian notion that words are indeed our common currency, for adults and children alike, but have different 'accent' and signification dependent on our particular socio-temporal location. Genres, too, are seen by Bakhtin to condense out of the normal orderings and patternings of speech, evolving into literary form as a secondary phenomenon (Bakhtin, 1981: 288; 1984). From this perspective, to separate children's literature from other literary forms will always be something of a socio-political manoeuvre, let alone trying – as Rose more expressly does – to isolate a more particular construction of writing for children from the whole historical landscape of children's literature. Some areas that Rose wishes to set aside, such as poetry and nonsense (alongside nursery rhyme and folklore), have already been mentioned. Drama is more problematic, though. Rose addresses the way that the play, *Peter Pan*, was carefully distinguished from pantomime in an attempt to keep children's theatre innocent; she also notes the infamous exposés of child prostitution in late Victorian England, but has little to say about the actual collaboration of adults and children in children's theatre, where the child can be read as more of an 'artful dodger', to use Marah Gubar's (2009) term for the anything but innocent, passive child figure (Goethe's Mignon has already been mentioned; cf. Walkowitz (1992) on actual 'Pantomime Waifs'). If these omissions are telling, what Rose chooses to include also leads to confusion, as, for example, in her claim that 'Barrie ... did not write the play until twenty-four years after its first production' – as though the acting scripts (of which there were many) were not *written*, hence do not count. Rose actually means *published* rather than *written*. Moreover, she then pronounces that, as the play of *Peter Pan* was published first in a volume of collected plays, it 'had nothing to do with children' – before declaring, significantly in a parenthesis, that 'this was the main publication although in the same year it was printed on its own' (Rose, 1984: 6).[7] In both cases, versions that were produced more for oral use – that is, for stagings of the play – are conveniently neglected. And, of course, it is in the acting scripts that alterations and amendments were **dialogically** negotiated.

The omission of a more oral, plebeian tradition in histories of children's literature has been quite common till recently, so in some ways Rose might be forgiven, but less so when it comes to 'Peter Pan' itself. She certainly follows the standard line in tracing the origins of children's fiction back to Rousseau, John Locke and the (male) Romantic child, which, in a Whiggish way, tends to produce its own truth effects; namely, the argument that '*Peter Pan* comes at the end of a long history, one which can be traced back to the beginnings of children's fiction' (ibid.: 8). However, not only was this end in Edwardian England rather premature (and Rose herself discusses more recent work), but it also starts the narrative at a point that suits Rose's case (i.e. children's fiction as having a Romantic birth). With this genealogy (to use Michel Foucault's (1977) helpful term), the child can easily be read as being at one with nature, beginning as a blank slate outside the complexities of language, hence requiring vocabulary that is simple and transparent. But as I've already hinted, such a history neglects many other discourses about the child, besides omitting a number of marginalised forms that have also contributed to the development of what we now see as children's literature (which is not to say that this oral tradition should be seen 'in the sense of some spontaneous and unspoilt form of expression which speaks for itself', to borrow Rose's apposite words (1984: 40): folktales and chapbooks (Neuberg, 1977; Spufford, 1987; Lynn and Preston, 1996), jokes and games (Thomas, 1989), Bible stories (Bottigheimer, 1996), penny dreadfuls (Turner, 1957), comics (Barker, 1989), and so on – some of which, as Rose herself observes (but does not challenge), might tell a different story (see, for example, Leeson, 1985; Myers, 1995; Cox, 1996; Hilton et al., 1997; O'Malley, 2003; Ruwe, 2005). In Bakhtinian terms, none of these forms is seen as ossified; rather, they are fluid and interfused, as are discourses about the child (its biology, sinful/innocent nature, educational potential, etc.), all informing ways of writing (or paging) the child, in some of which the child's answering voice can be discerned.

Andrew O'Malley, for one, has detailed some of the countervailing tendencies involved in the attempt by an emergent middle class to appropriate and redefine the child as part of that class's struggle to consolidate its position and to distance itself (and, in the process, the child too) from older, plebeian interests; that is, from more communal pleasures, from the bawdy and scatological, the supernatural, the romance and suchlike – all of which were the common fare of chapbooks. In other words, the late eighteenth century saw a huge struggle over what the child should signify, which O'Malley teases out, reacting against earlier oversimplifications of this narrative which, as he puts it, 'tend to draw attention away from the material conditions in which children's books were (and continue to be) produced' (O'Malley, 2003: 20).

His argument is subtly nuanced, showing how notions of self-improvement and self-regulation, of deferred gratification, of accepting one's place in the scheme of things, being deferential to one's superiors (and to adults in general) were all themes of this burgeoning literature; but he also posits that such notions were never fully secured. For instance, in what he terms 'hybrid' or 'transitional' books, like those of Newbery or Marshall, O'Malley draws attention to the 'residual' chapbook elements. *A Little Pretty Pocket-Book* (1744), for example, still features the chapbook hero Jack the Giant-Killer, albeit in more sanitised form (O'Malley, 2003: 23). *The History of Little Goody Two-Shoes*, aside from championing middle-class virtues also has its fantastic, fairy tale elements. We see Little Goody teach some birds to read, then gradually extend her power over the non-human world to other animals, which carry out chores for her at her school. As O'Malley comments on these developments:

> Her powers of instruction have by now reached supernatural proportions, and her magical empathy towards animals coincides much more closely with popular chapbook constructions of reality than with either those of novelistic realism, of [*sic* – 'or' is intended] the level-headed, practical, middle-class figure Goody originally embodied. (Ibid.: 25)

Goody ends up 'a hero of almost mythical proportions to the under-privileged of her community, receiving the sort of adoration reserved for such chapbook figures as Robin Hood or King Arthur' (ibid.: 25). In his conclusion O'Malley notes that '[c]hapbooks, and the plebeian culture they articulated, continued to thrive throughout the nineteenth century, even within the middle-class nursery' (ibid.: 135).

While O'Malley is certainly right to see children's books as material objects embedded within a new socio-economic configuration – that is, capitalism – it would be wrong to lose sight of other discourses that were also reconfiguring the child at this time and, indeed, later on, into the nineteenth century (seeking to invite it in, and to secure it, to adopt Rose's terms): discourses of religion, pedagogy, gender, biology, evolution, anthropology, and so forth. So while the English middle class was to become relatively secure under Victoria, the threat to the child (and the threat of the child) would continue to surface in various guises, with equally fervent attempts to 'normalize' this figure (to use O'Malley's Foucauldian terminology). The 'space in between', then, is one of intense activity, with neither the uniform adult (who 'comes first'), nor the equally uniform child (who 'comes after'), ever fully secure (Rose, 1984: 1–2). Harry Hendrick, for example (who usefully details the range of versions of 'the child' circulating in nineteenth-century Britain), quotes a telling instance from 1855, where a certain M. D. Hill complains about a troublesome youth who 'knows much and a great deal too much of what is called life', concluding: 'He has consequently much to unlearn – he has to be turned again into a child' (cited in Hendrick, 1990: 43). It is a curious comment, mixing notions of a 'natural' childhood with a simultaneous recognition that it is a socially constructed state, one which, given the right circumstances, can be engineered.

So, following the lead of O'Malley and others, it is suggested that rather than continue to rehearse grand narratives about the origins of children's fiction/literature, we need to probe more carefully the materiality of texts and their often conflicting and unstable discourses. In broad terms, we can discern attempts, on the one hand, to conceal the above instability, to make children's texts more sober, realistic, class specific, gendered and moral ('**monological**', in Bakhtin's terms), but, on the other hand, there is inevitably a recognition – even if it is only to nip it in the bud – of behaviour that disrupts such fixity of purpose: in nonsense, fantasy, the oral, the plebeian, the feminine – in short, in anything 'other' (which makes most texts 'dialogical' to some degree, and some overtly so).

While we can talk about the early construction of a children's literature only in broad terms, our knowledge becomes increasingly detailed as we move towards the present, although an oral dimension persists. On the composing side there are, on the one hand, the amateur improvisations by parents, especially at bedtime (often a time of carnivalesque licence, as Nicholas Tucker (1990) has argued), and on the other, the more polished, professionally produced texts that have developed out of such personal storytelling. *Alice's Adventures in Wonderland* (1865), of course, and *The Wind in the Willows* (1908) are two well-known examples, but there are others, although their oral background is often lost sight of. Thus it is of particular note that Rose can claim that '*Peter Pan* was not originally intended for children' because '[i]t first appeared inside a novel for adults ... *The Little White Bird*' (1984: 5). In other words, Rose prioritises a written, published text (1902), making this the defining moment, rather than Barrie's earlier oral storytelling to the Llewellyn Davies' children, in which children's pre-birth existence as birds featured. The privately published photo-story, *The Boy Castaways of Black Lake Island* (1901), also featuring the children, is likewise neglected in Rose's statement above, albeit she later – and rather contradictorily – concedes that it 'almost constitutes a second source book for *Peter Pan*' (1984: 29); indeed, we might want to observe, one that precedes the 'primary' source, a novel for adults.

On the consumption side there is the continual process of adults (parents, teachers, and so on) customising and editing their readings for children (something again, in which extracts from *The Little White Bird* could well feature – and did so officially when Barrie published this story-within-a-story separately, as *Peter Pan in Kensington Gardens*), let alone children themselves reworking stories they read and hear. Mention of the latter moves us from what might be termed the more top-down oral elements to those that are more peer generated: from such things as initiation and insult rituals to riddles, jokes, playground rhymes and the like (as recorded by Iona and Peter Opie, 1959; Turner, 1969; Schwartz, 1989; Sutton-Smith, 1995). This rag-bag category of material became consolidated as children's own largely as a result of the increasing separation of the child from adult culture, a process that was itself linked to the development of formal education systems.

So, while Rose is eloquent in writing about how different social classes of child were addressed in different published versions of 'Peter Pan', she has little to say about the dialogical influence of more oral, 'lowly' elements in the work's gestation – as noted above and as detailed by Andrew Birkin (1979). For instance, in Barrie's own dedication of the play '[t]o the Five [Llewellyn Davies' children]', he declares that '[t]he play of Peter is streaky with you still', claiming that it was written 'by rubbing the five of you violently together' (Barrie, 1995: 75). Aside from the personal, oral background that helped shape the play, there are other, more plebeian influences which tap into folklore and popular tale, and into the carnivalesque tradition of pantomime, with its outlandish costumes, its profanities, its celebration of the body and its pleasures ('some unsteady fairies … on their way home from an orgy' (Barrie, 1986: 95)) in innuendo and cross-dressing, and its history of collective (rather than individual) authorship/production – many of which qualities seem to survive in Barrie's novelisation ('"If you believe", he shouted to them, "clap your hands; don't let Tink die"' (ibid.: 164)).

More generally, then, I am suggesting that there are competing discourses at work in any text, some of which might more conventionally be accented towards 'adults', some towards 'children', but I am also keen to emphasise that this apportioning is always open to contestation (as I've posited already in relation to *The Little White Bird*). However, given children's frequent association with 'the other', with the colonised rather than the coloniser (a link Rose makes, which Nodelman (1992a) has also explored), subject positions taken up by readers of a text are more likely to be aligned with an underdog, with someone weaker or marginal (though often later empowered). This 'someone' might be a character deliberately constructed to be so (lesser, innocent, childlike), but it could as readily be someone read in this manner by the audience (the miniscule Gulliver, the isolated Crusoe, a maltreated horse). As children's fiction has come to be seen in increasingly generic terms, of course, adults more readily feel that they can unproblematically address this 'child'. Rose is certainly right that this being does not come so easily within the adult grasp, but seems to overstate her case when she deems it 'impossible' in principle to do so. Like the rest of us, the child becomes a language-using being, forced to take its place in the Symbolic via what Lacan calls the '**vel of alienation**'; that is, a Hobson's choice: subjectivity or non-existence. The child, then, has both a socio-cultural and an embodied sense of its location in society, from which vantage point it will respond, dialogically, to the various fictions proffered, liking some and rejecting others; and, no doubt, liking some simply because fellow children say they like them.

There are further implications that arise from viewing children's literature in this way, which help to explain another matter that Rose addresses; namely, why modernism had such little impact on children's fiction:

> When *Peter Pan* was being written, this concept of language had been challenged not just by Freud, but also by a shift in the adult novel which started to turn its attention to the throes of the written word. Meanwhile, children's fiction held out, and *Peter Pan* passed through unscathed (the most innocent object of all). (Rose, 1984: 65)

Before considering this issue in detail, though, it is worth noting that when Rose speaks of the 'adult novel' she, too, means not simply 'adult' but, specifically, works favoured by an upper-middle-class intelligentsia (Virginia Woolf's (1966a) 'highbrows'); in other words, it is the modernist literary novel to which she refers – not novels for adults in general (which, one might claim, are equally an 'impossibility'). The latter were, in the main, seen as middle or low brow; and, it should be observed, were far more popular, extending from authors like H. G. Wells and Arnold Bennett – the latter being singled out in an essay by Woolf (1966b) – down to more ephemeral works, such as the output of Ethel M. Dell and Sax Rohmer (cf. Bloom, 2002). For most 'adult' novel readers, modernism (as an artistic project – not modernity itself) passed them by, just as had earlier cultural movements, only having an effect through a gradual osmosis. But it would be wrong to see this lack of engagement as simply ignorance on the part of the majority; for, as John Carey has argued, in celebrating their elitism the proponents of modernism positively dismissed the masses; and, of course, children were part of this great excluded. The pointed manifestos of Henry James (1979) and others, such as George Moore, are key moments in this process of producing aesthetically crafted fictional works that were seen as specifically beyond the reach of women and children; as Moore puts it,

> all I ask is that some means may be devised by which the novelist will be allowed to describe the moral and religious feelings of his day as he perceives it [sic] to exist, and to be forced no longer to write with a view of helping parents and guardians to bring up their charges in all the traditional beliefs. (1885, quoted in Hughes, 1978: 547–8)

Thus it was not so much that 'children's fiction held out', as Rose put it; rather, it was modernism that deliberately distanced itself from what it saw as the restrictive world of writing for children – itself linked to earlier notions of family reading and strongly plotted stories, as celebrated in the works of Robert Louis Stevenson and others.[8] However, there is an irony here, in that the adult novel, in turning its attention 'to the throes of the written word', found some inspiration precisely in the work of children's writers, and in Carroll/Dodgson (once again) in particular. As Juliet Dusinberre (1987) has eloquently argued in her pointedly titled book, *Alice to the Lighthouse*, this was especially the case with Virginia Woolf. From Carroll, Woolf learnt how events could be represented imagistically, how language itself could become part of the story rather than a transparent window on an underlying reality – again, contrary to Rose's pronouncement, above, that children's fiction 'held out ... unscathed'. Once more, a dialogical (or intertextual) notion of literary influence is likely to make these connections more apparent, instead of seeing adult and children's literature operating in separate spheres (and, of course, all these works had an adult authorship in common).

As is clear from the above quotation, Rose brings in modernism as a stick to beat what she sees as reactionary writing for children (although Barrie would seem a poor choice, with his playful, almost postmodern approach to literary creation, hence querying notions that he was incapable of writing the definitive text of 'Peter Pan' – Jack, 1991). And this is why it is important to situate Rose's own work in its context, which chimed with many concurrent concerns about language that modernism seemed to address. The 1970s and early 1980s were a time when French theory was having its first major impact on English literary studies, with many British academics themselves going to study in France (Rose being one). Many of the emergent ideas first appeared in the film theory journal, *Screen*, which combined the psychoanalytic work of Lacan with Althusser's Marxism and Brecht's notion of *Verfremdungseffekt* (i.e. 'alienation effect' – the process of disrupting notions of verisimilitude). As the series under which Rose's book was launched, 'Language, Discourse, Society', pointedly declared on its dust-jackets:

> Working from recent advances in linguistics, semiotics, psychoanalysis and theory of ideology, this series is committed to forwarding an adequate account of the effective reality of meaning, sign, subject in the relations of signifying practices and formations.

It was edited by Stephen Heath and Colin MacCabe, the latter being particularly famous for his 1974 essay criticising the 'classic realist' text (MacCabe, 1974), wherein the narrator effectively controls the story and its interpretation through 'telling' rather than 'showing', suturing all the discourses into a unified hierarchy that is particularly evident in a story's ideological closure (the 'happy ending'); and where characters and their actions are seen as reflecting reality – rather than being linguistic constructs – especially in the way that the characters are depicted as having stable and knowable selves. Classic realist texts were seen as helping to endorse the reader's/viewer's own sense of agency and autonomous selfhood. As Tony Pinkney (1989: 21) puts it (albeit rather facetiously):

> The 'classic realist' text confirmed the subject in a position of ideological plenitude, papering over social and psychic contradictions; the avant-garde text, packed chock-a-block with alienation-effects, would disrupt and disseminate such fixities. ... Ideology in its Althusserian version expanded to devour the entire terrain of lived experience – which only the dessicating [*sic*] algorithms of Theory or the 'internally distantiating' violence of the Modernist work could break free of.

Catherine Belsey (1980), following Barthes's categorisation of texts into the 'readerly' and the 'writerly', also speaks disparagingly of the 'classic realist' text against which she juxtaposes the 'interrogative' text, which foregrounds exactly the issues of language and identity that concern Rose. And, for many, a new hierarchy (or canon) of texts was established, with James Joyce's linguistic experiments being placed at the pinnacle – as

MacCabe celebrates in his monograph *James Joyce and the Revolution of the Word* (1978), which also appeared in the 'Language, Discourse, Society' series, and was itself dismissive of earlier, realist readings of Joyce (it is also worth noting, of course, that Carroll's *Alice* books were a big influence on Joyce, being some of the most common intertexts in *Finnegans Wake*).

For the attentive reader of Rose, much of this should sound familiar – particularly the call for a fiction that draws attention to the written word (rather than seeing it as transparent); that recognises language's role in constructing reality, in conferring a gendered sexuality and in giving the illusion of a stable identity; and that rejects the notion of a closure wherein all discourses neatly cohere, providing readers with a sense of security in a solid world into which they can easily situate themselves. Finally, and most importantly, all these writers are united in celebrating the modernist (i.e. interrogative) text as the one that achieves such disruptive, progressive effects. The exclusivity of Rose's position comes across at a number of points, but perhaps most overtly when she calls for a different reading of Freud. Although she suggests a more open, poststructuralist interpretation of his work, her emphatic wording ironically hints at a more prescriptive agenda – 'We have been reading the wrong Freud to children. ... We have been reading the wrong Freud to children' [*sic*] (Rose, 1984: 12–13) – as though Lacan's polemical, linguistic 'return to Freud' was the answer for literary critics, children's writers and parents alike.

Since this time there have been a number of other developments, aside from those in children's literature studies. Modernism, for example, has itself been recognised as a far broader and more complex phenomenon ('modernisms', as Peter Nicholls (1995) describes the cultural zeitgeist). Secondly, work in cultural studies especially, where theoretical insights have been melded to the experiences of groups of readers/viewers, has involved a modification of the rather exclusive stance taken previously; in particular, there has been more openness towards popular or 'low culture'.[9] Lastly, as numerous studies in this area have shown, despite the conservative form of much 'low' culture, it does not follow thereby that it is politically and ideologically moribund – any more than highbrow, modernist texts are by definition progressive (those of Wyndham Lewis and Ezra Pound come to mind). Many, indeed, have identified dissident and utopian qualities in the former, especially where account is taken of their modes of consumption (e.g. Bakhtin's work, besides that of Jameson, 1979; Bourdieu, 1984; Radway, 1987; Modleski, 1988; Bloch, 1998; Dyer, 1992; Zipes, 1992). Bakhtin's work (some of whose key texts were not translated into English until the 1980s), as mentioned earlier, has been especially influential and, following on from the above, it can be argued that his approach shows that literary texts are inherently 'interrogative' in the way that they draw attention to their origins in conflicting and competing discourses, with readers abetting this process by providing their own answering words, populating texts with their own intentions and accents.[10]

This openness seems to be the case regardless of how 'monological' an author might intend a work to be, as this extract from 'Symon's Lesson of Wisdom for all Manner Children', part of the fifteenth-century *The Babees' Book*, exemplifies:

> Child, climb not over house nor wall
>
> For no fruit nor birds nor ball.
>
> Child, over men's houses no stones fling
>
> Nor at glass windows no stones sling.
>
> Nor make no crying, jokes nor plays
>
> In holy Church on holy days.
>
> And child, I warn thee of another thing,
>
> Keep thee from many words and wrangling.
>
> ...
>
> And but thou do, thou shalt fare worse
>
> And thereto be beat on the bare erse. (Townsend, 1976: 4–5)

While authority can be seen wagging its finger, the author simultaneously provides a list of pranks for the child's delectation (in terms of what Foucault (1981, 101–2) would call a 'reverse' discourse). There also seems to be a recognition by the speaker that his list of prohibitions might backfire, hence the physical deterrent made explicit at the end – though its coarse phrasing might undermine this message too. So, though the child might be mute in this rhyme, the adult certainly writes in anticipation of a child response (of its 'answering words'). In fact, we might note similarities with more recent stories which end thus: those of twentieth-century American and British comics, where children are regularly seen engaging in delinquent behaviour before finally being 'upended and made to sparkle from behind', as James Kincaid (1992: 365) colourfully expresses it. Once again, while such ideological closure might be seen to re-establish parental authority (admittedly, in far more open, dialogical texts), it is unruliness that is celebrated for most of the strip (a time of carnivalesque licence);

moreover, the final, punitive frame is often itself ambivalent: on the one hand, authority triumphs over the humiliated child but, on the other, a pair of buttocks moons cheekily at such authority.

So while there are countless attempts to construct monological texts, they are always subject to rupture in the ways that I have suggested (if that is, one accepts Bakhtin's pragmatic theory of humans being forever refracted through language, just as language is itself refracted, or inflected, by socially located beings). Contra Rose, then, Barrie's 'Peter Pan' is by no means exceptional in its seeming failure to cohere, to achieve a mono-logic of address.

In conclusion, then, I have argued that Rose's work, revolutionary as it has been, needs to be examined more critically by children's literature scholars, and itself be put into historical context. It does not, I have argued, represent closure, the end of children's literature and children's literary criticism because of some impossible, insurmountable aporia, as some have suggested.[11] To become fixated on the area's impossible status is, in effect, to hold on to remnants of a Romantic child figure: a being that somehow stands apart from the general language commun-ity so that it either cannot be addressed (unlike more mature readers) or, if it can, its responses cannot be known (Rudd, 2004; Gubar, 2009: 31). To turn this round, children's fiction thereby becomes peculiar as one of the few forms of communication unable to address the child. Of course, a Bakhtinian approach does not presume to determine the success of any such communication (and children's literature proffers very different versions of childhood and its cultures), any more than it outlaws texts that sometimes seem to migrate from one readership to another – as 'Peter Pan' arguably has, or *Gulliver's Travels*, or, indeed, 'Harry Potter'. Almost 30 years on, with the huge growth of interest in children's literature, and with the area's simultaneous loss of exclusivity in the crossover phenomenon, we are perhaps more attuned precisely to the area's possibilities – although Rose must be given credit for drawing our attention to the problems of what had previously been seen as a straightforward and unchallenging area of literature.

Other returns: the Romantic child rules!

At the outset of this chapter I talked about how Rose's work had been much cited but often with little heed paid to it, and it is certainly surprising how many critics continue to see the child as not only a knowable thing, but one that has persisted in its uniformity over space and time, and, indeed, stretches from infancy to adolescence. In this section I want to note some more recent examples where this seductive figure persists, albeit, tellingly, in a period that labels itself 'post-theory'.

Thus Jerry Griswold (2006: 4) can unproblematically claim that 'there are a chosen few [children's authors] who can speak to [the children] where they are'. Indeed, these authors are seen as so good that, rather than turning to children themselves, we can simply study their literature, as it 'provides an especially good place for the study of childhood and the ways in which the young see the world. There we can glimpse and come to comprehend (or recall) what it feels like to be a kid ... ' (ibid.: 125). However, one might question the uniformity of these 'kids' who extend, in his analysis, from picture book characters to those in the PG-rated *Antz*. In what ways, indeed, might Struwwelpeter (Shock-Headed Peter), Pollyanna, Pippi Longstocking, Sendak's Max, McKee's Bernard and the Little Mermaid be regarded as the same?

The various qualities that Griswold discerns in children's books are then cited as evidence of what children are really like, neglecting any notion of them being constructed through language by adults. Hence, he claims, '[i]mages of flight and lightness in Children's Literature ... appeal to the young because they confirm the worldview of childhood' (ibid.: 99). But what about the prevalence of vampires and similar dark things? Are they also there because they are part of a child's worldview? Or, indeed, what do we make of the tendency in children's books for children to be orphaned, for parents to be summarily removed?

Turning to another issue, Griswold informs us that, '[m]ore than adults, children are fascinated with the issue of size and particularly with smallness. Only in Children's Literature is littleness so frequent a topic' (ibid.: 51). Leaving aside that particular obsession that men are seen to have with size, once again Griswold seems to have forgotten that it is adults that like to point up the smallness of children, frequently with the aid of diminutives (Little Red Riding Hood, Little Red Hen, Little Mermaid, Tiny Tim). Indeed, Griswold perpetuates this conception in his very title, 'kid' being a belittling term associated with animals. Might this trope, then, again coming from adults (and men in particular), be used in order to put children in their place, as indeed adults (men) have done with other, less privileged groups (a wife as 'the little woman', service operative as the 'little man' or 'boy', etc.)? In a particular irony, Griswold, in discussing the appeal of cosy places in children's literature, claims that 'every snug place is Plato's cave of ideas' (ibid.: 25), forgetting, it seems, that in Plato's allegory the cave is precisely a place of illusion, where the prisoners are held captive in chains. It is only when one of them escapes that he finds the real world outside. One might then make more of Griswold's inversion of this allegory, in the way that it captures exactly what adults have tried to do with children in their fiction: to give them a make-believe world which adults pretend is the real one, hence confining them to childhood (Nodelman, in particular, seems to take up this idea, as we'll see in Chapter 4).

More recently, Maria Tatar in *Enchanted Hunters* (2009: 164–5) makes similar claims about a uniform, universal child:

> In order to attract children to books, you need to know something about what is going on in their minds. Adult authors have always understood that and even the earliest specimen of words and images designed for the young ... suggests a clear understanding of what appeals to children. But adults have not always acted on their intuitions, and the move to child-centered stories and to tales that validate mischief, energy, élan, and curiosity, is relatively recent.

As with Harvey Darton, quoted above, there is a notion that earlier children's literature did not really capture what children wanted (although, if one contrasts adult books of the eighteenth century, say, with contemporary material, the dubious basis of such comparisons becomes obvious). Though there *are* records of children's reactions to texts from earlier times, Tatar does not quote them, but instead rehearses the standard shift from instruction to entertainment: Carroll first 'veered off the beaten path, but Barrie used an even higher-octane formula to change direction ... to revel in the lawless world of the child's imagination' (ibid.: 178).

Lastly I'd like to mention two exemplars of what is known as 'emancipatory' criticism, Mary Galbraith and Joseph Zornado, both influenced by the work of Alice Miller (2002) on 'black pedagogy'. Galbraith (2001: 199) does at least mention Rose, but seems to misread her: 'The postmodern critiques of adult representations of childhood have done a great service to the field by promoting methodological skepticism about "the real child" (Rose, Lesnik-Oberstein)'; but they are then accused of being 'inherently delusional' (ibid.: 191) for failing to see, beneath these 'distorting interests of adults' (ibid.: 199), an existentially authentic childhood. Children's literature, however, 'has tapped into a particular child's deep-structure fantasies and revealed something profound about the SELF of that child – the child who grew up to create this work of literature' (ibid.: 194–5).

It is hard to see how adult authors for children can have such unmediated access (which is then conveyed to us in an equally unadorned way), but I'll ignore that problem here. Rather, I want to conclude my comments on Galbraith by noting how she is, in many respects, more closely aligned with writers like Mrs Trimmer than with those who celebrate the liberating aspects of fantasy. For, Galbraith declares, the 'emancipatory interests' of a child can only be undermined in 'unrealistic fantasies of childhood independence and power, ... promoting the view that children can overcome the failure of adults by rising above their own needs or by receiving unique favors from the universe' (ibid.: 195).

In developing her emancipatory struggle, Galbraith refers to Zornado as an ally, but his position is more complex. His book, *The Invention of the Child*, along with many of his reference points (Althusser, in particular), initially suggests a form of social constructionism, potentially in line with Rose. However, as the word 'invention' perhaps intimates, this construction is seen in ahistorical terms, as a once-and-for-all event, which he locates in prehistory, some 10,000 years ago during the Agricultural Revolution.[12] Since this time, the child's condition has remained largely unchanged (though, we are informed, it has deter-iorated in the last 400 years). Unlike the child in the work of Philippe Ariès and others, there has been little cultural variation, whether it be Shakespeare's childhood or Sendak's being considered; moreover, Zornado confidently asserts that '*all* literary production is a reproduction of the author's experiences as a child at the hands of the adult world' (Zornado, 2001: 43).[13]

Despite the 'basic biological and emotional needs' (ibid.: xiv) of the child, adult culture is 'blind' to them: 'the child learns to forget the felt experiences of the real conditions of her existence' (ibid.: 4) under a regime 'determined solely by the adult'. Only when 'the individual lets out the rage that is within him' can the 'real relationship to the conditions of ... existence' be possible (ibid.: 11). For someone influenced by the anti-humanist, Althusser, there is a strange voluntarism here, both on the part of adults (who determine the child's ideological world) and the child (who can seemingly escape the Ideological State Apparatuses – ISAs – through what sounds like a bit of primal scream therapy).

For Zornado, then, ideology constitutes a 'rape of the child's original mind' (ibid.: 40), but it can be overcome, restoring 'the child's intuitive understanding' (ibid.: 215):

> The empty consciousness is the spontaneous consciousness, acting spontaneously not according to plan [*sic*], but according to the compassionate

heart that is always already available when not bound by iron bands of ideological indoctrination and emotional repression. (Ibid.: 216)

This is reminiscent of Rousseau's notion of the child born free, but then enchained; or, in Althusser's terms, 'interpellated', except that, for the latter of course, there is no escape; ideology is 'an omni-historical reality' (Althusser, 1971: 161), despite being differently shaped according to particular historical ISAs. For Zornado, in contrast, ideology is a more blunt instrument and, curiously, something that (again unlike Althusser) he distinguishes from 'relations of power' per se: 'The depiction of relations of power in these stories [*Babar the Elephant, Curious George*] comes with an ideological bullet that ... penetrates flesh in the same way "real" bullets do' (Zornado, 2001: 128). The bullet metaphor, in particular, is reminiscent of the old 'effects' school of media research, where the passive child is indeed 'hit' by ideology, it being very much a one-way process (see Chapter 3). In this case, Burning Babar might be even more dangerous an exercise, like setting alight an ammunition dump!

Conclusion

In this chapter I have examined Rose's provocative thesis, agreeing with many of her tenets but rejecting her conclusion. Were one to accept the latter, I have suggested, one would thereby concede that children are, indeed, special beings, rather than joint speakers of the same language, all of us locked into the Symbolic. However, I have also drawn attention to how seductive this idealised image of the child is – and I deliberately use the word 'seductive' here to draw a contrast with Rose's usage, where she refers to 'children's fiction ... as something of ... a seduction' (1984: 2). The image is seductive, but adults seem more seduced by it than do children – as, indeed, some critics, quoted earlier, recognised: 'the idea of a boy who never grows up' is probably not 'as appealing to children as it is to parents' (Townsend, 1976: 106).

In terms of the Imaginary, though, this idea proves remarkably resilient. And I am not against any of us savouring it, cooing at the behaviour of children, just as we can enjoy the anthropomorphism of a fox's cunning or a cat's curiosity. But we need to recognise that it is only this – an idealised image – and not let it obscure the realities of childhood, both past and present (Kincaid, 1992; Higonnet, 1998). To indulge the former exclusively can allow one to become fixated on the lone paedophile and miss the homely family as the key site of abuse, with 65 per cent of adults (based on data from 21, mostly industrialised, countries) claiming to have experienced sexual abuse as children, the majority of it from close relatives. In 2002, an estimated 150 million girls and 73 million boys 'experienced forced sexual intercourse and other forms of sexual violence', with another million being pushed into pornography and prostitution, and a further 53,000 being murdered. As a final depressing statistic, an estimated 218 million children, worldwide, have to work, with 126 million of these doing so in hazardous conditions (Usborne, 2006).

2 Peter Pan and the Riddle of Existence

In the previous chapter I returned to Rose's thesis about the 'impossibility of children's fiction'. Though critical of it in some respects, I also endorsed much of her 'case'. In this chapter I want to return to its main subject, Peter Pan, for two main reasons. First because of the remarkable coyness of many critics in engaging with this work from a psychoanalytical perspective, even though, as Rose herself says, 'it is too easy to give an Oedipal reading of Peter Pan' (Rose, 1984: 35). There seems more to it than this, however, as though the text itself, like Neverland, resists such a reading. This reaction might seem strange, given the play's historical location, emerging at the very time that the unconscious was itself 'coming out' (in the 1890s) as a result of the pioneering work of Freud and others. The second reason for returning to Barrie's text is because it provides a very useful vehicle not only for undertaking a psychoanalytical reading, but for explicating some of the basic Lacanian concepts that I have used in structuring this book.[1] And this, of course, is also the second chapter that I have included in the 'Imaginary' part, for it deals with the way that the child figure is idealised. Peter Pan (the boy who would not grow up) is one of its key avatars, though also one that undercuts such a notion – as we shall see.

Let me begin, though, by looking at one of the few attempts to examine Barrie's *Peter Pan* from a psychoanalytical perspective, which comes from Michael Egan. He picks up on the prescient imagery of Barrie's work; the way, for example, that Mrs Darling, once the children are in bed, likes 'to rummage in their minds and put things straight for next morning', just as though she were 'tidying up drawers', putting 'the naughtiness and evil passions ... at the bottom of your mind' (Egan, 1982: 18). She enacts the role of parental superego. However, Mr Darling, the children's father, is seen to let the side down, acting more like a child himself in his reluctance to show the children how to take their medicine. 'Father's a cowardy custard,' as his son, Michael, remarks (Barrie, 1986: 32).

Egan pursues the Oedipal implications of this, noting how the children, lacking a proper father figure, escape into a fantasy realm, Neverland, where a more formidable father takes up the cause of patriarchy; namely Captain Jas. Hook. Clearly, in the novel, these two figures, Mr Darling and Hook, are not as closely interlinked, but in the play, as is well-known, a single male actor has played both parts since the work's first production in 1904. Also in Neverland, though, there is Peter Pan who, as the children's champion, plays out the Oedipal battle against this father figure, Hook. Peter Pan eventually overthrows Hook and replaces him. Thus we witness Peter sitting in Hook's cabin wearing 'some of Hook's wickedest garments ... with Hook's cigar-holder in his mouth and one hand clenched, all but the forefinger, which he bent and held threateningly aloft like a hook' (ibid.: 192).[2] Egan (1982: 54) then concludes his analysis: 'Having destroyed the Oedipal father the triumphant son becomes the Oedipal father. [Peter Pan] takes his place completely'. As I have commented elsewhere, 'Egan's argument ... becomes curiously truncated in its conclusion, as though Egan himself had been cut off in discursive stride' (Rudd, 2012c: 60). However, the main reason that Egan doesn't take his reading further is because this line of argument simply does not work, for Peter Pan never (never, never, in fact) does become 'the Oedipal father'. This is where Lacan's reworking of the Oedipal scenario proves more helpful and allows us to explore some Lacanian terms.

The main thing that Lacan does is to remove the biological essentialism from Freud's interpretation of the Oedipal scene: it has nothing to do with the penis and is, therefore, not delimited to males. Instead, Lacan interprets it in linguistic terms, wherein we experience castration in at least four ways. First, we feel ourselves sundered from some earlier sense of connectedness, especially from the mother. Second, and relatedly, this sense of connection arises from the fact that, whereas we formerly felt words were tied to things (in Saussurean terms, signified and signifier were united), now a gap seems to have opened up: these two parts of the sign have been parted (cut, sundered), such that we seem to be in a realm of substitutions, stand-ins and shadowy approximations. Third, words themselves – unlike the total immersion we experienced in the 'real' world (or even in our images of it) – are discontinuous: they have gaps between them across which we have to 'make sense' (it is not instantly there). Lastly, as a result of this splitting, we experience a sense of lack, or want of being (*manque à être*) which, ever after, we strive to overcome. And, for Lacan, *lack* is simply the other side of *desire*. Thus, adults look back wistfully to this former state. In the words of *Peter Pan*: 'On these magic shores children at play are for ever beaching their coracles. We too have been there; we can still hear the sound of the surf, though we shall land no more' (1986: 19).

Egan's analysis, then, stalls in the same way that the cocky boy himself does, in that Peter refuses to traverse this Oedipal stage: 'there never was a cockier boy' (ibid.: 41), we are told, and Peter will not forego this cockiness for anything. My play on words aside, though, it needs stressing again that Lacan is not talking about bits of male anatomy here (as detailed above), any more than he talks about actual castration – hence Lacan's preference for a word that represents this process in more symbolic terms; namely, the **phallus**. This is a complex concept that I will kick into touch for the moment, but let me just note that it is not something that boys, rather than girls, possess: for Lacan, we are all in a state of lack, therefore nobody *has* the phallus, though it *is* undoubtedly desired by all, and tends to be attached to the powerful and authoritative.[3]

I shall return to address Peter's actual status in a moment, but first let me briefly elaborate on Lacan's main claim that we exist within three orders, the Real, the Imaginary and the Symbolic. The Real consists of the brute 'stuff' of the universe: animals are at home in it but we are not. It is a space of sensory immersion and immediacy, a continuum of 'thinginess', unconceptualised, running around us and through us – and, indeed, we are very much part of it. However, we are also distanced from it, and this process of distanciation occurs in two stages. First, we start to experience ourselves as having a distinct boundary, and as bearing an individual name. This is what is initiated by Lacan's famous '**mirror phase**', where the child is presented with itself in a mirror and sees not a jumbled mass of movement and feeling but a more coherent being to which attention is drawn by others ('Who's a pretty boy, then?'). Thus something *outside* the child is reflected back to it in idealised terms; and this **ideal ego**, as Lacan terms it, is then built upon in many of the ways through which the child has its image presented to it. Whereas the 'ego psychologists', as they have been termed, see this 'I' as something to be fostered and strengthened, Lacan takes a very different view. He thinks the ego gives its owner only an illusory sense of unity, idealising something false and fictional (e.g. striving to live the 'American Dream'). Although we will always find such idealisations seductive, we should try to avoid being captivated by them. Peter Pan, of course, is just one such idealised image that our culture celebrates: the dream of eternal youth and innocence. And, in Barrie's words, Peter is seen as just 'the kind of boy the public wants' (Barrie, 1926: 99). He is completely irresistible, such that the Never Bird even gives up her nest, 'deserting her eggs' (Barrie, 1986: 124) for Peter's sake – as, of course, do generations of Wendy women, too, who go and spring-clean for him.

If Peter seems to incarnate the Imaginary, Captain Hook epitomises the Symbolic. This final order is one we move into as we come to realise that we cannot remain within the Imaginary, wedded to the mother, complementing her. And what causes this shift is the recognition of a third party: the father. The child realises that the mother's desire is not entirely for him or her, but lies elsewhere, with this father figure. Given Lacan's linguistic emphasis, moreover, it is the father function, the Name of the Father (the *nom-du-père*), that is significant. This figure puts an end to the cosiness of the mother–child dyad through a negation: No! Thus Lacan exploits the punnish link between the *nom* and the *non-du-père*. The child technically has a choice at this point ('the vel of alienation'): to accept this diktat and forego the mother, or not. For most people, however, it is a non-choice. It is, to use Lacan's own example, like being confronted by a brigand demanding *'[y]our money or your life!'* (Lacan, 1977b: 212). Could you make a bargain to hang on to the former while forsaking the latter? Most of us therefore accept that we must give up the mother and, in return, are granted a place in the Symbolic, the realm of language, of signifiers. On this basis we become split subjects (represented thus: $), distanced by language from things in themselves; that is, we play with signifiers (letters, sounds, etc.), the full experience of the signified (things, concepts) being barred from us.

In representing this, Lacan takes Saussure's original algorithm and inverts it, recognising that, in our everyday lives we deal with people through language, by swapping signifiers:

signifier
signified

We have a notion that somehow, beneath these noises, sense can be made, but we are not sure exactly what it is; and, when confronted, all we can do is utter more signifiers. Of course, words always lead to other words, and words also sound like other words, and words have connotations and metaphorical associations, so meaning is always fuzzy; it always has more potential – an excess – than is suggested on the surface (signifier). For this reason, Lacan makes much of the bar between the two; in other words, there is no simple, one-on-one mapping, the signified being something 'real' that the signifier, like the surface of a lake, simply reflects. Instead, to pursue the metaphor (as we often do), there is far more going on in the depths of this lake, which the bar conceals: material is refracted, distorted, fluid. 'What lies beneath', then, to borrow an apposite film title, is always subject to interpretation and analysis.

In developmental terms, then, we have a notion that a gap has opened with this sundering of symbol from thing. Whereas our wants were once instantly met, we imagine, gratification is now deferred, as we clumsily seek to articulate our wishes signifier by signifier, albeit never quite obtaining a sense of total satisfaction. In other words, whereas we think we were once in a state of full being, we now experience *lack* ('want of being' - *manque à être*); or, to turn this round, we have instantiated a *desire* to have that fullness back.

Hook certainly experiences this want of being, even his name evoking his status as a castrated being with his missing right hand.[4] In Lacanian terms, Hook's name is metonymic; that is, the word that encapsulates his *whole* person actually names but a *part* of him; and, beyond this, it is a name that itself points to a lack: an absence.[5] For Lacan, the signifying chain of language itself unfolds metonymically, as we strive to express ourselves, our meaning, completely, but always fail, hence the continual need for more words. However, though our sentences unfold in this way, as a result of our entry into the relatively incomplete Symbolic, a residue lurks outside this, exerting continual pressure on the signifying chain to mean *more*. In other words, our movement into the Symbolic has created the unconscious, a realm of *metaphorical* association, and one where slips (as of the tongue) at the level of the signifier can trigger meanings that derail the progress of the signifying chain.

If Hook encapsulates the Symbolic in his flawed being, then, he also demonstrates its relative emptiness with his stress on 'good form' – 'form' suggesting surface appearance, codes of behaviour, niceties of expression, and so on, beneath which there is a hollowness (again, exploited by McCaughrean (2007) below). Hook certainly has the social graces, with his classical, Etonian education (in earlier versions of Barrie's work he was, in fact, a schoolmaster) and in 'the elegance of his diction' (Barrie, 1986: 72–3). In Lacanian terms, then, Hook is the one seen to possess the phallus (he is the proper patriarchal father, as noted earlier). But as also mentioned, the phallus is a complex concept in Lacan's work. It is associated with power and authority, unquestionably, but it is just a *symbol* of these, a stand-in, behind which there 'stands' precisely nothing (which is why the phallus is usually veiled).[6] In Spielberg's (1991) version of the story, *Hook*, Dustin Hoffman portrays this mixture of phallic posturing (with his feathers and pointed moustaches) and underlying effeteness, which is certainly justified by Barrie's original stage directions: 'In dress he apes the dandiacal' with his 'hair dressed in long curls ... his eyes blue as the forget-me-not' (Barrie, 1986: 108) and he has a general 'touch of the feminine' about him (ibid.: 122).

Ludo, ergo sum ... not![7]

Armed with these basic ideas, we can now make more sense of Peter Pan's position, and of the whole realm of Neverland. For it would be a mistake to see Peter Pan as a perfect being – despite his own proclamations about incarnating 'youth' and 'joy', about being 'a little bird that has broken out of the egg' (ibid.: 187). Mabel Lucy Atwell's attractively cuddly illustrations, in fact, in no way capture the Peter Pan of Barrie's text. Peter might have 'all his first teeth' but he is also 'clad in skeleton leaves' (ibid.: 24); he has nightmares (ibid.: 205), cannot bear to be touched, and has no time for mothers (those who not only offer love – fine! – but want it reciprocated: impossible!). Neverland, too, is no paradise: it is a realm where images of death stalk the landscape. We have the pirates armed to the teeth, as might be expected, with characters like Cecco who carved his name 'in letters of blood' on the back of a prison governor (ibid.: 71), and Smee, with his cutlass called 'Johnny Corkscrew, because he wriggled it in the wound' (ibid.: 77); and then there is Hook himself, who chooses one of his own pirates to demonstrate how 'the hook shoots forth, there is a tearing sound and one screech, then the body is kicked aside' (ibid.: 73). Likewise, the 'redskins' are armed with 'tomahawks and knives', and Tiger Lily 'staves off the altar with a hatchet' (ibid.: 75). The Lost Boys, too, go hunting with their daggers, wearing 'the skins of bears slain by themselves' (ibid.: 69), with Peter being the worst offender; for besides the fact that 'they get killed and so on', when the Lost Boys 'seem to be growing up', Peter 'thins them out' (ibid.: 69).

But of most significance is the fact that these images of death, and especially of cutting and castration, cluster around Peter, Neverland being his realm, such that it only 'woke into life' when it felt 'Peter was on his way back' (ibid.: 68). Even in name this realm is disturbing: it might have fantastic, imaginary connotations, but it also invokes that negation characteristic of the Symbolic, the 'No', or *non-du-père* of the patriarchal father. In fact, the name itself has suffered its own metonymic trimming, with bits sliced off it since its conception:

> Peter Pan's island was called the Never, Never, Never Land in the first draft of the play, the Never Never Land in the play as performed ... the Never Land in the play as published, and the Neverland in *Peter and Wendy*. (Hollindale, 1995: 311)

The shadow of castration haunts Peter throughout, most overtly exhibited in Nana's attempt to catch him: 'slam went the window and snapped [his shadow] off' (Barrie, 1986: 25).[8] Lacan speaks about how such images of castration can persecute someone who is moving out of the Imaginary into the Symbolic. He speaks about *le corps morcelé* or 'fragmented body', involving 'images of castration, emasculation, mutilation, dismemberment, dislocation, evisceration, devouring, and bursting open of the body ... "imagos of the fragmented body"' (1977a: 11).[9] The Symbolic cuts through these formerly wholesome images; it 'manifests itself ... as the murder of the thing' (ibid.: 104). But Peter Pan, of course, is determined to avoid being 'hooked' by the Symbolic in this way.[10]

Peter thus finds himself in a 'no man's land' between the Imaginary and the Symbolic. As Solomon Caw remarks in *Peter Pan in Kensington Gardens* (itself extracted from the adult novel, *The Little White Bird*, Chapters 13–18), Peter is 'half-and-half ... a Betwixt-and-Between' (Barrie, 2007: 206): he has moved away from this oneness with the mother, but gone no further; consequently he hovers uneasily between *being* and *meaning*; that is, he has initiated the Oedipal process but not completed it. In Lacanian terms, this process involves two stages, one of *alienation* and one of *separation*. In alienation, as observed above, the child has come to realise that it cannot be all for the mother, that her desire lies elsewhere. Of course, as we desire only because we lack, the child realises that the mother too is incomplete, and the child seeks to be the very thing that could make her whole again (what Lacan terms the **'imaginary phallus'** – sometimes referred to as the 'maternal phallus'). Peter is stuck between this aspect, alienation, resolutely refusing to give up his cockiness, and separation, which involves that negation by the father: the 'No', or actual castration. Peter therefore remains full of himself with no room for anyone else; hence his narcissism ('oh, the cleverness of me!' (Barrie, 1986: 41)), and hence his irresistibility to others, noted earlier – though, ultimately, because he is so self-absorbed, he must disappoint everyone, which is the feeling that unites Wendy, Tiger Lily and Tinker Bell (ibid.: 133).

Earlier I mentioned that some people refuse what Lacan terms the vel of alienation (the either/or choice of subjectivity/non-existence), and Peter Pan is one of them. In clinical terms, he exhibits the structure of perversion (where the Symbolic is recognised but disavowed). As Bruce Fink (1995) indicates, such people are positioned between alienation and separation in the Oedipal struggle: rather than accept the position of *having* the phallus, they hold to the notion of *being* it.[11] In this they are not just suffering perversions but, as Lacan liked to pun, are *père-versions*, or versions of the father. Thus Peter Pan delights in playing the 'Great White Father', watching the redskins 'prostrating themselves before him' (Barrie, 1986: 127) and speaks of himself in the third person. Wendy, too, though unsympathetic, remains loyal to him, declaring 'Father knows best'.[12] Peter certainly likes donning the phallic regalia, then, although he resolutely refuses the price of admission; as he says to Mrs Darling, 'Keep back, lady, no one is going to catch me and make me a man' (ibid.: 206).

He is certainly not a man, but neither is he a woman, nor a transvestite, as Marjorie Garber has suggested, having picked up on the fact that, traditionally, Peter is played by a woman in the play; the reason for this is, she argues, '[b]ecause a woman will never grow up to be a man' (Garber, 1992: 168). Peter, however, will grow up to be none of the above; more straightforwardly, he will not grow up period (which is where Spielberg's sentimentality in *Hook* ultimately triumphs, making the story into one about the importance of adults keeping in touch with their inner child).

The reasons for Peter Pan not growing up (allowing Robin Williams ultimately to return to his whacky child-adult self) are less than straightforward, though. As noted before, Peter cannot grow up because he has not entered the realm of the Symbolic, being perched on its threshold only. However, as was also noted, he continually experiences images of mutilation (which threaten the Imaginary) and he seems aware that the Symbolic 'materializes the agency of death' (Lacan, 1973: 53); as Barrie (1986: 13) cynically expresses it, the age of '[t]wo is the beginning of the end'. But Peter Pan has not stepped over this threshold: he remains a liminal being ('limen' being the Greek word for 'threshold'), such that death cannot disturb him. One of the play's most famous and chilling lines expresses this: 'To die will be an awfully big adventure!' (Barrie, 1995: 125);[13] and at the end it is mooted that, equally, 'his cry might become "To live would be an awfully big adventure!"' (ibid.: 153). However, this could only occur if he entered the symbolic order, which is also an intersubjective realm, the very thing that Peter stands apart from. It is significant, then, that just before this stage direction Wendy has stated her wish to 'take' him and 'squdge' [*sic*] him, at which point Peter 'draws back'. He has no wish to enter the Symbolic, to – as quoted earlier – have them 'catch me and make me a man' (Barrie, 1986: 206).

Peter Pan, then, is unique in refusing to be a 'signifier for other signifiers' – as Lacan described our condition in the Symbolic.[14] He refuses to renounce what Lacan terms his *jouissance* (blissful, almost painful joy), which most of us forsake when we submit to our position under the Law of the Father (in the Symbolic); rather, Peter still has 'ecstasies innumerable that other children can never know'. However, he is thereby alone, hence condemned to be observed 'looking through the window at the one joy from which he must be for ever barred' (ibid.: 202).[15] He cannot die, certainly, but this is because he cannot live, either. He is not of that realm of 'the agency of death'. In Lacanian terms, then, Peter Pan exists in a liminal state 'between-two-deaths' (Lacan, 1959/60). It is of significance, then, that he does not want to be touched, reminding us of that phrase of Jesus's, '*Noli me tangere*' ('Do not touch me'), addressed to Mary Magdelene (John 20:17) after Jesus's death but prior to his ascension. Peter is dead in the Real (if ever he had an existence there) but lives on in terms of the Imaginary (as noted earlier, as an icon of the *puer aeternus* or eternal child, fresh out of its egg – and its ego) and the Symbolic (though never at home there). Like the primal father, then (see Note 12), Peter Pan is best described as *ex-sisting*, to use the term Lacan borrowed from Martin Heidegger. Fittingly, this word is linked to ecstasy, or *ek-stasis*, meaning to stand outside oneself. To be outside the Symbolic is to be in an impossible place, then, but one that the Symbolic order is especially good at creating (especially as words do not map onto actual things). It is a realm also inhabited by, say, unicorns, vampires and zombies, and, therefore, it should have come as no surprise that Joel Schumacher's teen film, *The Lost Boys* (Schumacher, 1987), made Peter Pan's tribe into undead vampires, long before this figurative representation of the adolescent became so fashionable.

It was not a fanciful move, either (unlike, say, the 'mashup' of Jane Austen and zombies (Grahame-Smith, 2009)), for the references are clearly there in Barrie, the title of Chapter 3, 'Come away, come away!', being a direct quotation from W. B. Yeats's poem, 'The Stolen Child' (1889). This poem details the fatal attraction to mortals of the 'leafy island' of the world of fairy, access to which results in a loss of the comforts of home, like 'the kettle on the hob' (Yeats, 1962: 5–6). Michael Hearn (1988: 19–20) has assiduously traced these links between fairyland and 'the Isles of the Blest, the Fortunate Isles, the Land of the Young, the Plain of Happiness [which ...] is also known as the Land of the Dead. It is the home of perpetual Spring, eternal youth'. It is hardly surprising, then, that Peter helps the 'children who fall out of their perambulators' (Barrie, 1986: 46), even digging their graves in Barrie's earlier version of the story (Barrie, 2007: 268–9).

In terms of Lacan's three orders, then, Peter Pan stands at the edge of the Imaginary, on the border of the Symbolic, but refuses to take that ontological leap into the realm of existence. He ex-sists instead. The former offers him a place as a signifier but only in exchange for his being, his *jouissance*. The Symbolic will also condemn him to mortality, of course, whereas, as long as he is celebrated for being Peter Pan (virtually guaranteed), he can reign immortal in the Imaginary.

Barrie's is thus a salutary tale for those of us trapped within more mortal coils, who sit more healthily in relation to the RSI (Lacan's 'heresy'). And it is Wendy who shows us the compensations of the Symbolic. In being a signifier for other signifiers we are given a relative place in this order; indeed, we exist only in relation to others – to relatives, parents and progeny. Moreover, through story we have the chance to weave these threads together, into texts, into memories, to which – the word is significant – we can then 'relate'. Wendy thus 'weaves and stitches the lost boys back into the Symbolic, just as she initially tries to "stitch up", or suture Peter Pan after he is separated from his shadow' (Rudd, 2012c: 64).[16] And so, in concluding this discussion of Barrie's creation, we might say that

> Neverland is ... a nice place to visit, to establish the contours of one's desires, but it is only safe in the hands of a traditional spinster – that is, one who holds on to, and can interweave, the threads of life; in other words, a storyteller or bard. One who can trace genealogies, establish one's place as a signifier within the family plot, which also means accepting one's final plot, one's life sentence. Neverland, then, is nice to visit, but one certainly would not want to live there, precisely because it would result in one's being 'barred': locked out of human existence and trapped within one's narcissistic and illusory mirror image. *Peter and Wendy* – barred or bard – the title presents us with this existential *vel*, or non-choice. 'Neverland' thus has one final connotation, functioning as an imperative, or directive: fly over it, dream about it, read of it, desire it, but whatever you do, don't settle there: never, never, never land! (Ibid.)

Of course, there have been numerous other versions of Peter Pan circulating since Barrie's creation, and they continue to be produced, right down to Geraldine McCaughrean's official sequel, discussed below. Probably most well-known are the film adaptations, with P. J. Hogan's (2003) perhaps deserving special mention in the way that it does not flinch from many of the darker aspects of Barrie's original, mutilation and death being ever present. At the climax, Hook explicitly taunts Peter with Wendy's decision to 'grow up'. The pirate then envisages Wendy's future, telling Pan that '[t]here is another in your place. He is called ... husband. ... You die alone ... and unloved. ... Just like me'. Clearly, we might criticise some detail: Peter has no interest in being a husband, a matter that he has clarified with Wendy earlier, to her disappointment; moreover, death holds no fear for him anyway ('an awfully big adventure'). What would be more disruptive to his existence would be to be 'unloved'. For this is what the slightly vampiric Peter feeds on, what preserves his imaginary being – his being as imaginary phallus, in fact – and without which he would, like some of the Neverland fairies, be just an ex-Pan. Wendy therefore demonstrates her love for him with her 'thimble'. As she puts it, 'This belongs to you ... and always will'. The full-on snog is not something that the untouchable Peter would usually tolerate, we know, but he is – arguably – unconscious for much of this osculation. As another character comments, 'That was no thimble. That was her hidden kiss'. Indeed, it is the 'kiss of life'. At this, poor Hook, facing the growing chorus of 'Old! Alone! Done for!', resignedly drops into the 'gently smiling jaws' of the waiting crocodile (the contrast with Spielberg's (1991) *Hook*, mentioned earlier, is quite stark here). 'Cut', one can almost hear the director shout.

The winter of his discontent: Peter Pan unravelled (but not unveiled)[17]

It is interesting to observe how Geraldine McCaughrean has dealt with some of these disturbing issues in her official sequel, *Peter Pan in Scarlet* (2007). It would have been all too easy to try to tame Barrie's cantankerous text, but McCaughrean is far too good a writer for this. Indeed, the narrator unflinchingly surmises that, as a result of the devastating impact of the First World War, Neverland has become altogether a darker place:

> flying debris ... – shrapnel and bullets and such – made holes in the fabric between Neverland and this world. Dreams leaked out through the holes; grown-up mess leaked in. And that's when the summerlands were spoiled. For a few ticks, Time moved on where Time was never meant to, and summer turned to autumn, and draughts slithered in, and friends grew cold. (McCaughrean, 2007: 273)

Thus it is now a more autumnal realm, making its images of putrescence more stark, as in the 'birdcages or crab-pots' on the shore that turn out to be 'the skeleton ribcages of mermaids, with here and there a backbone or a hank of yellow hair' (ibid.: 48). McCaughrean has not held back, either, from giving Peter lines that are as fitting and chilling as his earlier claim that '[t]o die will be an awfully big adventure'; thus, striding out across a 'narrow ice-bridge', Peter reworks this infamous line with an existential, Hamlet-like twist: 'A quest, Tootles? Yes! To be or not to be. *That* is the quest!' (ibid.: 169). The most interesting re-creation in the book, though, is Hook. He is still the main representative of the Symbolic, of patriarchy, while simultaneously showing up its precarious nature. McCaughrean has played up his more feminine side, which, it is shown, has partly been thrust on him thanks to his fate at the end of Barrie's text; namely, after being consigned to the belly of a female crocodile, which he describes in his 'valet's voice ... as gentle and springy as a lamb' (ibid.: 131) as being a '[l]ightless, airless tomb awash with digestive juices', feeding on a diet of eggs, such that he has been reduced to 'this SOFTNESS of a man! A thing like a sponge ... all ... frizzled to wool' (ibid.: 188–9). His new name, Ravello, fits him like a badly knitted glove, with John at one point referring to him as 'a very tall cardigan' (ibid.: 64). It suits him precisely because he is continually unravelling, coming apart, lacking any definite contours, with his shadow, trailing behind him, 'like a leak from the Quink ink factory' (ibid.: 186). Such links with the Symbolic are again apt, especially as Ravello is repeatedly trying to tempt the boys with stories about their possible futures. From the outset, then, Ravello, whom we first meet as a circus-master with cages full of wild animals, has disturbed Peter, as the latter unwillingly contemplates the idea of being trapped within the prison-house of language as a 'barred' subject, reduced to a signifier:

> The thought of sleeping in a cage ... struck horror into his freewheeling soul. The thought of animals caged was almost as bad. It appalled him to think of wild creatures penned up behind bars. It was almost as if they were trapped inside him – those bears and tigers and lions – pacing up and down, pushing their plush noses between the bars of his ribcage, so that he wanted to tear open his chest and set them all free ... [*sic*] A terrible foreboding settled over his heart .... (Ibid.: 64)

And, indeed, Ravello is always tempting the Lost Boys with his 'yarns' about growing up – tempting them in a manner that seems almost a parody of Rose, in that Ravello seeks to undo that 'which fixes the child and then holds it in place'. In contrast, Ravello attempts to make 'the child ... an outsider to its own process' and, thereby, not 'unashamedly ... take the child *in*' (ibid.: 2) but, rather, draw the child *out*. Slightly is thus lured with the prospect of becoming a musician:

'Oh yes!' said Slightly. 'I would *love* to be one of those when I grow up!'
'Then who can prevent it?' said the Ravelling Man, and his eyes flashed
with pure delight before he turned away. (Ibid.: 115)

And Slightly does, indeed, grow, such that Peter once again evokes the
phallic imagery of the symbolic prison-house:

Peter drew his sword – 'Oh, please, Cap'n, no!' – and with the swordpoint
drew a portcullis in the air, complete with rope and wheel and cruel iron
spikes. Then he raised the portcullis, drove Slightly backwards through it
on the end of his sword, and lowered the grill again, shutting him out.
(Ibid.: 128)

Later, Peter is himself almost 'hooked' by Ravello's tantalising variations
on this perennial question, 'What do you want to be when you grow up?';
for, as we are told, once contemplated, the child 'is halfway to being an
adult', as Ravello all too readily knows: 'He has betrayed childhood and
Looked Ahead' (ibid.: 193). Fortunately, Slightly's timely intervention
('Don't answer him!' (ibid.)) saves Peter, who, as we saw earlier, is
resolutely resolved to stay a 'Betwixt-and-Between' (Barrie, 2007: 206).

In the course of this story, then, we witness a more dangerous Hook,
whose bluff and straightforward piratical ways have been replaced by
more devious ploys. His previously phallic appearance, noted earlier,
and reaffirmed by McCaughrean at the end ('the hard, sharp shape of
the old ... Hook' (McCaughrean, 2007: 269)), has for most of this story
been lost to what can only be described as a flaccid, Medusa-headed,
shapeless mass. Interestingly, he now uses wiles more traditionally
gendered feminine in order to try to stitch Peter Pan into the Symbolic.
He obsequiously attends to Peter Pan's clothing, carefully dressing 'the
marvellous Peter Pan' (ibid.: 88) in a manner that flatters what is already
an over-inflated ego, eventually getting his hooks into Peter by trapping
him in Hook's own, former apparel. The use of Hook's 'old school
tie', with all its symbolic associations, is particularly effective, ending
up hanging round Peter's neck like a noose, such that, 'however hard
Peter wrenched at the white tie round his throat, he could not slip its
knot' (ibid.: 184). Hook's ploy is reminiscent of the evil queen's in *Snow
White*, where she over-zealously traps the girl within her bodice and
thereby seeks to reduce her to a passive and lifeless thing: the doll-like
toy of patriarchy.

As in Barrie's version, the line between playing and reality is shown
to be perilously thin. There we also saw Peter playing at being captain
after Hook's demise, dressing up in his clothes and crooking his finger in

a hooked manner. Clothes, like manners, maketh the man, as is shown, though this saying might also be read in semiotic terms: signifiers gesture towards particular signifieds, though we wouldn't want to be held captive by any particular association. But this is what Hook attempts with his question about growing-up, effectively seeking to locate the respondent within a particular niche in the Symbolic: to be a signifier for other signifiers. One is reminded of the dæmons that the characters have in Philip Pullman's (2008) *His Dark Materials*. These familiars become fixed at puberty, also fixing the disposition of their owners. Moreover, there is also the disturbing image of castration in Pullman's trilogy, whereby the church tries to sever characters from their dæmons through the process of intercission.[18] McCaughrean has Ravello employ a similar device in his removal of the boys' shadows. As they struggle up Neverpeak mountain, he 'kindly produced a knife and cut loose the Darlings' sticky shadows' (ibid.: 150). Peter resists at this point – '"I keep my shadow!" Peter snarled, stamping on Ravello's blade' (ibid.: 151) – only later to relent:

> 'Do it, then! Be rid of it! It's a nuisance and it weighs me down and I never liked it!'
> In one lithe movement, in one painless motion, with a blade not even visible within the sleeve of his cardigan, Ravello sliced away Peter's shadow. (Ibid.: 163–4)

Once again, as indicated earlier, similar imagery is present in Barrie's work, but one feels in McCaughrean's book that the dangers are more real, for in her reworking the removal of their shadows actually prevents the characters from flying: they have been grounded, rendered more incomplete.[19]

Brilliantly, McCaughrean also suggests that the real cause of Peter's near death experience is not a result of the autumnal state of Neverland following World War I, nor Ravello's interventions, but a bit of London fog, brought in by Wendy, from a cold she had: 'I might have killed Peter, and all for a silly sneeze' (ibid.: 223), as she puts it, which puts us in mind of the flu epidemic that succeeded that war and is estimated to have killed between 20 and 40 million people; that is, more than died in the war itself. In fact, it is thought to be the worst pandemic ever. Molly Billings (2005) appositely quotes a verse sung by children at the time:

> *I had a little bird,*
> *Its name was Enza.*
> *I opened the window,*
> *And in-flu-enza.*

In keeping their windows shut, then, mothers like Mrs Darling were certainly being wise, barring what would more likely have been the deathly intrusion of the skeletally attired Pan.

Conclusion

In this chapter I have offered a reading of Barrie's *Peter Pan* using some Lacanian concepts, which should now also be clearer. I have also shown how this enigmatic imaginary figure continues to haunt us with his annual returns – like some uncanny double of Jesus, of course, who also has some links with Christmas! Peter Pan seems to represent his pagan antithesis, offering a more disturbing version of the hereafter, besides being associated with the heathen theatre and all its illusions, rather than the church. Even his name, as Jack has noted, is, like the Greek god Pan, a hybrid creation: we have 'Peter', with its grounded, religious associations (the rock on which Jesus founded his church), linked to 'Pan', that hirsute, goat-associated (not lamb-linked, like Jesus) hedonist. McCaughrean has certainly managed to keep juggling most of the balls that Barrie first tossed into the air.

Armed with this way of examining texts, which – let me stress again – always recognises that signification will not be curtailed, we will now look more carefully at the register of the Symbolic.

Part II

The Symbolic

3 Holes and Pores: Slipping Between the Cracks of Social Criticism

Having discussed Rose's case about how the figure of Peter Pan, the eternal child, is deployed in children's literature to cover the various ruptures that make us the 'split' subjects of the Symbolic – that is, at how *Peter Pan* figures as an imaginary, idealised being – let me now look more closely at the divisions that exist within the latter, the Symbolic: of gender, race, and so forth. In my Introduction I voiced concern that criticism of children's literature often gave one a sense of déjà vu; and that sometimes children's literature critics adopted tactics reminiscent of the stepsisters in *Cinderella*, trying to shoehorn texts into ill-fitting footwear. I also suggested that, as a result, a rather procrustean reading of a work sometimes emerged, in which the vibrancy of the primary text was hobbled.

Critical readings are always open to this accusation; and, of course, as educationalists (in the broadest sense) we are no doubt keen to turn students into better readers, which usually involves making them more 'critical'. Thus Karin Littau (2006: 115) notes how, in studies of readership, 'resistance is assumed from the start'. Speaking about Janice Radway's study of romance readers in particular, Littau observes how readers were prompted towards adopting more politicised readings. However, as she comments,

> My hunch is that this 'passionate detachment' would destroy these women's pleasure in reading romances ... . Or, to put this differently, the negation in this pleasure is the negation of everything sensible or affective, in favour of alerting the mind to capabilities beyond such enjoyable traps. (Ibid.: 137)

She appositely quotes the feminist writer, Lynne Pearce, on the pleasures of giving oneself up to a book, of being 'off-duty' (ibid.: 140) – and I am sure this is something to which most of us can relate. A number of other professional readers have similarly confessed to illicit enjoyment; for instance, John Bayley (1997: 128) admits that '[p]rimal reading is a thoroughly irresponsible activity', although it 'can persist, and very often does so secretly'. Or, as, Grahame Greene (1969: 13) admitted:

> Of course I should be interested to hear that a new novel by Mr E. M. Forster was going to appear this Spring, but I could never compare that mild expectation of civilized pleasure with the missed heartbeat, the appalled glee I felt when I found on a library shelf a novel by Rider Haggard, Percy Westerman, Captain Brereton or Stanley Weyman which I had not read before.

Finally, here is Ebony Thomas (2009: 80), a black critic and reader, 'coming out' over her affection for L. M. Montgomery:

> Although removed from me by race, ethnicity, nationality, denomination, generation, and time, there is no author so important, no body of work so seminal, and no personal philosophy so integral to the woman and scholar I am becoming – indeed, have become. Maud's timeless words and unforgettable heroines are so much a part of me that I cannot remember a time when I did not narrate my internal biography with anecdotes from their fictional lives.

Bluntly, the question comes down to the following: are we content to expose children to the world of books (adult and children's), as so many of us, as avid young readers, probably were, or do we want to try to control this reading, to try to inoculate children against devouring books indiscriminately and illicitly, though often passionately? This contrast in approach seems to be hinted at even in the titles of our two most seminal introductions to children's literature, both from 1992: Perry Nodelman's *The Pleasures of Children's Literature* (1992b) and John Stephens's *Language and Ideology in Children's Fiction*. Not, of course, that I am inferring anything beyond their respective titles.

My own concern arises after spending much time researching children's responses to the work of popular children's writers often dismissed, such as Roald Dahl (Rudd, 1992, 2012a) and Enid Blyton (Rudd, 2000). Regarding the latter, I spoke candidly about the difficult questions I was then asked, such as, 'Is Blyton bad for you?' The framing of such questions, however, was itself problematic, as I then noted:

In its baldest form it suggests that Blyton deliberately encoded certain unsavoury discourses (racist, classist ideologies) into her texts, which readers then 'decode' and uncritically internalize. Such a view conceives ideology as a 'thing' that 'gets' its audience. Readers are envisaged as being blindly hit by it, such that the simple act of reading the texts is enough to constitute the effect, whether it be the sexism, racism, or whatever. Children are seen to be particularly vulnerable, imbibing ideology before they are rational enough to realise what hit them. (Rudd, 2000: 192)

I then enumerated the problems with this view of ideology:

First, precisely because it sees being rational as the solution; talisman-like, reason is seen to ward off ideology ... rather than itself being ideologically inflected ('reason' as a particularly male, unemotional and abstract pursuit of truth). Second, this model presumes, *a priori*, that certain texts are ideological, whereas others are not; and generally, it is works of popular culture that fit the former bill, whereas 'artistic' works rise above it. However, as has again been argued, this itself is an élitist, ideological construct. Third, this approach sees children as particularly passive and prone to ideology (women less so, men least); in which case, children worldwide, over several generations, have clearly been cultural dopes, choosing to read and re-read texts that, if the official view is to be believed, undermine half of them for their gender, and insult many more for their ethnicity or class. Fourthly though, if children are really so passive and prone, then presumably the effects cannot be too serious, for another text can just as easily come along and send them on a different path. Only an unrelenting diet of Blytons, with no other input (no TV or comics, no education), might then be problematic. (Ibid.: 193–4)

I still subscribe to this view, and question the bizarre notion that 'rational' adults somehow stand outside ideology, somehow immune. The problem is most elegantly expressed by Jean-Paul Sartre, who, in writing about Paul Valéry, stated: 'a petit bourgeois intellectual, no doubt about it', but added: 'not every petit bourgeois intellectual is Valéry' (Sartre, 1963: 56). In other words, there are pleasures in texts that can persist despite (or even because of) their ideological shortcomings.

In order to explain Blyton's immense appeal (which can certainly be disrupted by asking readers to hold fast to their gender, class or colour before entering the building), I turned to works of adult popular appeal that have also, often, confounded strict sociological profiling. *Dirty Harry* (Siegel, 1971) was a case in point, seen as a reactionary, if not a 'fascist' film, but one that was still remarkably popular with minority ethnic groups (Donald, 1992). I also drew on Valerie Walkerdine's experiences of watching *Rocky II* (Stallone, 1979), where she moves from a position of initial revulsion (the video of it was being watched in a working-class home where she was conducting some research, with the father continually replaying his favourite moments). When Walkerdine later watched the film on her own, she confessed: 'No longer did I stand outside the pleasures of engagement with the film. I too wanted Rocky to win. Indeed, I *was* Rocky' (Walkerdine, 1986: 169). The escapism, rather than the violence and sex-stereotyping, prevailed, which allowed her to theorise about why so many black audiences also celebrated Rocky's victory over his black adversary: 'Although it is easy to dismiss such films as macho, stupid and fascist, it is more revealing to see them as fantasies of omnipotence, heroism and salvation' (ibid.: 172; cf. Zipes, 1992: 119–23).

Stephens is certainly conscious of these, more narcissistic readings of texts, but clearly sees them as things to move beyond:

> The implications for subjectivity and for ideology inhere principally at the level of significance [in narratives], as readers move beyond the primary stage of specular recognition of 'story' to the deeper mirrorings of meaning. Here, the reading subject, as in an actual world pragmatic exchange, may negotiate meaning with the text or be subjected by it. (Stephens, 1992: 48)

One text he examines is *Thunderwith* (1989), a popular teen-romance at the time of writing, and one in which the benefits of literacy are stressed. However, Stephens (1992: 49) is critical of the way that the work conceptualises reading in terms of 'idle engagement' – terms similar to Bayley's 'primal' and Pearce's 'off-duty' ways of reading, above. Stephens particularly objects to the way that the works of Tolkien and Susan Cooper are singled out, as though exemplary:

> Now, the books of Tolkien and Cooper are profoundly ideological in their purposes, and reading beyond the primary 'sense' ought to lead to recognition of this. What, for example, should a reader make of a book which implies that the best way to think about the world is to do so from the perspective of a conservative upper-middle class English male? (Ibid.: 49)

It is the 'ought' and the 'should' that I worry about, if not the whole notion that Tolkien's work coheres around his class background (which was, itself, far less elevated, and more complicated; cf. Zipes (1992: 141–59) and Eaglestone's (2005) collection for some useful, alternative stances); that, in short, in reading such fantasy one must thereby align oneself with a particular class and national position – especially given his trilogy's incredible success in such a diversity of cultures (like *Dirty Harry* or *Rocky II*, in fact).

In a later, much quoted paper, Stephens discusses how generic expectations can handicap attempts to rewrite gender scripts. He comments:

> There is a tendency for traditional stories and genres to devolve always back into patriarchal discourse, and as a consequence, as has often been remarked, a female reader may be expected to identify with a [male] selfhood that defines itself in opposition to her; she is required to identify against herself. (Stephens, 1996: 20)

This passage has certainly been 'remarked', for these are actually Judith Fetterley's words (1978: xii), most effectively denoting an identity against her good self! This aside, Stephens seems too readily to envisage a core self that is, in this case, feminine, being effaced by a more masculine one:[1]

> Identification with focalizers is one of the chief methods by which a text socializes its readers, as they efface their own selfhood and internalize the perceptions and attitudes of the focalizer and are thus reconstituted as subjects within the text. (Stephens, 1996: 81)

This stance allows him to read *Five Children and It* (1902), for instance, as expressing the 'explicit and heavy-handed approach of Nesbit' in bringing the child to order: 'the Psammead is a projection of the desire process of socialization, and ... the children themselves are unwittingly benefiting from it. And that assumption is the most superior and condescending of any in the book' (Stephens, 1992: 137, 132).[2]

This is not to argue that any one approach is correct, but I am suggesting a need for more openness; for an approach that avoids finding texts, after being sieved through a particular theoretical grid, as either progressive or reactionary – and I say this in the light of many readers who also read 'otherwise'. To reiterate, then, the work of Stephens and his colleagues (e.g. Bradford et al., 2008) is exemplary in many ways, making us aware of the way that texts operate in technical terms, but I come back to the problem that I mentioned earlier: that Valéry always seems to end up as the petit bourgeois, just as Tolkien is reduced to being a 'conservative upper-middle class English male'.

This evaluative approach is also to be found in Zipes's work at times, where he envisions 'us' – that is, adult children's literature critics – functioning in a manner similar to Lenin's vanguard party. We are the so-called 'proletarians of the university' who, 'working from marginalized positions ... take the side of the powerless, the children, to speak for them, to include them, and to fight for their rights ... to improve the manner in which we acculturate children' (Zipes, 2001: 73). Not only does the class parallel seem inappropriate, but the whole notion that 'we' are the enlightened ones is worrying.[3] Here, for example, is Robert Moore (1978: 34), writing slightly earlier, and again, with the best of intentions, I am sure:

> Fairy tales … reinforce unhealthy and destructive images for the reader. It is not enough to dismiss these negative elements as reflections of the times …. Concerned parents and educators should work to liberate homes and schools from such potentially destructive materials and to provide children with more progressive and equally enjoyable fare.

Had Moore's wish been granted (it resonates with Kohl's view of Babar, above), Zipes might have found his own readership significantly reduced!

I now want to turn to two more extended examples where I feel that texts have been closed down rather than opened up. Firstly I will examine Daphne Kutzer's reading of Milne's 'Pooh' stories, following which I will examine a more recent classic, Louis Sachar's *Holes*, this time offering a more Lacanian reading, before contrasting my interpretation with that of two other critics.

Empire vs 'fanpire' fiction

In *Empire Fiction*, Kutzer claims that 'whereas adult fiction may … question the reigning cultural code of behavior, children's fiction rarely does so'. It is more about acculturating children, being 'highly conservative, interested in preserving the past rather than in preparing children for a realistic adult future' (2000: xv). It is Kutzer's final statement that I will begin with, for she seems to suggest that 'preparing children for a realistic adult future' is somehow progressive, when, for many, this sort of preparation is seen in negative terms, being associated with a crass utilitarianism, whereby children are primed for their future roles, whether in the economy, in the class system or as appropriately gendered subjects. From this viewpoint, fantastic writings are to be shunned as distractions, if not overtly dangerous (as Galbraith also viewed them, see p. 36). The Romantics, who were generally in favour of the fairy tale and chapbook traditions, were therefore very critical of such realistic approaches, which they laid at the feet of that 'cursed Barbauld crew', as Charles Lamb famously called them in a letter to Coleridge in 1802, after looking unsuccessfully in a bookshop for traditional tales.

In practice, though, the division between these two modes, the realistic and the fantastic, was never so simple, for the language and tropes of the one (the Romantics) always interfused the other (the utilitarians).[4] Such textual dialogism seems to me to be equally the case with 'empire fiction', which cannot be characterised as intrinsically conservative any more than it is straightforwardly 'realistic'. This is why I have somewhat frivolously coined the neologism, 'fanpire' fiction, to suggest, rather than the 'empirical' connotations of the word empire, the presence of a 'fantasy' element, but one that also infects these writings of empire in a vampiric manner. So, whereas Kutzer claims that '[t]he arcadian paradise of children's fiction provides an imaginative space where social and cultural disruption is not only impossible, it is barely acknowledged' (ibid.: xvi), I find the possibility of disruption ever present – though not necessarily acted upon (cf. Zipes, 1987; Auerbach and Knoepflmacher, 1992).

I thus want to argue against Kutzer's presumption that children are 'colonized by the books they read' (ibid.: xvi), despite this long being the utilitarian's dream (once again, it is there in Rose's claim about children's fiction aiming to 'unashamedly ... take the child *in*' (1984: 2), though she recognizes that it does not necessarily succeed). Moreover, it is not just that Kutzer sees children as 'colonized' but, in line with Edward Said's view of those so labelled (expressed in *Orientalism*, 1978), they are also seen to be passive recipients of the process: 'Just as colonial subjects were voiceless – their lives are described for us by Westerners, not by themselves – children are also voiceless, depending upon adults to describe their lives for them' (Kutzer, 2000: xvi).[5] This is similar to how Said talks about the Orient being an 'Other' that we, in the West, have created for our own purposes, producing a generally stereotypical and derogatory view of the East. However, as others have pointed out, there are problems with this stance. First, it clearly does render the Orient passive, as claimed above, unable to speak for itself, and thus ironically disavows the views of those that *have* written from an Eastern perspective. Second, it touches on an intransigent, epistemological problem about how we might ever talk about a more *authentic* Orient if we only have Western definitions to go on. In other words, where can Said stand in order to claim that the Western notion of the Orient is wrong? Where might there be more reliable evidence, and how might this knowledge be mediated to Western minds?

A more poststructuralist approach seems helpful at this point. First, it recognises and accepts an epistemological relativism (there is no, one, authentic version of anything, only partial ones – and they are decidedly plural and always dynamic). Second, it rejects the hierarchical divide between coloniser and colonised; that is, the West is not seen as standing imperiously aloof, creating its Other; rather, its very identity not only depends upon the Other, on that which it is not (uncivilised, primitive, superstitious, etc.), but is ineluctably linked to it. Empire, in other words, is always tainted (or made complete, whole) by fantasy. Always more than a geographical or administrative area, empire exists as what Benedict Anderson (1991) terms an 'imagined community', believing itself imperious, invincible, benevolent, an island entire unto itself, yet forever compromised, forever in need of shoring up these convictions through fantasy. The parasitic relationship that the term 'fanpire' expresses, then, whereby the colonisers always worry that they might be contaminated by the colonised, that their identity might somehow be in danger of being leeched away, is thereby productive.[6]

My model, then, is based more on the insights of such critics as Bakhtin, Derrida and Homi Bhabha (1994) who, albeit from very different perspectives, argue that communication is itself always open to derailment; therefore colonisation can never (ideologically speaking) be taken as read; or, in Bakhtin's terms, language can never be monological: it is always excessive, always opening up onto a more disturbing dialogism. So there will only ever be *versions* of the Orient, or indeed of the child, as of anything else. But to construct either the Orient or the child as thereby 'voiceless' is precisely to sidestep this ongoing negotiation of meaning; implicitly, it is an acceptance of the coloniser's grand narrative, whereby power inheres at the centre and the margin is impotent. In contrast, I am suggesting that both the Orient and the child can – and do – write back; or, to change metaphors, can read against the colonising grain. The text itself, 'neither living nor nonliving', as Derrida puts it (see Note 6), playing up these vampiric associations, then becomes temporarily inhabited by the reader, who feeds off its juices, making them his or her own.

Before I finally turn to the Pooh books, however, I want to point to what seems a particularly significant omission from Kutzer's historical analysis: Carroll's *Alice* books (1865/71). Somehow these have been steered around, with Kutzer moving straight from Ballantyne's *The Coral Island* (1858) to Kipling's work. This omission occurs despite such critical works as, for example, Daniel Bivona's, arguing that *Alice* is surely 'the most impressive comic critique of British ethnocentrism in the age of imperialism' (1990: 71), where the Victorian child repeatedly confronts otherness, yet makes little attempt to understand it on its own terms. Instead, Bivona argues, Alice tries to make Wonderland fit her own cultural paradigm. Thus she presumes that the 'natives' don't know how to play croquet properly, rather than considering that they might simply play it differently. With the caterpillar, Alice also tries to impose her normality, presuming that metamorphosis is unacceptable, that to be three inches high is to be vertically challenged, and so on. Generally Alice acts like the worst sort of imperialist, barging in where she isn't invited:

> 'How am I to get in?' asked Alice again, in a louder tone.
> 'Are you to get in at all?' said the Footman. 'That's the first question, you know.' (Carroll, 1970: 50)

And, at the tea-party, she berates the March Hare for not being civil in offering wine when there isn't any, to which he retorts, 'It wasn't very civil of you to sit down without being invited' (ibid.: 57). At the end, Alice's sister takes this process a step further, making Alice's narrative more mundane and explicable in terms of an English pastoral frame of reference. To quote Bivona (1990: 72):

> Alice's sister can be held responsible for the generations of bowdlerized readings of *Alice*, readings which emphasize how 'wonderful' were Alice's adventures, ultimately responsible, in effect, for encouraging the cultural marginalization of *Alice* as 'delightful children's literature'.

I will challenge this viewpoint later (Chapter 5), when I offer a rather different interpretation of *Alice*, but my point here is that I think Kutzer's choice of texts has its own impositions, if not a certain imperiousness.

The purloined Pooh: imperialism in the 100 Acre Wood

Let me now consider Milne's Pooh books, which Kutzer regards from the outset as disempowering for the child, given the narratorial stance:

> Milne undercuts Christopher Robin's power in these books. Yes, they are Christopher's toys, and the stories are presented as products of Christopher's playful nursery imagination, but in important ways, they are not Christopher's inventions at all, but Milne's. Milne is literally the creator of these stories, of course, but beyond that he inserts his adult voice and adult control over both the fantasy lives of the animals and the imaginative life of his son. (2000: 95)

We might respond to this by arguing that Milne's narrative technique is actually quite ingenuous in that he makes it plain that it is an adult telling these tales. Thus, in response to Kutzer's claim that 'Christopher Robin has been colonized by the adult narrator. He is not free to tell his own stories,

or to have the starring role in them' (ibid.: 96), we might ask in what sense
this storybook character could be more liberated: by having the stories
feature Christopher Robin more prominently, by having him narrate them
in the first person? Wouldn't this, in fact, make the fictions more of a 'soliciting … chase, or seduction', as Rose (1984: 2) terms it, concealing the adult
writer – Nodelman's 'hidden adult' – from the child reader?

Kutzer also makes the claim that:

> Milne asserts his narrative power … not only over Christopher Robin, but
> also over the reader, telling the reader what the reader is thinking and is
> going to say, denying the child reader a question of his/her own. (2000: 96)

Here Kutzer extends the narrator's control beyond Christopher Robin –
who is described as being 'as colonized and voiceless as any native in
India or Africa' (ibid.) – to the child reader, who is represented as a
singular entity, rather than a collection of people as varied as are adults,
comprising different ages, backgrounds and competences. Contra Kutzer,
I would suggest that, rather than narratorial control, the beginning of
Milne's text expresses the very opposite. The different 'I's and other
deictic shifters make the opening of his book one of the most complex
for any child to process. If anything, it seems that Milne's work displays a
sense of insecurity, as Barbara Wall (1991: 180–4) also contends: a certain
embarrassment about a grown-man talking to children.

The first volume opens with Pooh coming down the stairs, 'bump,
bump, bump', before we are told that he is 'ready to be introduced
to you' (Milne, 1965: 1), meaning us, the readers. In the next line, the
narrator speaks in the first person: 'When I first heard his name, I said,
just as you are going to say, "But I thought he was a boy?"' (ibid.). The
first two 'I's in this sentence refer to the narrator, but the third is meant
to be a question that the implied reader might ask, which then becomes
a different 'I' – 'So did I' – in the following line, this first person being
Christopher Robin. On the next page, a fourth 'I' is added, as 'a growly
voice' says, 'Now I am' (ibid.: 3). From this point on, Christopher Robin's
textual interjections are placed in parenthesis, in italics, but it is still very
complex and certainly confounds any notions of language transparently
telling the story. Once again, in this text language actively participates,
demanding to be taken notice of – often literally, as in such signs as the
one declaring that Pooh lives 'under the name of Sanders' (ibid.: 2), a sign
that we see him dutifully sitting beneath, or with the 'Trespassers W' sign
outside Piglet's house, which Piglet assumes must relate to his ancestor,
'Trespassers William'. Tying signs to their referents is a perennial

problem in the Pooh books: the relation of names to things, which can shift with alacrity. Apart from the confusion of Pooh living under this other name (Sanders), he is also simply 'Edward Bear' at the outset, who, we are informed, adopted the name of a swan: 'we took the name with us as we didn't think the swan would want it any more' (ibid.: ix), playing on the standard notion of 'taking' someone's name. He is then given another name, 'Winnie', from a zoo bear – although it is stressed that this must not be used on its own, as Pooh is male, hence he is 'Winnie-*ther*-Pooh', '*ther*' remaining unexplained. Indeed, we are summarily informed that this 'is all the explanation [we] are going to get' (ibid.: 1). However, only a few pages later, after the introduction of 'Sanders', we observe Pooh blow a fly off his nose, and are proffered another explanation of his name: 'And I think ... that *that* is why he was always called Pooh' (ibid.: 17).

Without elaborating further, the point should be clear that Milne is playing with the conventions of language, with the way that signs represent things (as with the North Pole and Heffalumps, too), showing language's slippage in the way that these things do not stay in place (again, confounding Rose's claims about the transparency of language in children's literature). And this is reinforced by other qualities of the tales, such as the use of upper-case letters, the parapraxes, the neologisms, the unorthodox graphology, the misspellings and the sound-driven 'hums'. Rather than being the all-powerful coloniser, then, Milne (or the narrator) appears to be remarkably 'uneasy and tentative', as Wall (1991: 181) expresses it. For me, then, Milne seems to be troubled by this relationship, unsure as to where he stands in relation to the child and to language.

This uneasiness would seem to explain Milne's difficulty in figuring Christopher Robin, in making him something more than another stuffed toy with a set role to play. Kutzer, however, makes a different move. Having said that Christopher Robin is 'as colonized and voiceless as any native in India or Africa' (2000: 96), she then argues that he 'morphs from colonized to colonizer' (ibid.: 98) over his own animal kingdom (she persists in calling them 'animals' rather than stuffed toys). And this 'play ... prepares him for the adult role of imperial ruler of children or of child-like colonial subjects' (ibid.). This is quite a shift for a character earlier referred to as the mere puppet of the narrator, as someone who does not even know what is going on (Kutzer earlier wrote that Christopher 'himself does not remember the stories: they are not his stories, but an adult's stories' (ibid.: 96), though this is true of almost all children's literature, of course). However, it is also an essential move if Kutzer is to make a case for Christopher Robin being a putative imperialist.

In order to argue that he is doing little more than making up games
with his toy animals – which are really the father's imaginative bedtime
stories told to his son about Christopher's toys – Kutzer needs to show
that some of the animals represent the colonies (for some reason, Kutzer
uses the ambiguous term 'imperial animal' here (ibid.: 99), which would
more logically suggest the British bulldog or, perhaps, the British Lion, a
creature that would be even more complex to deal with!). She thus makes
several interesting moves in the course of her argument:

> Empire, by the twenties, no longer presents the possibility for high
> adventure and heroic deeds: empire has been literally domesticated into
> nursery toys, stuffed tigers and kangaroos and elephants. The real world
> might be increasingly anxious about the state of empire, but in children's
> books we get the comforting image of an empire totally tamed .... We are
> a long way from Ballantyne's *The Coral Island*. (Ibid.)

This statement, unfortunately, is simply incorrect. Kutzer seems
unaware of the prolific work of other writers of this period. Aside from
the countless ephemeral characters from the comics, serious writers of
empire were thriving, as recorded by Graham Greene earlier, plus the
likes of John Buchan, Anthony Hope, Herbert Strang, P. C. Wren and
the very influential creation of Captain W. E. Johns, 'Biggles' (written
between the 1930s and 1960s). Johns claimed to 'teach a boy to be a man
... teach sportsmanship according to the British idea ... decent behaviour,
team work, loyalty to the Crown, the Empire and ... rightful authority'
(quoted in Trease, 1964: 80).[7] Perhaps one of the most telling comments
on Johns's work, though, comes from a compulsive reader who had what
Kutzer likes to term 'direct experience with empire' the Kenyan writer
Ngugi Wa Thiong'o (1992), who only later realised his contradictory
position; namely, that his elder brother was in the Mau Mau, fighting
to oust the British while he was enjoying the exploits of Biggles, seeking
to overcome just such insurrectionists. Further evidence, if needed, of
the persistence of undomesticated 'high adventure and heroic deeds', is
paraded in Orwell's famous essay, 'Boys' Weeklies', in which he bemoans
the fact that 'boys' fiction' (and comics especially) was still, in 1940,
'sodden in the worst illusions of 1910' (Orwell, 1957: 203).

Leaving aside this question of the domestication of empire, though,
what of Kutzer's claim that the empire is explicitly represented in the Pooh
books by 'stuffed tigers and kangaroos and elephants'? Tigger, she tells us,
'is a tiger, the emblem of India', and is altogether too bouncy, or 'uncon-
trollable' and 'upsetting', suggesting 'wildness' and having 'potential[ly]

life-threatening qualities' (Kutzer, 2000: 99). He is also 'childlike' and capable of 'disruption' (99–100), all of which are qualities that link him to India. Therefore, Kutzer claims, he 'must be domesticated through the ministrations of Kanga, the only one of the animals who behaves, always, like an adult' (ibid.: 100). This claim, again, is contentious, with Peter Hunt nominating others, 'Owl, Rabbit, and Eeyore', for 'the grown-up world' (Hunt, 1994: 112), and Anita Wilson (1985: 168) limiting the grown-ups to 'Rabbit and Owl' (though I, personally, would also add Kanga). Kutzer then makes the claim that Tigger's going to stay with Kanga is equivalent to convicts being 'sent … to Australia in the hopes they might repent' (2000: 100). Kanga, it seems, represents the more remediable side of empire. (Of course, the real problem that Britain exported to Australia was not the tiger, but the rabbit – an issue that is addressed in postcolonial terms in John Marsden and Shaun Tan's *The Rabbits* (2008) – but one that would over-complicate Kutzer's narrative.)

However that may be, let me go on to consider the Heffalump, which Kutzer terms the 'third invisible imperial animal' (ibid.: 99). Clearly, if it is anything, it can only be the *first* invisible imperial animal; the others, contentious as they might be, are certainly *visible*. She goes on to describe the Heffalump as a 'stuffed' animal. I have already suggested that it is problematic to speak of any of these toys as 'stuffed animals' (we are not dealing with taxidermy here), but it seems even more peculiar to call a non-existent beast 'stuffed' (the others do actually exist as stuffed toys, now housed in New York Public Library). The Heffalump's existence is surely as tenuous as the Woozle's (which we might, according to Kutzer's logic, interpret as a kind of 'weasel', perhaps inspired by the villains of Milne's favourite book, *The Wind in the Willows*). On the other hand, I can see that the word 'stuffed' clearly suits her argument, allowing Kutzer to claim that, '[a]s stuffed animals, kangaroo, tiger, and elephant suggest that the wild natives of the colonies have been fully domesticated and de-clawed' (ibid.). (I have left aside the other move Kutzer makes here, which is to claim that the Heffalump is, unproblematically, an *African* elephant, hence 'an emblem for Africa' (ibid.: 101).)[8]

But even if we were to accept Kutzer's reasoning, that the characters are indeed imperial animals, another problem persists: the omission of Pooh. It is no good seeing the others as wild animals that 'have been fully domesticated and de-clawed' without seeing Pooh in the same way. But he is not: he is described as 'more teddy bear than grizzly'. Why is the logic reversed for him? Kutzer argues that, rather than *being* a 'wild animal', Pooh simply 'keeps company with wild animals (Kanga and Roo,

Tigger, Rabbit, and Owl) and with domestic animals (Piglet and Eeyore)'
(ibid.: 98). For Kutzer, then, Pooh remains, perennially, a stuffed toy – a
teddy bear – whereas the others, even the non-existent Heffalump, have
to shift from an initial state of being actual wild animals into this stuffed,
de-clawed existence. This is despite the fact that Pooh's 'feral' pedigree is,
if anything, the most sound: he is named after two wild animals, a swan
and a brown, furry bear from London Zoo, the latter having originated in
the colonies (in Canada, in fact). But with this move, at one stroke Kutzer
circumvents the most obvious flaw in her argument; namely that the bear
itself is not indigenous to England, is not a domesticated animal and could,
thereby, undo the logic of her case. For instance, when Kutzer claims that
'Pooh's greed … suggests the greed of imperial powers' (ibid.: 101), we
could instead read him as a worrying, savage other (cf. Nelson, 1990), who
is driven by bodily appetites rather than his mental faculties. Moreover, if
we choose to read food as a metaphor for sex, as many suggest we might,
Pooh could be seen as sexually voracious. Indeed, moving into 'Pooh
Perplex' territory (Crews, 1964), his obsession with getting his head stuck
in jars of 'hunny' could take on completely different connotations; we
could read this Canadian bear, like the Americans, as both oversexed and
over here! He is even someone that the xenophobic Rabbit would rather
not be 'at home' to meet.

Kutzer's whole analysis therefore seems overly contrived to me. The
'Pooh' books appear very far from being imperial texts; if anything, written
by the pacifist Milne, they address the opposite; they are about inclusion,
about different beings living together in relative harmony. After all, it is
not Tigger that *is* finally unbounced, or 'de-clawed'; rather, it is Rabbit
who comes to realise the error of his ways, learning tolerance:

> Tigger was tearing round the Forest making loud yapping noises for
> Rabbit. And at last a very Small and Sorry Rabbit heard him. And the Small
> and Sorry Rabbit rushed through the mist at the noise, and it suddenly
> turned into Tigger; a Friendly Tigger, a Grand Tigger, a Large and Helpful
> Tigger, a Tigger who bounced … in just the beautiful way a Tigger ought
> to bounce.
> 'Oh, Tigger, I *am* glad to see you,' cried Rabbit. (Milne, 1965: 123–4)

There are undoubtedly signifiers in the stories that suggest imperial
themes, but to shut them down to this univocal reading seems dubious.
'Tiger', after all, aside from signifying India, also signifies energy,
unbounded, uncontainable power, as represented in William Blake's
poem, 'The Tyger'. The figure of the lion (not in the Milne texts, of course)

is likewise a rich signifier, showing what Vološinov (1973) termed the 'multiaccentuality' of the sign. Clearly we would agree that the lion has strong African associations (used effectively in *The Lion King*), but could not deny its equally strong associations with the British Empire.[9]

Leaving aside the fact that I disagree with much of Kutzer's interpretation, it is the procrustean (or 'procrustimoney' perhaps) nature of such readings that is my real concern: trimming the Pooh books into little manuals of imperialism. My contention, as I have articulated earlier, is that she has '**quilted**' these texts in a particular way, constraining other 'lines of flight'.[10] Shifting to a Bakhtinian frame, it is an attempt to impose a monological or univocal meaning, whereas the language of these texts is already excessive (as has been openly paraded, above), derailing any attempts at a straightforward promulgation of empire or, indeed, colonisation of the child.

I am of course aware that I am talking about reading these texts from another adult stance only. What actual readers make of these works is a different matter. All that we can safely assert is that the readings are likely to be more diverse than those of adult critics, given that children are relatively inexperienced in using language and are, therefore, more likely to engage in what might be termed mis-readings. This process is itself figured in many children's fictional texts, where the answering words of readers are anticipated and sometimes made fun of; just so, 'customary procedure' becomes 'Crustimoney Proseedcake' (Milne, 1965: 45). The writer can either be seen as knowing and superior, or as more anxious and ambivalent about his or her possible reception; but he or she cannot control it. A writer's meaning is always subject to appropriation, to the parasitic action of the textual vampire, the fanpire: the reader who suckles on this 'neither living nor dead' matter, appropriating it for her or his own use whilst also being used by it, being its carrier. With this image in mind, let me move on to a more recent 'classic' text, one that seems more aware of how this process of signification works and how meanings shift in the process.

(W)Holed[11]

Louis Sachar's *Holes* is a novel where, more than most, we seem to move from a state of lack (being full of 'holes') to a state of knowledge or fulfilment (being a 'whole'). It is also a text that demonstrates the problem Freud and Breuer originally identified in hysterics: that they 'suffer mainly from reminiscences' (Freud, 1955: 58), an insight that Freud was later to develop in his paper 'Remembering, Repeating and Working Through' (1977b). Here Freud argues that individuals can become trapped in compulsive, repetitive patterns that stop them remembering properly, such that they cannot move on. For transference to be successful, then, a place (or space) has to be found where this blockage can be removed; Freud describes this place/space as 'a playground in which it is expected to display ... everything' (ibid.: 154) – which, I shall suggest, is what both the characters and the readers of this novel experience.

It is not, then, for nothing that the young Stanley Yelnats is Stanley Yelnats IV, for the whole family is trapped at a point back in their history, with Stanley compulsively repeating the mantra that 'his no-good-dirty-rotten-pig-stealing-great-great-grandfather' (Sachar, 2000: 7) is responsible for his sense of failure. The fact that Stanley's name is a palindrome reinforces this: he seems to be in stasis: he ain't going anywhere. Stanley's symbolic chain fetters him to a fate that seems destined to have him, and his progeny (a possible Yelnats V), forever going round in circles (and there are also hints of Dante's *Inferno* here, with the mindless hole-digging that the correction camp inmates have to endure). As both Stanley and the family in general put it: 'They always seemed to be in the wrong place at the wrong time' (ibid.: 8). The symbolic nature of their chains – the way they 'quilt' the Yelnats's family's reality[12] – is shown early on to be out of touch with Stanley's existence, such that he is not even properly aware of his own body image, hence his being bullied by a smaller child. Stanley acts simply as a functionary of the Symbolic. In Althusser's terms, this is how he has been interpellated, or 'hailed', and he accepts his lot.

All this is to change, though, with what Lacan terms an eruption of the Real. As noted elsewhere, the Real is the brute stuff of the universe: that which is not symbolised, therefore that which we cannot comprehend. However, there are times when our benign symbolic world is shattered, often when we are, precisely, rendered speechless. Such a moment occurs for Stanley when Clyde Livingston's trainers come crashing out of the sky and hit him on the head, disrupting his universe and resulting in him being relabelled a criminal (one of Lacan's own examples is, precisely, being hit on the head by something falling from the sky; in this case, a roof tile (Bowie, 1991: 103)). This event causes Stanley to confront his symbolic position, seemingly for the first time; he turns around and asks the famous Lacanian question – now often more associated with Žižek: *Che vuoi?*, 'What do you want with me?', or, as Žižek glosses it elsewhere: 'Why am I what I'm supposed to be, why have I this mandate?' (1994: 113).

Camp Green Lake turns out to be an excellent place for Stanley to be sent to, for it intensifies his realisation that the Symbolic is flawed, or porous: it consists of empty signifiers, holes. As Morpheus was to express it more famously in *The Matrix* (1999), 'Welcome to the desert of the real!' (which itself became the title of Žižek's 2002 essay on 9/11).[13] The props of Stanley's prior, mundane existence are absent in this place that belies its very name: not green, no lake. But the same is true of Stanley: he bears a name that has little to do with him, that also reaches back 100 years, to Stanley Yelnats I (who, obviously, needed no such enumeration). From the start, Stanley is made to query what things signify. 'Be careful,' the bus driver warns him, and Stanley wonders whether he means 'going down the steps' or just 'be careful at Camp Green Lake' (Sachar, 2000: 11). Stanley encounters a man who wears 'sunglasses and a cowboy hat' even when he's inside, who has a name that is no name: 'Mr. Sir' (ibid.: 12). It is simply two honorifics that, in emphasising the character's masculinity, simultaneously render it ironic and excessive.

Another member of staff, Mr. Pendanski, is more anxious to sustain the existing symbolic order, planning to have everyone use 'the names their parents gave them – the names that *society will recognize them by* when they return to become useful and hardworking members of society' (ibid.: 18–19). But he is thwarted. It is precisely this order that is being rejected, giving the campers a chance not to be enslaved, or cursed, by their history. Thus they all have nicknames (and it is ironic that Pendanski himself, a staunch believer in patronyms, is emasculated by being nicknamed 'Mom'). The inmates' new names are less arbitrary, more related to their current situation and to some attribute of the person (seemingly more situated in the Real but, in actuality, being metonyms of some sort). So the inmates become very annoyed when hailed by their traditional names, as Stanley learns early on: 'Theodore whirled and grabbed Stanley by his collar. "My name's not Thee-o-dore," he said. "It's Armpit." He threw Stanley to the ground' (ibid.: 20).

Stanley's name seems the most arbitrary, being most obviously a signifier for other signifiers, in Lacanian terms. In other words, he is named so because the Yelnats sons have, down the line, been so named. Pushed on this, it is said that '[e]veryone in his family had always liked the fact that "Stanley Yelnats" was spelled the same frontward and backward' (ibid.: 9). Stanley's very being, in short, is seen to be determined by nothing but a happenstance-like arrangement of letters. His new name, 'Caveman', though, suggests that he is, indeed, a man (rather than a boy); and that he is not simply a name but someone with a body, someone with a physical presence (Reynolds, 2002). The name 'Caveman' also conjures up notions of a pre-symbolic or pre-linguistic existence – of an attempt to get at the Real (which is apparent throughout, with the emphasis on the physicality of things: the senses, the smells, the thirst and pain) – while simultaneously pointing to the impossibility of finding any essence in a mere name (a cave is nothing but a hollow space, of course, although it can be filled with all manner of things; moreover, as we have seen with Plato's allegory, it is also a place of illusion that one must learn to see through).

It is not only the inmates' names that are confounded here, though; the whole place is unpredictable according to traditional notions of signification: 'Stanley took a shower – if you could call it that, ate dinner – if you could call it that, and went to bed – if you could call his smelly and scratchy cot a bed' (Sachar, 2000: 21). Then there's 'the rec room', which turns out to be the 'WRECK ROOM', as '[n]early everything in the room was broken; the TV, the pinball machine, the furniture' (ibid.: 43); and we shouldn't forget the lizards:

> … it is kind of odd that scientists named the lizard after its yellow spots. Each lizard has exactly eleven yellow spots, but the spots are hard to see. … The lizard … has big red eyes. In truth, its eyes are yellow, and it is the skin around the eyes which is red, but everyone speaks of its red eyes. It also has black teeth and a milky white tongue.
>
> Looking at one, you would have thought that it should have been named a 'red-eyed' lizard, or a 'black-toothed' lizard, or perhaps a 'white-tongued' lizard. (Ibid.: 41)

It is in the camp that Stanley has a chance to avoid being just a number in a series – that is, part of the succession of Yelnatses differentiated only by Roman numerals. This is where plot becomes important. As Peter Brooks (1984: 27) notes, plot is 'the active interpretive work of discourse on story', tying events together, giving them some sort of patterning or repetition: of showing how earlier events become meaningful when tied to later ones. Narrative, then, in its repetitive way, is concerned with a 'a going over again of a ground already covered' (ibid.: 97) – which is exactly what Stanley is forced to do, both digging and filling in holes – thus addressing his position in the Symbolic. Before this, Stanley seems never to have questioned his existence, whether in relation to his bullying or having no friends. He is like a robot, a complete functionary of the Symbolic, whereas, as Lacan notes, we are split subjects, existing between the Symbolic, the Real and the Imaginary orders, and not singularly located within any of these. We therefore don't quite fit (there is a hole, or lack, at the centre of our existence). The intrusion of the Real via the trainers, though, shifts Stanley's perception (he starts 'looking awry', as Žižek 1992b would say), and the process of dialectising the signifier, that is, of trying to personalise the Otherness of the Symbolic, achieving some sort of narrative coherence (as in transference), begins.

Stanley engages with plot (and with plots of land, come to that) – plot being, of course, about repetition, as noted earlier – but not in the compulsive way he has repeated family myths up to now. Suddenly Stanley has the chance to work properly through the events of the past – 'Remembering, Repeating and Working Through', as Freud put it – and thus move the whole family out of its rut. Just as Stanley reads the landscape, in '*anticipation of retrospection*', to quote Brooks (1984: 22–3), so 'we read in a spirit of confidence, and also a state of dependence, that what remains to be read will restructure the provisional meanings of the already read'.

As noted above, part of Stanley's problem comes precisely from the fact that he exists as just one of a series of Roman numerals, which are very unwieldy and unproductive: they get longer and longer, but are very difficult to do anything computational with. To do more, you need a zero – which functions as a place-holder, allowing patterns to emerge. The character Zero, then, is immediately of interest to Stanley, not just because the person's name is associated with nothingness (and therefore with the holes that feature throughout the text), but also with the fact that zero is the most versatile of numbers, providing 'a glimpse of the ineffable and the infinite', as Charles Seife (2000: 3) puts it, adding, 'through all its history, despite the rejection and the exile, zero has always defeated those who opposed it'. Robert Kaplan (2000: 66) also comments on the bad press that the number zero has received: 'criminals were the zeroes of society: we still call our losers zeroes', and it is particularly fitting that Hector Zero is the most marginal character in the book, having grown up almost completely at odds with the Symbolic: with no official papers, illiterate, unschooled, father unknown, mother missing.

In Lacanian terms, this means that Zero does not possess the traditional masculine structure; that is, he is not totally subsumed within the symbolic order, alienated by language; rather, he fits more the feminine position (it is noteworthy that it is Zero's *female* ancestry that is continually emphasised, not his male line at all). Zero's position is therefore one that points to the lack in the Other, allowing the individual 'to step beyond the boundaries set by language' and show 'that the signifier isn't everything' (Fink, 1995: 107); in other words, Zero points up the holes (in some ways, like Peter Pan, Zero seems to 'ex-sist': see p. 47. Zero is also the instigator of the plot, whereas Stanley is unaware even that there is one until this time (he discovers this retrospectively), just as Madame Zeroni earlier instigated Elya Yelnats's story. Thanks to Zero, the magical coincidences 'multiply' as isolated parts of the puzzle start to come together. From a lack of signification we henceforth move towards an excess.

Zero and Stanley are thus both prime candidates to undertake what Žižek, after Lacan, terms 'the act', that which 'restructures the very symbolic co-ordinates of the agent's situation: it is an intervention in the course of which the agent's identity itself is radically changed' (Žižek, 2001: 85). Zero's act occurs when he smacks Pendanski in the face with a shovel; then Stanley's shortly thereafter when he steals and wrecks the water truck (no matter that both are ultimately futile gestures: they mark a turning point). The two of them then journey to God's thumb, which, as others have noted, is overtly phallic (e.g. Wannamaker, 2006). But it is also an example of the Lacanian Thing, something that is beyond the limits of the possible with its uphill-travelling water. Bruce Fink helpfully traces the 'Thing' back to its Freudian roots, noting its close relation to the sublime, to notions of 'God'. As Fink informs us, 'the *finding* of the signifier must be understood as an encounter ... , that is, as fortuitous in some sense' (Fink, 1995: 115).

Lacan also notes that when objects are sublimated in this way, there is a sense of transcending death – which Stanley and Zero certainly experience, both personally and in the way that they are seen to be 'between two deaths' (Lacan, 1959/60). That is, their respective ancestors, though physically dead (in the Real), live on in the Symbolic, waiting to be finally laid to rest in order that the living, too, can move on. So, in properly working through their situation – or, in the terms I introduced earlier, in *remembering* with the proper affect, rather than compulsively *repeating* family myths – curses can be lifted.

Using Lacan's vocabulary, this act results in Stanley '**traversing the fantasy**', such that reality comes to be seen afresh, as the holed landscape of Camp Green Lake most certainly is. Stanley thus subjectifies his Otherness; that is, he takes responsibility for his place in the Symbolic: 'He couldn't blame his no-good-dirty-rotten-pig-stealing-great-great-grandfather this time. This time it was his own fault, one hundred percent' (Sachar, 2000: 148). Interestingly, this recognition of his position is not announced overtly, in what Lacan (1988: 246) would call '**empty** speech' (Stanley has just pinched the water truck and driven it into a hole); rather, it is conveyed in terms of free indirect discourse, suggesting a more thoughtful transference from speaker to reader.

This shift is also eloquently demonstrated in the verse of an old song that the Yelnats family recites. 'If only, if only' is its refrain – a song about longing and regret (or lack), featuring a wolf howling pointlessly at the moon:

> 'If only, if only,' the woodpecker sighs,
> 'The bark on the tree was just a little bit softer.'
> While the wolf waits below, hungry and lonely,
> He cries to the moo-oo-oon,
> 'If only, if only.' (Sachar, 2000: 8)

The tough bark suggests an initial resistance, just as Stanley experiences when he first starts digging his holes, trying to get beneath the hard crust. At the very end of the novel, the ensuing verse is sung by Zero's mother (someone even more marginalised in the Symbolic, but who, at this point, manages to speak – indeed, she has the last word):

> If only, if only, the moon speaks no reply;
> Reflecting the sun and all that's gone by.
> Be strong my weary wolf, turn around boldly.
> Fly high, my baby bird,
> My angel, my only. (ibid.: 233)

She points to the error of addressing the moon – itself, of course, only reflecting the sun's light (a bit like passing on information second-hand, or seeing your image as the real 'you'). The wolf is thus shown to have been trapped by an image of 'all that's gone by' (as has the Yelnats family) and is advised to 'turn around boldly' – which is precisely what Stanley has done through his 'act' (significantly undertaken in a place that has no mirrors – apart from the one that the Warden has, and she, also like her ancestors, is shown to be equally trapped in an imaginary past).

The excess of coincidences at the end of this novel has effectively shaken up the symbolic order, giving the reader a sense that things can be otherwise. It also means that the buck is passed back to us: 'You will have to fill in the holes yourself' (ibid.: 231), we are told. What is particularly apparent is that Stanley is not asserted as a sovereign 'I' at the end; rather, we have Stanley and Zero, an interdependent duo, with no discrimination in terms of colour – or indeed, gender.

I mention these two, seemingly unconnected points because my reading differs in these respects from two other critics, Karen Coats (2004) and Annette

Wannamaker (2006). Taking gender first, Wannamaker (2006: 29–30) argues that masculinity is championed at the expense of the feminine, with Camp Green Lake itself being a feminine wasteland consisting of 'holes and dried up lake, ruled over by the castrating Warden'. In contrast, I have argued that this is a space where the Real leans more heavily on the Symbolic, showing up the latter's porous nature. Such different emphases, or 'lines of flight', are certainly productive, but I would take issue with Wannamaker's reading of what she calls the book's 'final scene', where Clyde (the basketball player whose trainers land on Stanley) asks Stanley to cover his wife's mouth, showing the silencing of the feminine; his action, in effect, Wannamaker (ibid.: 31) states, points out that this is 'the way things "ought to be"' in a patriarchal society. Yet my response would be that this is precisely *not* the final scene of the book. The final scene, rather, occurs on the last page (as mentioned earlier), where Zero's mother is described, with 'her mouth [which] seemed too big for her face' (we had previously been told that her ancestor, Madame Zeroni, had 'a very wide mouth' (Sachar, 2000: 29)). This hidden figure is then given the last words of the novel; in other words, finally she is *not* silent: she sings (the verse quoted above), which is itself a corrective addressed to the patriarchal line of the numbered Yelnatses.

Coats, in contrast (who writes from a distinctly Lacanian perspective), is more concerned with addressing the racial questions raised by the novel, arguing that Stanley is 'in denial' about the significance of race, as shown in statements like the following:

> Stanley was thankful that there were no racial problems. X-Ray, Armpit, and Zero were black. He, Squid, and Zigzag were white. Magnet was Hispanic. On the lake they were all the same reddish brown color – the color of dirt. (Coats, 2004: 84)

Coats argues that 'Stanley is part of a larger conspiracy of white denial of the privilege that comes with being a white male' (ibid.: 133), which relates to his Latvian ancestor, Elya, being indebted to Zero's Egyptian forebear, Madame Zeroni. As Coats writes, '[i]t is this failure, this erasure or even mere forgetfulness of the debt to the Other for one's position as subject, that haunts Whiteness' (ibid.: 133–4).

Elya, she argues, is guilty of 'thinking only of himself and in exercising the privilege of the white male to travel and make his way in the world' and has thus 'failed in his responsibility to the Other' (ibid.: 133). Again, this is strange, as we have been clearly told that Madame Zeroni's son exercised exactly this privilege in travelling to America (Sachar, 2000: 30). Coats, however, argues that it is when Zero digs Stanley's hole for him that Stanley becomes aware of the slave/overseer relationship (with which X-Ray taunts him) and of his need to take responsibility for his white privilege by looking after Zero and fulfilling the original promise that his ancestor had made.

Personally, as I said earlier, I find that it is the whole order of things that is challenged in this holey place, whether it be lizards, race (it doesn't seem irrelevant, for instance, that it is the black youth X-Ray who is top-dog) or gender (the female Warden is in charge of Mr Sir). We have also had the dangers of loose signification pointed out to us in other areas: in the Yelnats's family history, for instance, as it turns out that Elya never really stole a pig; moreover, Madame Zeroni is not 'one-legged', either, but simply lacks a foot. Finally it does not say that she was a Gypsy, but Egyptian (Sachar, 2000: 29), it being a common fallacy that gypsies originated in Egypt, whence the name 'gypsy' derives, whereas they actually emigrated from India. There is, then, some ambiguity here: if she is Egyptian, the designation 'black' is contentious;[14] but it is equally so if she is a gypsy, as her prophetic powers might lead one stereotypically to expect. It seems to me that, as elsewhere in the novel, we are being shown the holes in our signification – that is, in the Symbolic – which we have already met in terms of colour when it was asked why the lizards came to be described as yellow-spotted.

In short, gender and race – like other harmful discourses from the big Other (the Symbolic) – are queried, or put 'under erasure' at Camp Green Lake. And readers, in traversing the fantasy, in experiencing the transference both to and from the Camp, will also have undergone the joys and delays of plot as it advances and retards our understanding, offering anticipatory fore-pleasure, arousing desires, before delivering a final sense of mastery. But we should also have an awareness that, without some way of plotting our stories, our lives can seem empty, tales told by idiots, signifying nothing: zero. And yet our desire for 'wholeness' can often be excessive, too, hence suspect: the more we fill in the holes showing how stories and their characters are plotted, the more the porosity increases, the flaws become more evident – and the coincidences stretch our credibility. Finally, this book seems to suggest that we might look at how we ourselves are storied, and how we can be re-storied, too: how, rather than be resigned, things can be re-signed. Such are the energetics of plot.

Conclusion

In the above readings I have pressed for a more open-ended approach to criticism, one that does not wish to deny others, or only so when they seem to shut down interpretation and, thereby, delimit the pleasure, or energetics, of reading, which is why I have suggested this more 'heretical' approach. Though I have adopted a broadly Lacanian framework in my own interpretations, in that I have argued that such an approach helps open up a text, I am also guided by Lacan's attention to 'the letter of the text' (Fink, 2004), where meanings undoubtedly arise and multiply, but always from the ground up, rather than being imposed from above. In the process, the *jouissance* of a text can be released, as the censorious monologic of the Symbolic is defied.

4 Hiding in the Light: Perry Nodelman and the Hidden Adult

Introduction

This is the second chapter that I have framed in terms of the Symbolic. Whereas the previous one was critical of sociological readings of texts, this one considers a far more ambitious work: *The Hidden Adult* (2008) by Perry Nodelman, in which he attempts to define the whole field of children's literature (Rose, of course, attended to just a subsection of this – children's fiction – which she saw as impossible). Both Rose and Nodelman are united in seeing this seemingly safe, imaginary realm as concealing more significant, symbolic concerns, but whereas I emphasised the imaginary appeal of the Peter Pan figure in the first two chapters (emphasising its Romantic roots in Rose's work, also), here I want to continue probing the way this figure has been dismantled. So, whereas Rose tends to emphasise the seeming innocence and evasion of adult concerns in children's literature texts (the Imaginary), Nodelman considers these adult concerns to be more overt. His claim is clear, straight from the title of his book, that there is always a 'hidden adult' in children's literature. However, unlike Rose (whom Nodelman 2010 warmly credits), he is far more precise (and less negative) about the nature of this adult presence. As he puts it, a text of children's literature 'implies an unspoken and much more complex repertoire that amounts to a second, hidden text', which he terms a 'shadow text' (Nodelman, 2008: 8).

In this chapter, then, I want to explore some of Nodelman's key issues and their implications. While it might seem unbalanced to single out his work in particular, it is for the best of reasons, for, like Rose, he is clearly one of the most influential and prolific critics in the field and should be credited with the way he has helped shape the provenance of children's literature studies. He has been seeking to define our area of study in an impressive range of publications reaching back to the 1980s, which is something that his magnum opus, *The Hidden Adult*, brings together, and it certainly problematises some of the key concerns that I share: around the adult–child binary, around children's literature being a genre, and, as we saw earlier, its very possibility as a branch of fiction. But I do have some problems with his model; in particular, with his central notion of this hidden, 'shadow' text. It seems to me that it is unclear exactly what this shadowiness comprises – and this is nowhere more manifest than in his discussion of picture books, which is where I shall begin my reading.

Shadowiness of shadow texts

So, like Peter Pan with his shadow, I have problems in figuring out exactly how Nodelman's shadow texts relate to the more overt, surface texts that he discusses. Where, indeed, is the join? At times he invokes a shadow text when discussing the more detailed knowledge that an adult might bring to a text; at other times it seems to involve spotting the connotations involved in textual interpretation, such as inferring certain outcomes from textual gaps; and yet it is also invoked to speak about the underlying ideological messages of a text and even more specialised theoretical readings of works.

In order to unpack this, moving further into the shadowlands, so to speak, I'll begin with Nodelman's analysis of one of his six chosen texts: Ezra Jack Keats's *The Snowy Day* (1962). Nodelman begins with the most superficial level of shadowiness, where a reader is required to draw on additional knowledge in order to fill in textual detail and provide emotional colouring. In picturebooks, Nodelman claims that the pictures 'operate as a visual equivalent of the shadow text' (2008: 11).

There is, straightaway, another complication here (which I did not mention above), for Nodelman does not designate the pictures as themselves comprising 'text', unlike some other writers in this area (e.g. Lewis, 2001). Thus he informs us that we do not know what the snow looked like from the text; rather, we discern this from the 'accompanying illustration' (Nodelman, 2008: 10). This follows his practice in his earlier book, *Words About Pictures* (Nodelman, 1988: viii), where it seems less of an issue to argue that 'the words and the pictures in picture books both define and amplify each other'. However, to associate the words with the surface text and the illustrations with the shadow regions seems to lose the whole process of 'interanimation', to use David Lewis's preferred term (2001: 35) for the word/picture relationship:

> Picturebook text is ... usually composite, an 'interweaving of words and pictures' as Allan Ahlberg puts it .... A text ... is something woven together, a cohesive patterning of inter-related strands that adds up to more than a mere accumulation of individual parts. (Ibid.: 33)

Returning to Keats's work, then, Nodelman's terminology allows him to claim that the text doesn't mention Peter's blackness (2008: 11), whereas I'd argue that the text displays it precisely: right on the surface in its pictorial elements (i.e. it is evident even to those who cannot yet decode written language). Such problems are more than terminological, I'd argue, especially when the hidden text is blatantly visible in the pictures, as we can see in a work like Pat Hutchins's *Rosie's Walk* (1968) or, even more pointedly, in wordless texts like Raymond Briggs's *The Snowman* (1978) – both of which Nodelman (1988) discusses. Using the former as an example, then, the verbal text simply describes Rosie the hen's rather pedestrian (in many ways) constitutional walk around the farmyard. What it does not mention is the fox in his various failed attempts to pounce on Rosie. Do we then say that this information is, despite being 'hidden in the light' (to adapt Dick Hebdidge's (1988) catchy phrase), part of the shadow text? For surely it is a central and overt part of the story, and planned as such all along. As Lawrence Sipe (1998: 107) avers, 'visual texts are on an equal footing with verbal texts'.

For me, then, if the term 'shadow text' is to have any mileage, it must be concerned with less obvious textual elements (whether verbal or pictorial), which, in the case of Hutchins's story, comprise such matters as the gender of the protagonist and antagonist (a female hunted by a male), the opposition of wild/uncivilised and domesticated/civilised (with the superiority of the latter), the hint of 'Little Red Riding Hood' as an intertext, with Rosie being someone who is not going to be diverted from her path; and, finally, the irony – which we can see explored more fully in a film like *Chicken Run* (Lord and Park, 2000) – namely that, whereas the fox is the *known* predator, there is a more invisible one, the farmer, who keeps hens for just one or, at most, two reasons.

Nodelman (2008: 13), however, claims that children 'need pictures to shadow them, to show and tell all that the written words cannot say'. But isn't it more the case that, without some words (either from the text or a parent), it would not be apparent what was meant to be in shadow in the first place (in Rosie's case, being shadowed by a fox)? The pictures, then, are overt in this case, with the words setting up the 'hidden text' (though, in practice, it emerges from a combination of these two signifying systems). If this were not the case, and the pictures always did the shadowing, there would be problems with wordless 'texts' like Raymond Briggs's *The Snowman*: the story would be forever hidden until a reader enunciated a narrative around it.

Returning to Nodelman's own example, *The Snowy Day*, let us look at a point in the text where the reader is required to go beyond factual knowledge, to make an inference. In the relevant picture, Peter is seen to have a dark patch on his jacket, which appears after he has gone into his 'warm house' having put a snowball into his pocket. Either the reader will infer that the darker patch on Peter's jacket signifies a melted snowball or he or she will perhaps put this together after the verbal text informs the reader that Peter had a dream about the sun melting the snow (something that is also visually depicted). (Of course, it might be that a child is simply told this information by a zealous adult reader.) My point, though, is that an understanding of this 'shadowy' element could come from *either* of the signifying elements, the verbal or visual text, or, indeed, from their juxtaposition. The overt visual text, I'd therefore argue, is not shadowy by default but, like the verbal text, will contain shadowy elements; and Nodelman provides what I would see as a stronger example when he speaks of this book's expressionist style of visual representation, which hints at an 'innocent eye', frequently associated with children (ibid.: 12).

Let me now move on to another of Nodelman's six exemplary texts: Carroll's *Alice*. In discussing this work Nodelman seems to stretch the notion of a shadow text even further. Whereas a shadow text can simply provide information about what things look like (ibid.: 15), it can also involve far more complex interpretations, which, I'd argue, go beyond what he elsewhere terms the text's 'implied sense' (ibid.: 9) – a phrase that I'll return to. He claims that '[*Alice*'s] simplicity evokes the complex shadow text that critics describe in their analyses of it', mentioning, as examples, 'Jungian archetypes' and 'postmodern conceptions of schizophrenia' (ibid.: 15). Significantly, he uses the verb 'evokes' here, which suggests to me something more than that which a text might *imply*; whereas his final example – of obscure allusions to contemporary politics – could more justifiably be *implied* by the text (as, indeed, Jones and Gladstone (1995) argue);

and, one might say, in Victorian times such allusions would have been far less obscure. But the former examples (archetypes and schizophrenia) seem to move us more in the direction of Stanley Fish's 'interpretive communities', with their more specialist critical repertoires. It seems that here we are dealing less with what a text *evokes* than with what an interpretive community is predisposed to find, just as very different shadow texts might be uncovered by linguistics experts (Fordyce and Marello, 1994), or philosophers (Irwin and Davis, 2009).[1]

However, while Nodelman is quite prepared to take seriously the often esoteric critical responses to Carroll's text (he refers to 778 citations from the MLA International Bibliography in 2006 (Nodelman, 2008: 15)), he is less charitable when it comes to his five other texts. Given his own, rather light-hearted examples at this point, though, this attitude is less than surprising. Thus he speaks about finding Jungian archetypes in *The Snowy Day*: 'I could identify the long stick Henry finds [*sic* – he clearly means the protagonist, Peter, here], and the firm but all-too-meltable snowball he tries to bring indoors, with his search for manhood'. Such interpretation is rather easily dismissed, as Nodelman himself concedes (ibid.: 16) – and, if anything, the stick and ball are more the props of vulgar Freudian interpretation. But there are, surely, more pervasive, ideological issues that shadow texts, which might certainly have been probed with more gravitas; with Keats's text, issues around class, gender and ethnicity, for instance.

Turning to other texts within Nodelman's chosen half-dozen, we find that all manner of critics have discerned other, possible, shadow texts within his corpus. For example, Maria Edgeworth's 'The Purple Jar' has been read in terms of the 'truly heroic' privileging of 'the Beautiful before the Useful',[2] of demonstrating the seductions of consumerism (McGillis, 2002; Denisoff, 2008), and, from a very different perspective, as being a lesson about menstruation (Robbins, 2005).[3] The key point I want to emphasise is that one either has a far more restricted notion of what a text implies, which might constitute a 'shadow text', or one recognises that texts are inexhaustible in casting shadows – forever being renewed by current cultural concerns, new 'lines of flight' as I've referred to them (e.g. around ecocriticism, ethical criticism, queer readings, and so on). In other words, it becomes less a question of a shadow text than an open-ended cultural dialogue that will have endless contributors to its conversations. This is where a more Bakhtinian approach to a text, which recognises that a word is only 'half-ours and half-someone else's ... open ... and able to reveal ever new ways to mean' (Bakhtin,

1981: 345–6), seems far more viable, as I mentioned in Chapter 1. Let me elaborate on the quotation from Vološinov, introduced there:

> I give myself verbal shape from another's point of view, ultimately, from the point of view of the community to which I belong. A word is a bridge thrown between myself and another. If one end of the bridge depends on me, then the other depends on my addressee. A word is a territory shared by addresser and addressee .... (Vološinov, 1973: 86).

At times, Nodelman seems to agree: that it is less about the shadow a text throws than about the fact that the addressee stands in a different place. Thus, after discussing the presence of a more knowing focaliser, Nodelman observes that, in Beverly Cleary's *Henry Huggins*, although such a presence is lacking, he finds himself automatically providing this more complex viewpoint. As an example, he mentions the scene where a policeman threatens to arrest Henry, commenting that, as an adult he knows 'that the policeman is joking' (2008: 25). But I'd argue that Nodelman is wrong in thinking that this is simply an adult perception. Picking up on the point Vološinov makes about the 'view of the community to which I belong', Nodelman's view is more particularly that of a white, Jewish, middle-class male (Nodelman candidly provides us with his profile (ibid.: 82–3)). For a young black reader from the community of the 'hood', or any underprivileged child from many areas of the world (the *favelas* that feature in *City of God* (Meirelles and Lund, 2002), for instance), such a view expressed by a policeman might be less than jokey. Indeed, we need only point to the experience of Henry Louis Gates Jr, a respected black academic arrested for trying to break into his own house in Cambridge (Massachusetts) in 2009! Of course, returning to *Henry Huggins*, one would hope that Henry's error would eventually be clarified; that, in his neighbourhood at this time, the police were nothing but friendly community figures (unlike, say, the way that William Steig anthropomorphises them as pigs in *Sylvester and the Magic Pebble* (1969) – a book that some US police forces at the time saw as having a less-than-hidden subtext).

Before moving on to a larger point about the 'hidden adult', let me make one more observation about this shadow text, to which I alluded earlier: Nodelman's use of the word 'implied' (2008: 8), which is frequently used in his definitions (as quoted earlier). The word 'implied', of course, brings most readily to mind the work of Wolfgang Iser (1974; 1978), who argued that the implied reader was the very person who could produce a meaningful reading of a work, especially by filling in its gaps or indeterminacies. But there is immediately a conflict between this and

Nodelman's conception in that, in Iser's sense, any implied reader would, by definition, be someone who thereby discerned the 'shadow text'; that is, the implied reader is the person capable of filling in the text's gaps. Nodelman does actually refer to Iser (2008: 9), but only in the context of a '"repertoire" of knowledge' – which also conjures up Stanley Fish's rather different notion of reader response.[4]

The larger point I want to make, however, is about the person that stands behind the shadow text, the 'hidden adult' of Nodelman's title, which actually overshadows a far more occluded 'hidden child'. For (returning to Vološinov's point) children will inevitably bring their own 'answering words' – their own shadows – to texts, which are not necessarily those of the dominant adult culture; indeed, they might well work against it. This is certainly what I found in my research on the British writer, Enid Blyton, where children were far more interested in enjoying what they saw as the pleasures of the text (being together, celebrating holidays, eating and enjoying adventures, being heroes) than in excavating what many adult cultural critics have unearthed from Blyton's work. If one only recognises the latter, as I wrote at the time (and also quoted in the last chapter), then 'children worldwide, over several generations, have clearly been cultural dopes, choosing to read and re-read texts that, if the official view is to be believed, undermine half of them for their gender, and insult many more for their ethnicity or class' (Rudd, 2000: 194). Not something that I find convincing.

This larger point becomes more clear when Nodelman discusses two components of his shadow text in terms of the text's 'unconscious' (an unfortunate choice, I think, but one that presumably alludes to Fredric Jameson's 1981 usage): 'a literary unconscious' and a 'political or cultural unconscious' (Nodelman, 2008: 205). These aspects, it should be noted, derive from the text per se, although he does recognise that ideology – and our general knowledge about the world (of policemen, etc.) – also informs our everyday life. But he then declares that children's literature texts

> can be read as intended only by those immersed enough in the ideology of
> their culture to properly read its traces in what the text actually says. ... It
> is interesting, therefore, that real readers of these texts often don't know all
> the texts imply. There is a sense in which the texts exist exactly to allow adult
> readers to share knowledge of the shadow with children. (Ibid.: 205–6)

There is surely a contradiction here, besides an unnecessary deferral to adults who 'properly read'. For I'd argue that it is precisely those who are immersed in their culture's ideology who, like the proverbial fish (though not the Stanley variety), do not see the water in which they swim. Patriarchy, masculinity, middle-class mores, heterosexuality and whiteness are the default – and therefore often the invisible, naturalised – values. It is precisely those who are less immersed – those who deviate from this norm (in which one would include most children) – who are more likely to see the faultlines (and be caught up in them). Once again, Nodelman's notion of a 'shadow text' seems to conflate these opposing notions. As I suggested earlier, to become a successful 'implied reader' can mean filling in all the gaps but, in that very process, consolidating one's ideological commitment to a text's values. As Terry Eagleton (1984: 69) depicts this process, it can suggest dutiful, compliant readers. Stephens makes a similar point, arguing that Aidan Chambers's 'description of a successful reading... envisages the reader's internalization of the text's implicit ideologies. What Chambers presents as an empowering act of interpretation is just as likely to be a process of subjection' (Stephens, 1992: 10).

Let me therefore draw on some actual child readers at this point, both to give an addressee's perspective and to provide a sense of how a reader might engage with textual implications. Here is a comment from three-year-old Lindsey, who has had Beatrix Potter's *The Tale of Peter Rabbit* read to her by her mother. On hearing the line, 'I am sorry to say that Peter was not very well during the evening', she enquired:

> 'Are *you* sorry?' ... as if this were my [her mother's] personal comment. I said no, and tried to explain the author's voice .... I said that the author was sorry, and Lindsey asked who the author was.
>
> 'Beatrix Potter,' I replied.
>
> 'Oh,' she said, and looked at me for awhile. 'Is he a bunny, too?' (Wolf and Heath, 1992: 67)

Whereas a more mature reader would be well aware of the function of a narrator, Lindsey found this sudden interjection intrusive (which, once again, shows how important it is to take account of the particular addressee: not simply to label all non-adults under the rubric 'child reader'). Indeed, without an actual reader to draw on, we might easily have claimed that this 'I' was part of the overt text, not something we would see as shadowy (as this reader found it). In other words, that which was formerly assumed to be omniscient narration turns out not to be (something that might surprise most of us), but neither is it a parental interjection: there is a hidden adult (or bunny, perhaps) operating in this area!

There is one more point to make about this, for I see no reason to defer to the adult's literary knowledge ('properly read') and ignore Lindsey's perceptive misreading (itself constituting another shadow text). Is the adult really sorry? she asks, thereby drawing attention to an adult form of words ('I am sorry to say') that tends to ironise the remorse, suggesting that the speaker might actually feel that Peter's indisposition is deserved. It *could* well have been a 'sarky' parental interjection. Lindsey's question, 'Are *you* sorry?', hints at this, as though she herself has adopted this parental tone, one wherein a child is asked to look within itself in order to discern whether its apology conveys genuine contrition or not.

Clearly, to conceive children's literature *as a genre* leaves out these confounding and messy aspects, and we lose precisely the fact that 'the word in language is half someone else's' (Bakhtin, 1981: 293). It is all very well to talk about the literary and politico-cultural unconscious of a text while neglecting the more conscious young readers who populate the text, not as *tabulae rasae*, but as active addressees, for whom books are but one aspect of an extensive cultural landscape, alongside their home lives, family relationships, peer interactions and other cultural media. Once again, Wolf and Heath (1992) are full of examples of how a text's implications and possibilities are explored in these more lateral but no less valid ways. Thus the young Lindsey, once again, found Sendak's *Where the Wild Things Are* not just a favourite book, but also something that

> fortified her with the intertextual ammunition to cope with her fears. 'Be still!' she would threaten the big, bad wolf as his cheeks filled with air. And she would shout the same words to me when I scolded or denied her something she wanted. (Ibid.: 35)

This, surely, is a legitimate way of pursuing the meanings and resonances of a text, but one that is both less adult-friendly and one that suggests we need not be shackled by this problematic concept of the shadow text. Instead, in a more Bakhtinian (and Barthesian) vein, I am suggesting that we need a model that gives us more room to move about in, one where the shadow play of signification – the lateral rather than the hierarchical process of reading – can be indulged; one which might also incorporate children's own readings. As I found in my research on Blyton, this can involve extending the reach of texts into games, fantasies, story-writing, rituals of reading (up trees, under bedclothes with torches, comfort eating), and so on. Interestingly, David Bleich (1986: 256), in his study of the ways readers read, found a distinct gender difference in how men and women responded to canonical texts, with women being more concerned with the affective aspects, seeing a text as more dialogically open, such that one could make inferences, extrapolate and relate it to everyday life, whereas men were more focused on the text per se, tending to rule out any deviations as digressions. Radway, again exploring female readers (of Romances, in this case), also found that the traffic was two-way, from world to text and back again, thus arguing in favour of seeing readers as agents who 'fashion narratives, stories, objects and practices from myriad bits and pieces of prior cultural productions' in order to capture 'the entire tapestry of social life' (Radway, 1988: 363, 367).

With children, who are learning the way the world is and what it means to be childlike, this two-way conversation is likely to be even more intense and often subversive as well. Thus, to turn to Lindsey's brother, Ashley (aged just under four), he gave what might be seen as a more gendered response when he suggested a revision to *Where the Wild Things Are*. After the line, 'but Max stepped into his private boat and waved good-bye', he stopped his father's reading: '"No, Dada," he admonished. "Not like that. It's: 'and Max stepped onto their private parts and waved good-bye.' Like that"' (Wolf and Heath, 1992: 44). One might proffer various interpretations of this, from the sheer scatological and phonological enjoyment of the phrase, especially with a child's realisation of what this euphemism connotes, to a more physical (and empowering) pleasure (especially if the child happened to be seated in his father's lap at the time (the text is silent on this point)), and, of course, one might work this up into a more full-blown Oedipal reading.

Before moving on, let me summarise the key points of this section. Nodelman (2008: 205) comments that 'texts can be read as intended only by those immersed enough in the ideology of their culture to properly read its traces in what the text actually says'. I've made the point that this defers to adults too much (particularly so in his subsequent sentences, quoted above). But beyond this I have other problems with his statement. First, there is the issue of knowing how books are intended to be read, which I have also broadly addressed. I do not believe we can ever know a text's intentions, and even if we could, it would be hard delimiting the text to such an 'intended' reading. Second, there is the matter of being 'immersed' in one's culture's ideology, which suggests that no one but an expert would be able to read a text from another culture or period 'properly'. Again, I don't think we need to conceive reading in this delimiting way, seeing a particular time-and-space-bound interpretation as more correct. And, aside from this (my third point), the word 'ideology' remains problematic, for someone who is immersed is, arguably, the one least likely to read a work 'properly'.

The adult–child binary

Mention of the power of the adult brings me on to my second major point: that, along with the idea of a text's intentions, and of it being read properly, Nodelman has a tendency to shape his readings of his six chosen texts in terms of an adult–child binary that is presumed already to exist, whereas I see these texts as merely setting up differentials between innocence and experience, immaturity and maturity. For example, Nodelman comments that, in 'The Purple Jar', the mother 'directly states her conviction that having knowledge – gained through careful examination of the world – is a corrective to the dangers of impulse and childishness' (ibid.: 33). But neither of these latter qualities is mentioned by the mother. It would indeed be hard to call Rosamond's act impulsive for she is offered, in the cool light of day, a choice between some shoes and a purple jar, and, at first, angles to be given both gifts, only then to agonise between them ('You can't think how these hurt me. I believe I'd better have the new shoes. Yet, that blue flower-pot ... '), and is seen to stand 'in profound meditation, with one shoe on and the other in her hand' (Edgeworth, 1918: 5). 'Childishness' isn't explicitly mentioned either; only the need to be wiser.

These might seem small points, but I find them indicative of the way that they enable Nodelman to set up what appears to me a false dichotomy (one that he can then more effectively challenge and destabilise later). Thus he goes on to claim that the tale undermines its message about a child deferring to adult knowledge and not acting impetuously in line with its desires. For, despite learning this lesson, Rosamond remains in her childlike state (2008: 34–5). However, as Nodelman subsequently acknowledges, there is only the *hope* that Rosamond be wiser in the future (ibid.: 35) – and, indeed, over the next 25 years of Rosamond's appearance in Edgeworth's stories (making her a 32-year-old in the end, were we counting), 'she never, significantly, finishes growing up', as Mitzi Myers informs us (1994: 61). This is surely the point: Rosamond is an early version of the naughty or troublesome child character (cf. Anne of Green Gables, William Brown, Dennis the Menace, Pippi Longstocking); so, the more tales she was to feature in, the more her child readers would, no doubt, glory in her behaviour. For example, Myers (ibid.: 72) quotes the popular nineteenth-century poet, Felicia Hemans, who described herself as

> little better than a grown-up Rosamond ... who constantly lie [*sic*] in bed till it is too late to get up early, break my needles, (when I use any,) leave my keys among my necklaces, answer all my amusing letters first and leave

the others to their fate; in short, regularly commit small sins enough every day, to roll up into one great, immense, *frightful* one at the end of it!

For many child readers, then, the enjoyment lies in the hope that Rosamond's 'getting of wisdom' will be forever deferred. Thus Nodelman's claim that childhood is defined in two contrary ways – one in which ignorance and impulsiveness is curtailed as a result of adult knowledge and one where it persists (2008: 35) – does not seem to be born out in Edgeworth's text, where we only seem to have the second.[5]

If anything, nineteenth-century children are shown to have rather too much in terms of adult knowledge thrust at them, as famously depicted by Bitzer in Dickens's *Hard Times*, describing a horse in his 'gramniverous' way. The uselessness of such dry, factual knowledge is, of course, amply demonstrated in that novel, as it is later, in Carroll, where we find Alice repeatedly rehearsing her garbled understanding of such things as 'The Antipathies' and 'Latitude or Longitude', which 'Alice had not the slightest idea' of anyway (1970: 28, 27). But Rosamond, far earlier, had also shown her eloquence on a variety of topics, such as 'cheese mites, hunting spiders, and snowflakes from Dr. Hooke's discoveries via the microscope' (quoted in Myers, 1994: 61–2). In short, it is not knowledge that is the issue; nor is it behaviour, for Rosamond's sister, Laura, who features in various Rosamond tales, is eminently well-behaved, yet is still seen to be a child. In other words, what Nodelman terms 'forms of knowledge' (2008: 35) are not really anything to do with adults per se, hence a child's adoption of them is not going to change her appreciably. This is convincingly shown in other tales printed in *The Parent's Assistant*, where 'The Purple Jar' first appeared (in 1796, and not in *Early Lessons* of 1801 as Nodelman (ibid.: 2) has it, though it *is* the later version of the tale that he draws upon); for example, the story 'The White Pigeon' features a Mr Cox, an 'alehouse keeper', a drunkard, fighter and thief who, despite being an adult, is shown to lack various of the superior qualities exhibited by the child characters and, specifically, to know less.[6]

Nodelman's insistence on this binary opposition of adult and child seems even more fraught with problems when he comes to discuss *The Story of Doctor Dolittle*:

> What are readers to make of Lofting, clearly an adult, expressing ... disdain for the wisdom of adults like himself? An adult cannot actually become a child again. That Dr. Dolittle does so makes Lofting's novel the most extreme form of wish-fulfillment fantasy, in which what is wished for is not only unlikely but actually beyond the realm of logic

or possibility. There is something perverse in wishing for what cannot possibly be – and something peculiarly self-hating, even life-denying about wishing to be what one so clearly is not. To think as one imagines a child thinks, to be simple, to know less – all this means is that one is less conscious of the brute horror of the bare truth, despicable and unbearable reality itself. (Ibid.: 44)

Nodelman ends by depicting Lofting as extremely negative, giving an acrid perception of a world that, as an adult, he cannot help but inhabit (ibid.). There is certainly passion here, causing Nodelman to ride roughshod over notions of the implied author in order to accuse Lofting, directly, of expressing a disdain for adult knowledge. But again, I fail to find any opposition between adult and child expressed in the books. Where, for instance, does Dolittle express a wish to 'become a child again'? If anything, Dolittle is more of a trickster figure, one who can move with ease between human and animal worlds, cross-dressing as a woman in one episode (*Doctor Dolittle's Caravan* (1927)), much as Toad does in *The Wind in the Willows*. But Dolittle is clearly shown interacting with adults too, quite successfully when required ('All the prominent people in town were there – famous continental opera stars, great composers, writers, painters, sculptors, as well as ambassadors, dukes, earls and a large gathering of lesser nobility' (Lofting, 1968: 172)); in fact, he is seen to be the head of his own 'family' of animals, overseeing their bedtime (ibid.: 163, 171, 174). He certainly does not wish 'to be simple, to know less'; rather, he wants most adults to know more, to avoid being so blinkered by 'conventional adult values'.

In the passage that Nodelman (2008: 43) quotes in relation to this point – which begins, 'People make me sick', and is spoken by Polynesia the parrot – it is quite clearly shown to be a criticism of *human*, not *adult* short-sightedness: humans' lack of recognition that they, too, are animals. As Dolittle puts it elsewhere: 'One of my chief complaints against people has always been that they had no respect for animals. But many people have a great respect for money' (Lofting, 1968: 194). Such passages bring to mind Swift's *Gulliver's Travels*, where similar views about humans are expressed by other races, like the equine Houyhnhnms; but most famous is the King of Brobdignag's view: 'I cannot but conclude the bulk of your natives, to be the most pernicious race of little odious vermin that nature ever suffered to crawl upon the surface of the earth' (Swift, 1940: 140). Just so, in Lofting, it is clearly not 'self-hating' or being 'less conscious of the brute horror of the bare truth' but actually recognising and despairing at human cruelty and short-sightedness with regard to animals. Thus Dolittle engages in activities like 'animal liberation' from caged confinement in pet-shops and making sure that travel conditions for animals are suitable (Lofting, 1968: 220).

But Nodelman's stance is linked to another aspect of his case, where he refers to other childlike figures, mentioning Chaplin and Don Quixote, with this caveat: 'those other innocents are adults who have remained childlike – and who are, therefore, like Dr. Dolittle, clearly removed from their intended audience, different – not so much to be identified with as to be admired and desired in a wish-fulfilling sort of way' (Nodelman, 2008: 53). It is difficult to know whether Nodelman here means that the 'intended audience' is primarily children (clearly not so with Don Quixote) or adults (not so with Dolittle). However, leaving this aside, his caveat is important, for earlier in his text he has assumed, 'obviously, that readers tend to identify with the characters through whose perspective they view the action', and notes that this tends to be actual 'child protagonists' or those who are childlike (ibid.: 18, 19). However, he then becomes more restrictive in his view: 'Because Dr. Dolittle is already an adult, and unlikely to change, it is more difficult for child readers to identify with him', readers being 'outside and detached from him already' (ibid.: 30–1). It is hard to see why this should be the case but, leaving this, too, aside, let me go back to the piece I quoted earlier, claiming that Dolittle is 'not so much to be identified with as to be admired and desired in a wish-fulfilling sort of way' (Nodelman, 2008: 53). Why, or indeed how Nodelman can make this distinction, I am unsure, but his use of the word 'identification' compounds the problem. As I've written elsewhere:

> Do we mean by it that we empathize with a particular character? Do we mean that we simply see likenesses between that character and ourselves, or is it that we wish there were likenesses? Alternatively, do we actually go further and seek to imitate a character's behaviour? These are all different, so should not be lost in a blanket term. (Rudd 2000: 194).

For me, a child can find a character attractive for all sorts of reasons, partly to do with focalisation, but also because of particular attributes, which are often connected to the relationship between the empowered and disempowered. As mentioned in Chapter 1, children are frequently drawn to the latter (the orphan, the youngest child, the isolated animal) but, equally, can be attracted by reversals of this state, where the child becomes empowered, outdoing adults him or herself, or has a heroic figure enact this role. Gulliver is once again interesting in this regard, playing both roles, and has thereby been repeatedly linked to children's literature. But the key point is that this more open way of looking at the attraction of particular characters requires not identification, which is seen as a relatively passive process, but a more active engagement, which Bakhtin's notion of 'dialogism' supplies. In Martin Barker's words, "'Identification" suggests that we are spoken for. "Dialogue" suggests we are spoken to' (1989: 260). Certainly, the example of Lindsey (quoted earlier) adopting the phrase 'Be still!' to empower her, is telling.

Finally, in terms of this juxtaposition of child and adult, I want to return to another of Nodelman's texts (excepting *Plain City*, I've discussed them all to some extent): *Alice's Adventures in Wonderland*. This requires more detail than I gave it (above) as I feel that it is the most mistreated in Nodelman's work. *Alice* is particularly interesting in that it involves adult characters almost exclusively, apart from Alice herself (though if one were to be strict, the puppy would have to be mentioned, plus a baby-cum-pig, and, of course, a caterpillar which, developmentally speaking, should not be very old, and should definitely not be smoking). In contrast to 'The Purple Jar', Nodelman argues that *Alice* shows how 'knowledge is what one desires', leading him to conclude that Alice wants to 'stop being a child' (Nodelman, 2008: 38).

His basis for this claim is the idea that adulthood represents a stable sense of self and a fixed notion of the world, whereas, for children, things are more fluid and open (Pullman's *His Dark Materials*, with its dæmons that become fixed at puberty, hints at a similar idea). Nodelman then makes the claim that, for Alice, this state of uncertainty is 'more utopian than nightmarish', although, on the following page, he speaks of Alice's adventures being frequently horrific and unsettling (ibid.: 40, 41), which is certainly more my perception of the novel. There are parallels, in fact, with Dante being led down into Hell by Virgil (Alice following the White Rabbit) and witnessing people engaged in fruitless, repetitive tasks, similar to Sisyphus trying to push a stone up a hill. In *Alice* we have, instead, the Mad Hatter et al. having to circle the table, endlessly taking their tea. Alice, I'd suggest, strives to hold on to her sanity, her mental coordinates of latitude and longitude, in a world where, as the Cheshire Cat terms it, 'we're all mad' (Carroll, 1970: 89). So I am even more perplexed when I read Nodelman's claim that Alice's 'one moment of certain knowledge about the Wonderland creatures is the assertion that ends her stay in this utopian land: "You're nothing but a pack of cards!"', which he describes as 'the exact equivalent of Rosamond's mother's certainty that her daughter's purple jar is nothing but a perfectly ordinary clear one'. When the respective child characters accept this adult form of knowledge, then, 'their fantasy worlds of desire must and do end' (2008: 40).

It is hard to see how Alice's cry is equivalent in certainty to the reasoning of Rosamond's mother, given that, of course, these Wonderland beings are no more a pack of cards than they are anything else (actual Gryphons, Mad Hatters or Mock Turtles). They are, rather, products of fantasy. This is something that Edgeworth would have found far from acceptable (and, as a matter of textual accuracy, Rosamond's mother does not claim this certainty about the purple jar; she merely suggests that Rosamond examine it first and might end up disappointed). Moreover, the only 'certain knowledge' occurs, surely, not with Alice's pack of cards pronouncement, but when she wakens from her fantasy to discover that the cards are actually 'dead leaves' (Carroll, 1970: 162). And, if there is any equivalent to Rosamond's mother, it must lie in the person of Alice's sister, the one who is 'gently brushing away' these leaves (ibid.); the one, in fact, who turns the wonder of Wonderland, like that of the purple jar, back into mundane reality ('the rattling teacups would change to tinkling sheep-bells' (ibid.: 163)), offering a more normal trajectory of development than that obtained from pursuing White Rabbits.

What is even stranger, though, is that Nodelman then comes round to entertain just the view expressed above, noting that Wonderland does indeed display the arbitrariness and insecurities of the adult world, its institutions, laws and language, such that 'many adults now think of *Alice* as a children's book unsuitable for children' (Nodelman, 2008: 41) – rather than, as might be a more logical next step, to see it as not really a children's book after all. But this would not then allow Nodelman to develop his notion that all his chosen texts contain 'two opposing views of childhood' (ibid.: 35) – a notion that I also queried in connection with 'The Purple Jar'. Moreover, Nodelman would then find it hard to advance his main thesis, developed later in the book. Namely, that the seeming simplicity of children's books conceals shadows, wherein lies a much fuller, more involved appreciation of the world; moreover, he claims, it is this very depth that gives children's books their surface simplicity, by implying, but not declaring, what is less obvious (ibid.: 206). But in order for the seeming simplicity of children's literature to make sense, he maintains, 'children must have access to at least some of the complexities' (ibid.: 207).

Shadow texts and hidden adults

Let me now stand back from Nodelman's argument slightly, and recap. First, I have argued that the notion of a shadow text, attractive as it seems, is actually itself very amorphous, shifting from a knowledge of concrete referents in the text to a text's connotative implications, and thence to an awareness of the literary and ideological issues that inform a text. I've also suggested that there is a particular problem in the difference between Iser's notion of being an implied reader, filling in the gaps a text proffers, and a reader thereby becoming, in Althusser's term, 'interpellated' by a text (i.e. ideologically captured by it, identifying with certain characters). These seem to be conflated in Nodelman's model. Relatedly, there seems to be a tension between the reader who sees the 'shadow text' and thereby swallows it, and what we might term, following Judith Fetterley (1978), the 'resisting reader', who goes against the grain of the text to some extent, not aligning her or himself with elements of a text's ideology. Which, we might ask, is the more adult?

And, more basically, are we right to frame the question along such 'aetonormative' lines?[7] I also particularly questioned the appropriateness of the term 'identification', suggesting that readers are more active and flexible in the way that they engage with texts.

I have further suggested that the adult–child dichotomy that Nodelman finds in these texts is actually a more procrustean imposition – as is perhaps most overtly shown in *Alice*. Nodelman's curious annoyance at *Doctor Dolittle* seems motivated by such a stance. But it is only by holding on to some notion of this child–adult binary that he can thereby map onto it his notion that children's texts (more than adult ones) have these overt and shadowy dimensions. They are thus locked into a binary opposition, where children have to see things in black and white terms, being either home or away, either ignorant or knowledgeable (2008: 62).

But why is there a need to map these texts in this way? That is, to associate the overt text with a position of childhood and the shadow text with adulthood? Especially as Nodelman quotes Mavis Reimer specifically criticising such a viewpoint (Reimer is speaking about *Tom Brown's Schooldays* in particular): 'The assumptions that there are only two reading positions available, that these are closely correlated with the ages of actual readers, and that "the child" can be linked with the simple and conventional and "the adult" with the complicated and innovative are insupportable' (quoted in ibid.: 209). But to my mind, rather than reframe his model, Nodelman tries to hold on to his binary while building in this complicating factor. Thus, while the overt text represents a simple childhood, he then asserts that child readers know about the shadow texts in their literature; in other words, they are not gullible or ignorant but simply pretend to be (ibid.: 214).

This reminds me of Thomas Kuhn's (1970) famous model of scientific revolutions, which, he argued, occur when the existing paradigm begins to creak as a result of its complications. He gives the example of the ever-more convoluted epicycles that became necessary to account for the Earth being at the centre of the universe, until Copernicus came along and suggested a far more straightforward model. So, rather than holding so firmly to his binary model, especially given Nodelman's belief in children's awareness of their texts' shadows, why not consider the idea that all texts indubitably have shadows (it would be hard to consider them otherwise), but that the shadows do not tidily correlate with an adult position. We could then talk about ironies, underlying plots, things not being what they seem, innocence giving way to experience, unknown relationships coming to the fore, and so on, without this extra baggage. Nodelman certainly entertains the idea that adult texts also have shadows, but contends that there's far less of an 'obvious disjunction' between them (2008: 14), *Alice* being the exception.

As I have said earlier, I would suggest that fictional texts (indeed, most non-fictional texts, too) always depend on a penumbra, following Jerome Bruner's (1973) contention that as humans we always go 'beyond the information given', making inferences, classifying, extrapolating and so on. It is also a central tenet of structuralist thinking that any term is always umbilically linked to its opposite, which is thereby invoked, even if not overtly present: masculinity gestures to what it is not, and the figure of the child gestures likewise. But rather than move towards a more post-structuralist way of thinking that would query notions of identity and identification, Nodelman seems to have his feet bound by this structuralist binary, resulting in some quite convoluted statements: '[c]hildren's literature subverts its subversiveness but also possibly subverts the subversions of its subversiveness' (2008: 287; see also p. 101 in this book).

But let me briefly play devil's advocate and consider Nodelman's claim that, though there are shadow texts in adults' literature, there isn't the 'obvious disjunction' (ibid.: 14). As I've said before, this all depends on what the shadow text involves (it ranges in his examples from denotative to connotative decoding, to comprehending more figurative elements, and thence to questions of ideological 'identification' or 'resistance'). And, beyond this, we really need to consider *which* adults we are talking about and *which* texts. I am presuming that Nodelman is considering a fairly sophisticated reader (from one of Fish's informed 'interpretive communities') rather than your average, unqualified school-leaver. This makes a huge difference to the claim. In the case of the latter, a work like Joyce's

Ulysses is likely to have a huge disjunction between overt and shadow text (knowledge of early twentieth-century Ireland and its politics, of Dublin in particular, of religion, of classical mythology, of modernism, of anti-Semitism, of *Hamlet*, of metempsychosis, and so on), although, for an English graduate, this disjunction will be far less. In short, without specifying the reader, such claims are fairly meaningless (Andrew Melrose (2012: 39), for instance, quotes a statistic claiming that half the UK workforce (*c*.16 million) 'has the average reading age of a child of around 11–12 years old', which is what the average tabloid aims at).

In terms of texts, too, there's a huge disparity between *Ulysses* and the sorts of popular fiction that most adults consume. This is in no way to disparage the latter, but if we are to take seriously the sorts of readings that Nodelman mentions in connection with *Alice*, we should equally attend to cultural theorists' readings of James Bond (Eco, 1979) or popular romances (Radway, 1987; Modleski, 1988). Once again, I think we would find a huge disjunction between most adult readers and what we might call the shadow hunters.

There's also the question of 'truth' that Nodelman mentions. He argues that adult texts, unlike those for children, 'don't usually presume to tell less of the truth than their writers know'. In other words, books for children are reticent about particular issues, though it might well be that traces of these issues remain, which, suggests Nodelman, could well be 'a defining characteristic of children's literature' (2008: 142–3). This idea seems rooted in a Romantic conception of literature as revealing the 'truth' about things, with writers being the ones 'in the know'. In contrast, I would argue that truths are always constructed within texts, and are always subject to being reined in from saying too much. One thinks of Ezra Pound hacking swathes out of *The Waste Land* for T. S. Eliot, or, of the revelation that Raymond Carver's best short stories were heavily edited and rewritten by Gordon Lish. Whether one sees the truth as always inhering, in a sort of Platonic way, or being the result of a particular ordering of words (and their shadows), is a moot point. But beyond individual cases, I would argue that all texts deliberately hold back. Certainly, until modernism, there had long been a tradition of reticence when discussing sexual relations, let alone more everyday bodily functions. And some genres, of course, are founded on such notions of reticence, like Mills & Boon/Harlequin Romance novels, or, to go back a few centuries, the Romances of the Courtly Love tradition. It is a convention of much science fiction, too, that emotional matters are sidelined in favour of the technology, the action. But more generally, I'd say that one could go through the entire history of literature pointing out how each new literary movement criticises its precursor for not telling the truth properly: Victorian realism in redressing eighteenth-century adventure and sensation novels; naturalism's critique of Victorians for ignoring huge areas of society and their living conditions; modernism's more swingeing critique; second-wave feminists criticising most of the canonical writers for misrepresenting women, let alone lesbians, gays, writers of colour also lambasting earlier distortions; post-feminists reacting against their rather over-serious precursors, and so on.

To return to my main point, then, I do not see there being a larger disjunction between overt and shadow texts in children's books, and – the key issue – I do not see this as being aligned with the respective positions of children and adults. In most books, I would argue, the plots work by setting up a position of relative innocence, naivety or character flaw, fairly early in a novel, from which a process of learning and revelation occurs. In fact, Aristotle developed a terminology that is used by critics to this day to account for this, with what he termed *anagnorisis*, the point at which a character moves from a state of ignorance to knowledge, and *peripeteia*, a sudden reversal of events, fortunes and the like. Thus, to take a well-known example, in Jane Austen's *Emma*, the protagonist, through whom much of the novel is focalised, is shown to undergo this journey from ignorance to knowledge, initially seeing herself rather superior and justified in her actions, while we, through the shadow text, have this view ironically undercut, and Emma's haughty snobbishness is revealed. We are not thereby 'adults'; this is simply the nature of the narrative process, and particularly so in the novel as it developed in the West, which (tradi-tionally) is plot dependent (hence Aristotle's model, derived from Greek drama). It is not for nothing, then, that the most common form in which novels are written is the 'narrative past', where the narrator is (usually) the one 'in the know'. (As a coda, of course, I would add that, while we endorse Austen's construction of a truth, we do not thereby criticise her for 'holding back' on the inequities of the French Revolution, or indeed, of the Industrial Revolution, colonisation or slavery – *pace* Said, 1994).

Likewise on the issue of home and away, which is certainly a charac-teristic of children's literature, but, as Nodelman also realises, exists far more widely in culture, acknowledging Joseph Campbell's *The Hero with a Thousand Faces*. Yet it is also a staple of the traditional novel, as Brooks (1984: 110) has noted: 'Most of the great nineteenth-century novels tell this same tale', namely 'the narrative of an attempted homecoming: of the effort to reach an assertion of origin through ending, to find the same in the different, the time before in the time after'. As Brooks argues, this process usually takes place through repetitions that spell out the sorts of variations on a theme to which Nodelman also refers as characteristic of children's books.

Hiding in the light?

Standing back a little further from Nodelman's text, I now want to pull the various strands of my argument together. I have suggested that Nodelman's model is unnecessarily complex and convoluted, if not sinister at times with its maskings, bluffs and double-bluffs:

> children can be understood to need to pretend to be better than they ac-
> tually are and occupy a childhood they don't actually experience only
> by continuing to be what they actually are in spite of or because of the
> pretense. They are necessarily double and divided – both that which they
> mimic, childhood as envisaged and imposed on them by adults, and that
> which underlies and survives and transgresses that adult version of child-
> hood. (2008: 187)

Of course, one could argue that Nodelman is simply talking about textual constructions of the child, but he is evidently not;[8] he persistently alludes to real children who 'learn childlikeness from children's books' (ibid.: 13). However, he is also careful to steer clear of ideas about children's actual likes and needs, drawing instead on adult notions of what these are (ibid.: 188). But it is of note that he restricts himself to the expertise of 'adult writers, editors, and librarians' (ibid.) rather than offering more widespread views about childlikeness, though these must clearly inform how the child is storied (as becomes clear elsewhere, when he discusses the 'political and cultural unconscious' of a text, which derives from everyday life).

This, rather limited, almost incestuous view of childlikeness is problem atic. It makes one wonder where children who do not read children's books (i.e. the majority) learn it. Clearly, notions of childlikeness are phenomena that are far more culturally embedded – unless it is being suggested that children's books are unique in presenting this more innocent view of childhood, one that is otherwise out of line with children's experiences of the world. I suggest not, and would also suggest that Nodelman doesn't think so either, otherwise he would not talk so readily about children identifying with childlike characters. But if this is the case, is Nodelman suggesting that elsewhere in their lives children have this 'double and divided' (ibid.:

187) sense of existence? That they overtly mimic expected behaviour while, underlying this, a more transgressive disposition survives, as Nodelman proposes above? (This is not quite William Golding's *Lord of the Flies*, but that text certainly comes to mind!)

I'd suggest, instead, two things. First, that if we are going to read behaviour in this 'double and divided' way, then it is by no means peculiar to children. Erving Goffman termed it, as an early title of his proclaims, *The Presentation of Self in Everyday Life* (1990), arguing that we all have a public and a more off-stage self, the former abiding by the social niceties, the latter engaging in nose-picking, bum-scratching, belching and so forth. Once again, literature has for centuries had fun with this disparity (e.g. Swift's 'The Lady's Dressing Room', Joyce's *Ulysses*). But there's also the problem with Goffman's model that it suggests that the real self is the off-stage version, the one not on public display. This is where Judith Butler's notion of 'performativity' is particularly valuable; for it elides this difference, suggesting, in fact, that we are always performing, that there is no real off-stage where we can cease, in some sense, from acting. Butler, of course, is particularly concerned with gender, and the way we learn from birth how to deport ourselves in a gendered (and heterosexual) way.

Seen in these terms, we immediately divest ourselves of the doubletalk and see children as more straightforwardly performing childhood in line with the instructions conveyed repeatedly by adults (parents, education, the media, books) and, significantly, other children, who might suggest some more covert scripts, too. So, rather than arguing that children's literature's 'key lesson might be to teach children how *not* to know' (ibid.: 161), it could more simply be suggested that it delineates what it is socially acceptable to know. And this is something that has changed over time, as picture books like *The Story of the Little Mole Who Knew it was None of His Business* (Holzwarth and Erlbruch, 2002) demonstrate, and, at the other end of the spectrum, explorations of sex that we see in Judy Blume's or Melvin Burgess's work.

Second, I have also suggested that, even though the focus is on children's literature, it can only be discussed in a wider cultural context, and that the hidden adult is actually quite a visible figure, unlike the more occluded presence of the child, which is a far more messy and disruptive variable. However, dialogue is not impossible. Children's literature is most frequently likened to popular literature in being defined by its readership, and there is now a substantial body of empirical work to be drawn upon (indeed, I've referred to some of this work above). Moreover, studies of children's reading are growing too (reaching back to the eighteenth century, with Matthew Grenby's 2011 analysis of marginal comments in texts), which I have also mentioned. I am not in any way suggesting that Nodelman should become an ethnographer, but I do think that children must be part of any model (if only schematically) that seeks to define children's literature. Nodelman, however, takes a different view, arguing that children's literature can only be defined as

> a genre of literature whose defining characteristics can be accounted for by conventional assumptions about and constructions of childhood. The issue here is not what children do actually like or do need. It is how adult perceptions of what children like or need shape the literature that adults provide for children in ways that provide it with distinct markers that allow it to be identified as a genre. (2008: 188)

Obviously, I have disagreed with a number of these markers but, beyond this, I would argue that adults are not deaf to what children say and have said about their books (alongside other issues), and these will feed back into this form of literature. For example, the disappearance of prayers and hymns from children's books was surely at least partly influenced by children's behaviour, as Grenby (2011: 251) records:

> Mary Louisa Molesworth was not a subversive child ... . But even she remembered passing over the prayers and the hymns at the end of each chapter. It was apparently the almost universal practice. 'Did we not one and all skip that prayer?', asked Lucy Bethia Walford.

I therefore end up commending Nodelman on his heroic achievement, but would contend that defining children's literature in generic terms is equivalent to defining drama without reference to actual performances or, more generally, to audience reception. This seems especially the case in that he chooses to speak of the whole of 'children's literature' as a genre when his six exemplary texts are drawn solely from prose fiction. He does briefly address his omission of other forms, and hopes that others will venture there, but certain passages unfortunately underline Nodelman's fixation, as when he speaks about reducing the huge variety of children's literature (poetry, drama, nonsense, fairy tale, biography, religious writings, etc.) to – in his own words – 'a specific genre of fiction' (2008: 81).

Part III

The Real

5 Home Sweet Home and the Uncanny: Freud, *Alice* and the Curious Child

Introduction

This chapter is in the part of the book headed 'The Real', Lacan's third order of human existence, and the one that is probably most hard to conceptualise. As I said earlier, this is because it concerns that which lies resolutely outside signification (hence beyond the Symbolic and the Imaginary). Its existence can thus be felt only at times when we find ourselves 'lost for words', undone by events; in short, when we find that we are not at home in the universe. It therefore seems apposite to introduce this notion through the concept of the 'uncanny', or 'unhomely' (or, indeed, 'unhomey', as US usage has it), which, as Richard Gooding (2008: 392) remarks, 'has only lately begun to attract critical attention' in children's literature.

In making his statement, Gooding credits Coats (1997) as being one of the first to consider the uncanny in children's literature, also mentioning a special issue of the *Children's Literature Association Quarterly* on the topic (Trites, 2002).[1] However, Gooding neglects to mention a far earlier piece by Zipes (1983), which argues that the fairy tale is itself an uncanny form – a claim that I shall contend shortly. The uncanny itself, of course, has a much longer history, though cultural theorists have tended to link it to notions of modernity (Castle, 1995; Collins and Jervis, 2008). Undoubtedly, its presence is more prevalent in recent times, perhaps because 'it captures something that resonates with contemporary society', though this does make it 'in danger of losing all specificity' (Rudd, 2010c: 252) with areas such as 'uncanny studies' appearing (Collins and Jervis, 2008: 1), including the popular notion of the 'uncanny valley'.

While I think there has been some lack of specificity in the use of the term – as I shall indicate in considering Zipes's piece (which itself stages an almost uncanny return in his 2011 work, *The Enchanted Screen*, though still with little reference to continuing debates on the topic)[2] – I shall argue that the problems originate in Freud's own, very influential, 1919 essay, 'Das "Unheimliche"'. I will examine this essay in more detail after considering Zipes's work, before going on to suggest that a post-structuralist, Lacanian version offers a more profitable way of considering the phenomenon, which I shall then undertake in an analysis of Carroll's *Alice*. Finally, I shall return to Nodelman's work and, specifically, his claim that children's literature constitutes an 'attempted imposition of adult views of childhood on children'; that is, the notion that though *childhood* might appear safe, *children* themselves are seen 'as inherently and dangerously *unheimlich*' (Nodelman, 2008: 225).

Let me begin, though, with some advice found in Martin Gardner's classic, *The Annotated Alice*, which appositely carries an epigraph from Joyce's *Finnegans Wake*, a work that itself draws on *Alice* extensively: 'Wipe your glosses with what you know' (Carroll, 1970: 6). This advice seems particularly pertinent when considered in conjunction with Freud's 1919 essay, in which the bespectacled Sigmund finds repeated images of ocular devices (spy-glasses, weather-glasses, spectacles, eyes, etc.) in E.T.A. Hoffmann's tale 'The Sand-man'. These, he thinks, provide him with a key to the uncanny, expressing repressed anxieties about blindness and castration. But, much like the *Alice* books (and, indeed, *Finnegans Wake* itself), Freud's analysis proceeds in anything but a straightforward, linear way, mixing philology, personal anecdote, psychoanalysis and literature, and continually revising and rethinking its precepts en route. It always, therefore, appears less familiar than we once thought, making the concept live up to its *unheimlich* name. Indeed, those extra scare quotes that Freud places round that dangerous, titular word ('Das "Unheimliche"') should make us realise that this topic needs approaching with caution: 'Here be dragons!' it seems to suggest.

Mention of such creatures leads me to another epigraph, this time from Neil Gaiman's *Coraline* (2002) – the subject of Gooding's essay – where G. K. Chesterton is quoted: 'Fairy tales are more than true: not because they tell us that dragons exist, but because they tell us that dragons can be beaten'. However, this facility for overcoming the dangerous in the fairy tale – where, in Freud's words, 'the world of reality is left behind from the very start, and the animistic system of beliefs is frankly adopted' (Freud, 1985c: 373) – is what made Freud deny the genre's uncanny nature.

'Wish-fulfilments, secret powers, omnipotence of thoughts, animation of inanimate objects' were simply too commonplace in these tales (ibid.), and he gives as an example the Grimms' story, 'The Three Wishes', where wishes are thoughtlessly wasted on sausages that, after what we might term 'a domestic', subsequently need removing from the wife's nose (ibid.: 369).

Zipes's redundant uncanny

I will consider the rest of Freud's essay in more detail later, but let me first pause (in much the manner adopted by Freud) to introduce Zipes's own objection to Freud's assertion about 'fairy tales ... excluding the uncanny' (1983: 174). In fact, the way Zipes expresses this concern is unfortunate, making it sound as though the uncanny *might* have been present but for some unspoken prohibition, whereas, as the above quotation from Freud shows, more to the point is the fact that fairy tales are seen by many critics as failing to *evoke* the uncanny. Rosemary Jackson (1981: 90), for instance, argues that

> They are neutral, impersonalized, set apart from the reader. The reader becomes a passive receiver of events, there is no demand that (s)he partic-ipate in their interpretation. *Structurally, too, fairy tales discourage belief in the importance or effectiveness of action* for their narratives are 'closed'. Things 'happen', 'are done *to*' protagonists, told *to* the reader, from a position of omniscience and authority, making the reader unquestioningly passive.

Likewise, Max Lüthi, on whom Jackson draws for support, suggests that 'the fairy tale is the poetic expression of the confidence that we are secure in a world not destitute of sense' (quoted in ibid.).

For Zipes, in contrast, rather than the tales' divorce from reality rendering them immune to uncanny effects, it is the very disjunction of these tales from the everyday world that renders them uncanny: '*the very act of reading a fairy tale is an uncanny experience in that it separates the reader from the restrictions of reality from the onset and makes the repressed unfamiliar familiar once again*' (1983: 174). Though Zipes admits to 'modifying' Freud at times, his persistence in using orthodox psychoanalytical concepts (e.g. 'repression') makes his case problematic. For the moment, let me just note that, from what he writes above, it seems as though there is nothing in the fairy tale per se that is distinctively uncanny; rather, he seems to suggest that any text that releases readers from 'the restrictions of reality' should have this effect (e.g. fantasy in general).[3] For Freud, in contrast, it is precisely 'the setting ... of material reality' (1985c: 375) that makes the uncanny possible.

Zipes (1983: 174) even suggests that 'the complete reversal of the real world has already taken place before we begin reading a fairy tale on the part of the writer, and the writer invites the reader to repeat this uncanny experience'. I am not quite sure what he means in the first part of this sentence: that the writer will have experienced the uncanny first (not simply created it). If this is the case, then are we to understand that the uncanny is a product of this 'complete reversal of the real world', which suggests more than a straightforward separation 'from the restrictions of reality' to which he earlier refers? Moreover, talking about a 'reversal' will, for many readers, conjure up Bakhtinian notions of the carniva-lesque, as we see in the 'world turned upside-down' type of tale, where hierarchies are inverted, the poor are crowned, animals rule people, and the body is celebrated over the mind (Bakhtin, 1984). This type of tale has a long history in children's literature, from works like Ann and Jane Taylor's *Signor Topsy-Turvy's Wonderful Magic Lantern* (1810),[4] where the animal world becomes armed against the humans, through to Roald Dahl's more recent reversal in *The Magic Finger* (1974), or Anne Fine's in *The Chicken Gave It to Me* (1999) (cf. Rudd, 2009).

Putting these queries aside, though, Zipes makes much of the German roots of the term, *unheimlich* (literally, 'unhomely'), arguing that '[t]he fairy tale ignites a double quest for home', both from the reader and from 'within the tale itself', concluding:

> In both quests the notion of home or *Heimat* ... retains a powerful progressive attraction for readers of fairy tales. While the uncanny setting and motifs of the fairy tale already open us up to the recurrence of primal experiences, we can move forward at the same time because it opens us up to what Freud calls 'unfulfilled but possible futures to which we still like to cling in fantasy ... '. (Zipes, 1983: 175)

There are several problems with this that I want to discuss. First, it is difficult to see how a whole genre (the fairy tale) can be uncanny in its form, any more than fantasy can be, *ipso facto*, subversive, as Jackson tries to argue (see p. 146). For Freud, in contrast, the uncanny is something more specific, triggered (potentially) by particular items or feelings (as we shall explore later). But even if we were to countenance Zipes's notion that it is the initial move into a fairy tale that precipitates the uncanny, what, then, do we make of the succeeding uncanny 'motifs' (as Zipes calls them), given that we are already, according to him, within an uncanny space? This is my second problem with his reading: what, to use a tale that Freud himself mentions, might be the effect on the reader of Snow White's return to life from her inanimate, death-like state, given that we are already experiencing the uncanny as a result of 'the very act of reading a fairy tale'?

Third, in Freud's initial definition of the uncanny, he speaks of it comprising 'that class of the frightening which leads back to what is known of old and long familiar' (Freud, 1985c: 340). But in Zipes's reading, the frightening aspect seems to have disappeared. In fact, I'd argue that the uncanny itself has become largely irrelevant. This is particularly apparent in the quotation from Freud with which Zipes ends the above quoted paragraph. I have cropped it, but what is particularly salient is that Freud at this point is talking about the *ego*'s desires (nothing to do with the unconscious), such that Freud goes on to remark how 'none of this helps us to understand the extraordinarily strong feeling of something uncanny' (ibid.: 358). There is, then, no 'repressed unfamiliar' (picking up on Zipes's earlier words) in this tamed version of the uncanny, which might also explain Zipes's emendation of Freud's more psychoanalyti-cally inflected spelling of the term 'phantasy' in Zipes's quotation (it is what we might term a peculiarly non-Freudian slip).

So, to go back to my starting point, it is Zipes who is effectively 'excluding the uncanny' in anything resembling a Freudian sense, by associating it primarily with conscious wishes and homeliness. This said, reworking it in this way is certainly in line with Zipes's agenda of seeing 'home as liberation' (which he derives – more persuasively – from the work of Ernst Bloch), arguing for 'the liberating potential of the fantastic in fairy tales'. In Zipes's words,

> through the use of unfamiliar (*unheimlich*) symbols the fairy tale liberates readers of different age groups to return to repressed ego-disturbances, that is, to return to familiar (*heimlich*) primal moments in their lives, but the fairy tale cannot be liberating ultimately unless it projects on a conscious, literary, and philosophical level the objectification of home as real democracy under non-alienating conditions. (1983: 178)

Seen in these terms, the uncanny becomes a very mechanistic device, with 'unfamiliar symbols' doing the business (whereas, in Freud's model, context is all: there are no such symbols per se).[5] But even setting this aside, the idea that an experience of the uncanny somehow 'liberates' its reader is a strange one, given that the uncanny is, precisely, disturbing, unnerving ('that class of the frightening' etc.). Moreover, to talk of being liberated in order to 'return to repressed ego-disturbances' is even stranger. Clearly, it is the very material that the ego has repressed that disturbs people; so the idea that it might be re-accessed in some more homely fashion makes little sense; it is uncanny (disturbing) exactly because it was *once* familiar but is *now* frightening. As Freud notes, the once familiar womb, home to us all, is often transformed into a 'terrifying phantasy' about 'the most uncanny thing of all', namely 'being buried alive by mistake' (1985c: 366–7). In short, there is no way that this frightening experience could be put in the service of 'a conscious, literary, and philosophical ... objectification of home as real democracy under non-alienating conditions' (Zipes, 1983: 178). As Mladen Dolar (1991: 19) comments on ideological criticism of this ilk,

> it tries to reduce [the uncanny] to another kind of content or to make the content conscious and explicit. This criticism is always on the brink of a naive effort to fix things with their proper names, to make the unconscious conscious, to restore the sense of what is repressed and thus be rid of the uncanny.

In conclusion, whilst Zipes is usually keen to criticise the more cosy versions of fairy tales, such as those of Disney, when it comes to Freud's more disturbing ideas, he seems to have engaged in a similar domestication (although, as suggested in the next section, Freud himself laid the crumbs of this trail).

The Freudian unconscious

I now want to move on from Zipes's attempt to make the uncanny into something like a consciousness-raising tool, one that might help people undo repression and alienation, to look more closely at Freud's own model. For it is certainly the case that many of the problems critics have with the concept of *Das Unheimliche* (1919) derive from Freud's own essay. There is a contradiction at the heart of his uncanny analysis, in fact, that he has bequeathed to future researchers. In short, while he thought that he was identifying the repressed infantile complexes that precipitate the uncanny, he ultimately bypasses these in favour of a more socially amenable interpretation, one that pays but lip-service to repression, to the unconscious. As a result of this analysis, I will then draw on more recent developments that suggest a more fruitful, theoretically accommodating way of addressing the phenomenon of the uncanny – one that neither traduces Freud's work, nor reduces the concept to an epiphenomenon.

Freud begins his essay with a lexicographical examination of the term, the 'uncanny', from which he notes how the word, across different languages, moves in two, opposing, semantic directions, from the 'familiar and agreeable' to the 'concealed and kept out of sight' (1985c: 345). As Freud puts it, the term thereby 'develops in the direction of ambivalence, until if finally coincides with its opposite, *unheimlich*'; thus he reasons that the '*[u]nheimlich* is in some way or other a subspecies of *heimlich*', or the 'unhomely' is part of the 'homely'. Freud completes his lexicographical study by endorsing Friedrich Schelling's claim that 'everything is *unheimlich* that ought to have remained secret and hidden but has come to light' (ibid.).

From here, Freud enumerates some of the things that arouse the uncanny in us, which he later summarises – 'animism, magic and sorcery, the omnipotence of thoughts, man's attitude to death, involuntary repetition and the castration complex comprise practically all the factors which turn something frightening into something uncanny' (ibid.: 365) – apart from the fact that he omits some of the aspects he has already discussed (e.g. doubles), and proceeds, subsequently, to add others (e.g. being buried alive). Also, having started to introduce the factor of animism, he breaks off in order to discuss Hoffmann's 1817 tale, 'The Sand-Man', taking particular issue with Ernst Jentsch's interpretation, in which Jentsch argues that the automaton (Olympia, in the story) is 'one of the most successful devices for easily creating uncanny effects'; '[t]he thing', continues Jentsch, creates a 'peculiar emotional effect' (quoted in Freud, ibid.: 347–8). Freud promptly recasts Jentsch's notion of an 'emotional effect' into 'intellectual uncertainty', which, Freud avers, 'has nothing to do with the [uncanny] effect' (ibid.: 351). In contrast, argues Freud, the tale's main concern is 'something different'; namely, it is 'the theme of the "Sand-Man" who tears out children's eyes' (ibid.: 348). After spending some considerable time interpreting the story in this, his preferred way,[6] he confidently re-asserts his conviction that 'the idea of being robbed of one's eyes' is central, whereas Jentsch's claim about uncertainty is 'quite irrelevant in connection with this other, more striking instance of uncanniness' (ibid.: 351). A subsequent paragraph opens by reasserting that '[t]here is no question … of intellectual uncertainty here', rounding off, in case we had not been paying attention, by reiterating that such uncertainty is 'thus incapable of explaining' the phenomenon (ibid.: 352).

And yet, after all this, Freud then poses the question: 'are we after all justified in entirely ignoring intellectual uncertainty as a factor, seeing that we have admitted its importance in relation to death?' (ibid.: 370). On this occasion he is referring back to an earlier comment about mortality: 'our thoughts and feelings have changed so little since the very earliest times [... in] relation to death', such that 'almost all of us think as savages do on this topic', these primitive thoughts being 'always ready to come to the surface on any provocation' (ibid.: 364, 365). This, we might say, is a return to something that Freud has fought hard to repress but, as is evident, less than successfully. As has often been noted, Freud was at this period also wrestling with the notion of a 'death drive' (which he would shortly conceptualise in *Beyond the Pleasure Principle*, 1920), to which he briefly alludes in this current essay when he speaks of a 'compulsion to repeat' (ibid.: 361); however, he also seems keen to avoid its more powerful implications in relation to the uncanny.[7]

Having sought so convincingly to provide a psychoanalytic explanation of Hoffmann's story (contra Jentsch) – 'We know from psychoanalytic experience' – (ibid.: 352), Freud still finds 'the literary' aspects troubling. So, while '[i]t may be true that the uncanny ... is something which is secretly familiar ... which has undergone repression and then returned from it, and that everything that is uncanny fulfils this condition', it is also the case that '[n]ot everything that fulfils this condition ... is on that account uncanny', with Freud admitting that it is 'the realm of fiction' (ibid.: 368, 370) that is really problematic. It is this that leads him to mention the fairy tale, as discussed earlier, arguing that despite all sorts of outlandish events (wishes coming true (sausages!) and the dead returning to life (Snow White)), the effect is not ultimately uncanny. He therefore distinguishes between a sense of the uncanny caused by what is *repressed* as opposed to that which has been *surmounted*. The former concerns 'can be traced back without exception to something familiar that has been repressed'; for example, dismembered limbs, which for Freud bring to mind castration; or, being buried alive, also mentioned earlier, which is seen to evoke our 'intra-uterine existence' (ibid.: 370, 367). The latter type of uncanniness, in contrast, occurs 'when primitive beliefs which have been surmounted seem once more to be confirmed' (ibid.: 372) – such as our 'intellectual uncertainty' about death or about the animate being lifeless. It is the latter that creative writers can manipulate, although only when a 'writer pretends to move in the world of common reality'; then '[w]e react to his inventions as we would have reacted to real experiences' (ibid.: 374).

Freud might seem to have salvaged his case here, having held on to the *repressed* uncanny as still special, unaffected by 'reality-testing': '[w]here the uncanny comes from infantile complexes [i.e. repression] the question of material reality does not arise'; thus, '[t]he class which proceeds from repressed complexes ... remains as powerful in fiction as in real experience'; but he then adds, 'subject to one exception' (ibid.: 372, 374). And this is the matter of the 'severed hand', which, though associated with the castration complex, sometimes has no 'uncanny effect'. As to why, Freud declares, rather too precipitately, '[t]he answer is easy' (ibid.: 375): it all depends on which characters we identify with in a tale. But with this move, Freud has once again made his explanation dependent, not on the unconscious but, rather, on the storyteller's 'peculiarly directive power over us: by means of the moods he can put us into', guiding 'the current of our emotions' (ibid.). Jentsch's stress on the significance of 'uncertainty' (or, something that creates a 'peculiar emotional effect' as he termed it), previously decried, is now subtly reinstated.[8]

Freud's attempts are prodigious in seeking to give the uncanny a satisfactory explanation in terms of the new science of psychoanalysis, his master discourse, rooted in his key concept, the unconscious. But, as Dolar (1991: 6) puts it, despite the fact that Freud is 'gradually forced to use the entire panoply of psychoanalytic concepts: castration complex, Oedipus, (primary) narcissism, compulsion to repeat, death drive, repression, anxiety, psychosis, etc.', he is repeatedly thwarted by the power of literature, and of writers, to do two things: first, to create uncanny effects without recourse to repressed material (drawing on *surmounted* fears); and second, even where repressed material is present (castration anxiety – as with the severed hand), to avert its return thanks to the writer's power.

For those wishing to draw on Freud's influential concept, then, there are two options. The first is to reject Freud's psychoanalytical explanation entirely. In other words, to misappropriate his 'talking cure': In other words, making light of his 'talking cure'; we might say that Freud has effectively talked us out of it, showing (albeit not intentionally) that there are, indeed, quite *conscious* psychological mechanisms at work, including 'uncertainty' (that which he initially attempted to decry in Jentsch's work), which are produced largely because of the ability of the creative writer (and elsewhere, of course, Freud had conceded that 'before the problem of the creative artist analysis must, alas, lay down its arms' (Freud, 1985b: 441)). The second option is to accept that there really *is* something disturbing and uncanny about these phenomena, but to recognise that Freud, in his attempts at mastery (or his doubts about its adequacy), either misses or avoids these effects. As Steve Vine expresses it, Freud seems 'disturbed by [the uncanny's] *power to disturb one's power to recognize it*', and by the fact that psychoanalysis itself

> remains haunted by the repressed possibility that its own 'truths' *may* be
> forms of fiction – the truth or the fiction of 'castration' included – and that
> literature inhabits the body of its discourse as the uncanniest of guests.
> (Vine, 2005: 63, 66)[9]

In short, psychoanalysis, too, is ineluctably haunted by the uncanny effects of language. This is where a more post-structuralist reading of Freud can be instructive, rather than one that sees the uncanny as a phenomenon that can be deployed in the service of social liberation (and thereby reduced to a slogan). Whereas Freud claims that the '*Unheimlich* is in some way or other a subspecies of *heimlich*' (1985c: 345), then, we might now want to reverse this claim to state that the *heimlich* is a more fragile island set in an *unheimlich* sea; and that the 'master discourse' of psychoanalysis turns out to be no such thing, but is itself very much caught up in the ongoing process of signification. Another heretical notion, perhaps, but Freud's penultimate sentence in this essay has always struck me as moving in this less secure direction: 'Concerning the factors of silence, solitude and darkness, we can only say that they are actually elements in the production of the infantile anxiety from which the majority of human beings have never become quite free' (ibid.: 376).

Following Lacan's lead then, a number of commentators have sought a more open, linguistically informed basis for the phenomenon, based on Lacan's key proclamation that 'the unconscious is structured like a language' (Weber, 1973; Cixous, 1976; Dolar, 1991; Žižek, 1992b; Derrida, 1994a; Møller, 2005; Vine, 2005). Dolar consequently sees '[t]he dimension of the uncanny' as 'located at the very core of psychoanalysis' (1991: 5). Certainly, in these revised readings there is no need for what are ultimately tenuous and unsustainable distinctions between repression and surmounting,[10] or between the real and the fictional. In Lacanian terms there is, more straightforwardly, a 'common denominator', as Dolar phrases it; namely, the uncanny is about 'the irruption of the real into "homely," commonly accepted reality. We can speak of the emergence of something that shatters well-known divisions and which cannot be situated within them' (ibid.: 6). This is the Lacanian Real, which we experience at moments of crisis, when neither the Imaginary nor the Symbolic, our shields against the Real, function properly.

The uncanny is therefore less concerned with particular motifs than felt effects. It certainly involves such matters as 'seeing' and 'blindness', but these are not to do with any simplistic notion of castration; rather, they are concerned with the fact that our look is always partial, always distorted by desire and blind to a **gaze** that seems to emanate from outside our own, limited perspective. We can never see the uncanny in full view, then, because the 'narcissistic categories of identity and presence are riven by a difference', as Samuel Weber (1973: 1113) puts it, continuing:

> [The] uncanny is a certain indecidability which affects and infects representations, motifs, themes and situations, which ... always mean something other than what they are and in a manner which draws their own being and substance into the vortex of signification. (Ibid.: 1132)

But it is also, notes Weber, a

> defence against this crisis of perception and phenomenality, a defence which is ambivalent and which expresses itself in the compulsive curiosity ... the craving to penetrate the flimsy appearances to the essence beneath ... the desire to uncover the facade and to discover what lurks behind. (Ibid.)

Almost providentially, Weber ends this sentence by referring to the look of 'a simple woman' (ibid.: 1133). It is Hoffmann's Clara, rather than Carroll's Alice, that is being spoken about here, but it could almost have been the latter. Certainly, Weber's two, fuller quotations above seem to capture the tone of *Alice's Adventures in Wonderland* exactly.

Alice in Uncanny-Land

As Coats noted, there are few works in children's literature that effectively create uncanny effects, disrupting our symbolic coordinates, but the *Alice* books seem to be exceptions. Though Nodelman concedes that they are now often seen as not suitable for children, because of their 'hidden adult' shadow texts, I prefer to see these texts as disturbing in a more basic way, being not simply about the literary and ideological subtexts that the implied reader might discern. Indeed, *Alice* seems to me to dramatise how the whole process of signification falters when the signified slips beneath the signifier, as occurs quite overtly when Alice drops down the rabbit hole, this opening itself suggesting the dangerous porosity of the Symbolic. Previously, of course, we have seen her sitting with her older sister, presumably being looked after. But her sister is shown to be utterly captivated by the Symbolic, absorbed in a book that has neither pictures nor conversations; in short, nothing dialogical. At the end of the story, this sister will seek once again to perform an exercise in textual simplification, or monologism, shutting down the very signification opened up by Alice's vivid dreams with their endless and very vivid conversations.

One could, of course, argue that this story is just another fairy tale, in that the coordinates of reality are divested from the off; but the beginning – and, of course, the end also – is initially too naturalistic for this. Moreover, Alice herself (at least within the space of the tale) thinks that her journey is real, not beyond the reality principle: 'When I used to read fairy tales, I fancied that kind of thing never happened, and now here I am in the middle of one!' (Carroll, 1970: 59). Aside from a fairy tale, though, one could also argue that *Alice* is a portal fantasy, with the realm of Wonderland separated from the real world, except, that is, for the fact that the rabbit with the waistcoat and watch appears *before* we enter this realm. Of course, we are later informed that Alice's adventures have been nothing but a dream, but this does little to allay the fact that disturbing questions about identity and existence have been raised.

Alice certainly experiences the narcissistic crisis of not being identical with herself that Weber describes. In fact, as she falls down the rabbit hole, where the coordinates of latitude and longitude cease to signify (they only map the surface of the world, of course), so too does Alice find her entire being hollowed out – something that is doubled in her action of removing, during her descent, 'a jar from one of the shelves ... labeled "ORANGE MARMALADE"'; unfortunately, it turns out to be "empty" '(ibid.: 27). The signified is thus no longer at one with the signifier. It seems particularly pertinent, then, that at this moment she decides not 'to drop the jar, for fear of killing somebody underneath' (ibid.). Suddenly she seems to have developed an awareness of death and destruction, though she does not consider that the impact of her own body plummeting towards someone beneath might be problematic, either for the squashed or squisher. But Carroll's evocation of a jar crashing down from above is powerful and reminiscent of one of Lacan's own examples of 'the encounter with the real' erupting into our symbolic world (mentioned previously): of 'a tile falling on to the head of a passer-by' (Bowie, 1991: 103; see also p. 72 in this book). Entering Wonderland, then, seems to heighten Alice's awareness of mortality and the Symbolic's fragile state – something that is emphasised in Alice's thoughts: 'after a fall such as this' (itself a reference to a post-Edenic state), '"Why, I wouldn't say anything about it, even if I fell off the top of the house!" (which was very likely true.)' (Carroll, 1970: 27).

The uncanny images continue as Alice runs down a passage to arrive in a hall with many doors, including one small one, behind a curtain, that opens with a key. She tries in vain to squeeze through this door with her head, commenting on how it might help if she could 'shut up like a telescope', adding, 'I think I could, if I only knew how to begin' (ibid.: 30). Such imagery, coupled with the later swim in the pool of tears, has led a number of critics to suggest that these scenes are evocative of notions of the female body and birth, of an 'intra-uterine existence', once homely but now disturbing; the curtain, certainly, might suggest a garment being pulled aside, and the door through which Alice cannot yet squeeze could be seen to resemble a birth-canal (cf. Phillips, 1972). Moreover, as she herself says, if she only knew how to begin the process, she might succeed. One might also note that, before this, there is the scene where she bathes in her own tears, once again, in an amniotic-like environment reminiscent of the womb.

Similar birthing imagery occurs in the White Rabbit's house where Alice swells up until she completely fills his room, with her foot lodged against the chimney. In this instance, she has come to embody what had earlier been just a thought (thoughts becoming real, in fact), as she imagines her gross body, its parts moving steadily away from each other, such that she fears she might lose any contact with her feet ('Goodbye, feet!'), apart from sending them boots at Christmas, addressed to 'Alice's Right Foot, Esq.' (in a more traditionally Freudian sense of dismemberment, it is of note that this fetishistic extremity now turns out to be male), at the 'Hearthrug,/ near the Fender' (Carroll, 1970: 36) (near, in fact, a female hearth/chimney). This repetition is but one of many, though, with which I'll deal later, but it is worth noting that the imagery of birth continues alongside another repetition, where Alice once again finds herself back in the long hall (at the end of Chapter 7). This time, however, she successfully manages to squeeze through the little door into the garden, only to find that it is not the Edenic realm she had imagined, but one where images of castration and death lurk ('Off with her head!' (ibid.: 112)). The phrase *et in arcadia ego*, referring to the fact that death, also, resides in arcadia, comes to mind. But Alice has herself been implicated in this scenario earlier when, with her distended neck, she is accused by the Pigeon of being a serpent, and confesses that she is, indeed, partial to consuming eggs.

Home and death, or *Heim* and the *Unheimliche*, are thus close companions in this tale. Indeed, it seems significant that this story (unlike its sequel, which opens at the hearth, right foot intact) does not begin at home; in fact, Alice's parents are not mentioned at all: only her sister and her cat, the rather mortifying Dinah. Homely elements, in particular, are rendered unusually disturbing in this first book, with the domestic space of the kitchen in 'Pig and Pepper' being, rather, a site of violence and destruction. It is 'full of smoke', with pepper choking the air, causing the baby to sneeze and howl, let alone having 'fire-irons ... saucepans, plates, and dishes' (ibid.: 84) thrown at it; not only this, but the baby is nursed by the Duchess, who seems not to be its mother, although after its later transformation into a pig, Alice does remark that 'it would have made a dreadfully ugly child' (ibid.: 87), which would certainly tie it more closely to the Duchess who, in Tenniel's illustration at least, seems to be based on a portrait of Margaretha Maultasch (i.e. 'bag-mouth'), a fourteenth-century duchess said to be 'the ugliest woman in history' (Gardner, in Carroll, 1970: 82).

The only other, potentially homely scene in the book, the Mad Hatter's tea-party, also significantly occurs outside the home and, unlike most tea-parties in children's literature, is conspicuously devoid of consum-ables. On her arrival, then, Alice is offered some wine, only to be told that there is none. There is bread and butter, but it is of note that, in Tenniel's illustration, it is omitted, as though the illustrator inwardly recognised the austerity of this sterile and stagnant meal-time. Even the teapot, symbol of Victorian decorum and civility, takes on more sinister overtones (of being buried alive) as the Dormouse ends up stuffed into it (after an initial baptism of having 'hot tea' poured on his nose), perhaps in emulation of the creature's own story about people living at the bottom of a well (and, of course, of Alice's initial descent). The imagery is thus simultaneously womb and tomb-like.

But Alice, the dreamer, is not merely a bystander: she herself contributes to the disturbing atmosphere of Wonderland. She is the home-wrecker who floods the long hall with her tears and subsequently almost destroys the White Rabbit's house. The Pigeon is likewise explicit in accusing Alice of potential destruction, seeing the girl as a threat to both her nest and brood. (The Pigeon and her eggs are also, notably, the closest approxi-mation to a family that we see in Wonderland, where, otherwise, we are confronted with mostly isolated and antagonistic individuals.)

As other commentators have noted (e.g. William Empson, in Phillips, 1972), death lurks everywhere in this story. I have already mentioned several instances, but there are many others, such as that displayed at the end of the Mouse's 'long and ... sad tale', which ends, as everyone's own story must, in 'death', the calligrammatic tail disturbingly represented in a font size that becomes ever smaller until blankness alone confronts us (Carroll, 1970: 50-1). It is, again, a repetition of an earlier event, where Alice tried to imagine herself like a snuffed candle – conjuring up those lines from *Macbeth*, 'Out, out brief candle! / Life's but a walking shadow' – as she worried about shrinking to nothingness: 'it might end

... in my going out altogether, like a candle' (ibid.: 32). In the scene with the Pigeon, too, we are informed that Alice has 'to stoop to save her neck from being broken' (ibid.: 57).

These references to death, and the fact that they repeat, can also be linked to another powerful discourse in the book: the contemporary debate about Darwin's theory of evolution (obviously on Dodgson's doorstep in Oxford). The pool of tears, then, also conjures up another sea, that from which we all emerged, only to engage in what seems like a purposeless race, similar to the caucus-race in fact, with some species destined to become extinct along the way. The Dodo is the iconic example – its name also a pun on Dodgson's own name, which his stutter ('Do-Do-Dodgson') must have emphasised, and thus also pointing to Dodgson's own, personal short-comings when it came to the survival of the fittest (our close cousin, the ape, also features prominently in Tenniel's illustration).

It is this side of the evolutionary debate that is most prevalent and uncanny: an eruption of meaninglessness amidst the church spires of Oxford where, instead of the industrious bee earning its just deserts, we find instead the lazy crocodile merely opening his 'gently smiling jaws' as he 'welcomes little fishes in' (ibid.: 38). This meaningless fight for survival is repeatedly drawn attention to, mostly through the figure of Alice's beloved cat, Dinah, its name also punning on its predilection for being precisely this: a 'diner', especially on mice, in fact. Alice insists on sharing this information with the Mouse she meets in the pool of tears, just as she also tells him about a 'nice little dog' that will 'fetch things if you throw them' (ibid.: 43), adding that 'it kills all the rats and – oh dear!' The omission of the word 'mice' at this point is almost more disturbing than its mention, Alice's expression of regret emphasising the creature's euphemistic erasure. However, in another doubling, Alice herself later comes to appreciate the Mouse's perspective with regard to dogs, when she confronts an 'enormous puppy' which, she realises, 'might be hungry' (another diner), if not 'very likely to eat her up' (ibid.: 64).

All these aspects of the uncanny are, of course, interconnected; and the fears of castration and death ('Talking of axes,' said the Duchess, 'chop off her head!' (ibid.: 84)) are closely linked to attacks on Alice's identity, her formerly complacent ideal ego. So, the things that might normally guarantee Alice's existence, that might ground her sense of identity, become increasingly ineffective. She first tries the principle of sameness, seeking to establish continuity through her memory of herself (*was* I the same when I got up this morning? I almost think I can remember feeling a little different. But if I'm not the same, the next question is, "Who in the world am I? Ah, *that's* the great puzzle!"' (ibid.: 37)). She then tries the principle of difference, contrasting herself with other people; thus, Ada is seen to have her long ringlets, whereas Mabel 'knows such a very little'. But this too is fruitless: she only has the emptiness and repetitiousness of pronouns to hang on to, which insist on registering *sameness* only: '*she's* she, and *I'm* I' (ibid.: 37–8). Her store of knowledge (of geography, arithmetic and verse) also fails to define her; it simply 'doesn't signify' (ibid.: 38), as she puts it. Even the signifying plane of her body becomes somewhat arbitrary as she shifts in shape and proportion. So that sense of wholeness that one experienced at the mirror stage, as Lacan argues, is here repeatedly under attack, with anxieties about what Lacan (1977a: 11) terms '*imagos of the fragmented body*', among which he lists 'castration, mutilation, dismemberment, dislocation, evisceration, devouring, bursting open of the body', specifically noting that these are often present in children's play. Some of these images have been discussed earlier, motifs of death and castration explicitly, but images of fragmentation are also present in other forms, too: 'evisceration', for instance, is exemplified in Alice's tearfulness, where she ends up enveloped in her own secretions. At other times in the book, Alice displays more aggression in defending herself, as demonstrated, for example, when she kicks Bill the lizard up the chimney (Carroll, 1970: 61–2). It is in the chapter, 'Advice from a Caterpillar', though, that her inability to signify is at its most stark: 'Who are *You*?', he asks her, to which she can only stammer out, 'I – I hardly know' (ibid.: 67).

Another aspect of identity, also touched on earlier, comes with the doubling of characters, also a central feature of Freud's notion of the uncanny. A double, by definition, queries notions of individuality, and there are many examples in this text: the Mad Hatter and March Hare, the Duchess and the Queen, the Mouse and the Dormouse (each of whom regales us with a story), and then there is Alice herself, being 'very fond of pretending to be two people' (ibid.: 33), though in Wonderland her splitting becomes even more dramatic. But doubling goes beyond character to the repetition of events, which Freud treats as a different aspect of the uncanny, linking it to attempts to ward off anxiety-producing matters – and, ultimately, to an avoidance of the fact of death itself. One could see all the encounters in Wonderland recapitulating this basic horror of non-existence, as for instance at the mad tea-party, where 'it's always tea-time' (ibid.: 99), the party-goers' movement around the table evoking the equally fruitless swim in the pool of tears (which, in turn, might also conjure up associations with the vale of tears, or *valle lacrimarum*, emphasising the toil and sorrow of earthly existence that was seen to end only as one entered heaven). But there are also some more subtle repetitions that curiously lead us back to these earlier, hauntingly familiar spaces; for example, where Alice finds herself inhabiting the same position as the mouse in relation to Dinah when it comes to her confrontation with the dog (above). Elsewhere, and again as discussed before, the Mouse's 'long and sad' tale ends in death and blankness, which is echoed in the Cheshire Cat's disappearance, 'beginning with the end of the tail, and ending with the grin, which remained some time after the rest of it had gone' (ibid.: 90). Worryingly, it is the teeth of the predator that linger, reminiscent of the crocodile's 'gently shining jaws'.

Yet another feature that Freud thinks disturbing occurs when the inanimate comes to life – something that, it has to be said, is relatively common in children's literature. But in Carroll's story it does seem to have a darker twist, perhaps for two reasons. First because, not only do we see such things as playing cards come alive, but also because animate things, like the hedgehogs and flamingos, are treated as though inanimate. The cards are, effectively, the ones playing the game.[11] Second, and in a more Lacanian vein, language is itself shown to have a life of its own in this story. Critics (Sewell, 1952 being one of the first) have speculated that Carroll, forever the logician, disliked the prodigality of language, its fecund nature, and thereby tried to curtail its open, signifying movement by turning all figurations into literal, concrete manifestations. This process is most evident with the characters created out of sayings. The Mad Hatter, for example, is a realisation of the phrase 'as mad as a hatter', and the Cheshire Cat derives from the saying 'a grin like a Cheshire cat'. But such literal figuration occurs elsewhere too, as, for example, in the episode where the Hatter is accused of 'murdering the Time!' (Carroll, 1970: 99). In all these instances, Carroll attempts to shut signification down to a single meaning, a monoglossia.

Dodgson openly acknowledges language's prodigality in speaking about a later work of his, *The Hunting of the Snark* (1876): he 'didn't mean anything but nonsense!' he admits, but 'words mean more than we mean to express when we use them: so a whole book ought to mean a great deal more than the writer meant' (Gardner, 1967: 22). Similar statements are also voiced in *Alice*; for example, there's the Duchess's statement, 'take care of the sense, and the sounds will take care of themselves' (Carroll, 1970: 121), which, I have heard it argued, means that sense should take priority, or, in more modern parlance, that the signified should take precedence over the signifier. However, as this statement itself parodies another, about being careful with your money ('Take care of the pence, and the pounds will take care of themselves'), we can see how its very creation depends precisely on sound, on rhyme: it is undone! This knowledge of the distinction between signifiers and signifieds occurs elsewhere, too; for example, where the March Hare tells Alice to 'say what you mean', to which she replies, 'I do … at least – at least I mean what I say – that's the same thing, you know' (ibid.: 95). But, of course, it is not: the former prioritises meaning ('say what you mean'), the signified, whereas the latter foregrounds the signifier ('mean what you say'), that which is enunciated.

It is the latter that seems to 'rule' in Wonderland, where one can move blithely across different codifying systems without concern: 'the jury eagerly wrote down all three dates on their slates, and then added them up, and reduced the answer to shillings and pence' (ibid.: 146). Signification deteriorates from the moment Alice drops below the surface of the rabbit hole and has her own meaning hollowed out (she becomes not Alice but 'A-less', alas). The world thereby becomes uncanny, with words seeming to control things, to bring them into being, just as Freud speaks about the psychic seemingly controlling material reality. In *Through the Looking-Glass*, of course, Carroll would revisit this idea in the figure of Humpty Dumpty, who starts by proclaiming 'in rather a scornful tone' that '[w]hen *I* use a word … it means just what I choose it to mean – neither more nor less … . The question is … which is to be master – that's all' (ibid.: 269). However, he turns out not to be in control at all: words speak him, as he later comes to realise. I've commented elsewhere on this:

> So, as with the chicken and egg problem of which came first, Humpty Dumpty clearly sides with the egg: he wants to be in control of language, rather than recognise that it pre-exists, and thus pre-empts him. If his existence is called forth by the very rhyme that names, or nominates him, it just as readily ex-nominates him. (Rudd, 2010b: 113)

In *Alice*, even normally familiar words begin to erupt with strangeness – either from an excess or a disturbing lack of meaning; the signifying chain stutters and stalls: 'Do cats eat bats? … Do bats eat cats?' (Carroll, 1970: 28); 'Did you say "pig," or "fig"?' (ibid.: 90); 'important – unimportant – unimportant – important – ' (ibid.: 155). Like the shift of the *heimlich* into the *unheimlich* where, as Freud (1985c: 368) puts it, 'the prefix "*un*" is the token of repression', words slide and the process of semantic satiation occurs, where meaning starts to empty out of signifiers.[12]

I mentioned earlier the notion of the psychic seeming to overpower material reality, and this certainly happens elsewhere in *Alice*, where we have the Caterpillar's seemingly telepathic link with Alice:

'One side of *what?* The other side of *what?*' thought Alice to herself.
'Of the mushroom,' said the Caterpillar, just as if she had asked it aloud ... .(Carroll, 1970: 73)

More disturbing still, though, is the rather overly familiar presence of the figure of the narrator. He appears too close for comfort in those hugging parentheses that enwrap Alice's thoughts and statements:

> ... she was considering, in her own mind (as well as she could, for the hot day made her feel very sleepy and stupid) ... whether [to make] a daisy-chain ... when suddenly a white rabbit with pink eyes ran close by her.
>
> There was nothing so *very* remarkable in that; nor did Alice think it so *very* much out of the way to hear the Rabbit say to itself, 'Oh dear! Oh dear! I shall be too late!' (when she thought it over afterwards, it occurred to her that she ought to have wondered at this ...). (Ibid.: 25–6)

As ever in this story, these invasions have their echoes elsewhere, as, for instance, when the Duchess, whose voice Alice 'heard close to her ear' before 'she squeezed herself up closer to Alice's side', manages 'to rest her chin on Alice's shoulder', eventually 'digging' it in (ibid.: 120–1).

There is one other Lacanian aspect of Carroll's text to mention before moving on to consider the story's ending; namely, the way that language is shown to be forever caught up in a subject's desire and sense of identity, rather than being concerned with communication and reciprocity. As Lacan puts it, 'the function of language in speech is not to inform but to evoke' (quoted in Fink, 2004: vii). Certainly, the language of *Alice* is anything but an attempt to establish mutual understanding and inter-subjectivity (regularly subverting Grice's maxims of conversation, for example); rather, language is fractured and often vituperative. It reflects not simply Lacan's view of how language is deployed but is also reminiscent of Lacan's method of therapy, wherein, unlike traditional psychotherapy, he established the variable-length or short session (causing him to be thrown out of the International Psychoanalytical Association). That is, Lacan would terminate a session abruptly, often provoking unexpected responses, and preventing the too easy flow of the signifying chain, which, he maintained, permitted only vapid, 'empty speech'. He thought that his disruptions could provoke more 'meaningful' responses. Wonderland is thus the realm of what Lacan terms *la linguisterie*, translated by Fink as 'linguistricks', which emphasises 'the playfulness of the unconscious and the way it is always trying to trip the subject up, playing tricks on conscious thought' (Homer, 2005: 69).

We come, then, to the ending of *Alice*, with its dream explanation, about which so much has been written. It is often seen as a bit of a let-down (for Tolkien (1964: 19), at least, it thereby barred the book from the realm of Faërie, which 'cannot tolerate any frame or machinery suggesting that the whole story ... is a figment or illusion'). For Tzvetan Todorov (1975), too, a tale that might be disturbingly fantastic would be rendered merely 'uncanny' if the events were found to have a natural explanation.[13] Even a Lacanian reading might be constructed along these lines, with the last chapter demonstrating how Alice is finally recognised by the Symbolic: she is named by the Law (in a court, in fact) – except that by this time she has already realised the superficiality of this whole world. In other words, the realm of the Symbolic, the *nom-du-père*, really is the *non-du-père*: these creatures are mere signifiers – cards that are meaningful only in the way that they are structured within particular games and stories. The fact that these mere cards now turn into 'dead leaves', settling on Alice's face (Carroll, 1970: 162), should not escape us either; for her own period of animation is also time bound, as the reference to 'her riper years' at the end of the book underlines (ibid.: 164).

The attempt by Alice's sister to peg down these floating signifiers, to quilt them into the fabric of everyday life ('rattling tea-cups would change to tinkling sheep-bells' (ibid.: 163)), therefore does anything but explain away these events, reducing them to a one-to-one, signifier–signified relation.[14] For the cat is already out of the bag, so to speak; up in the air, in fact, and grinning inanely at us: like mice, the signifiers have already run loose and free. Alice awake is thus only the tip of the iceberg, for, in her unconscious, in the real of her desire (the figurations of Wonderland), she has already shown herself a formidable force of disruption. Once again, we observe the *heimlich* as an island of sanity in a world where the *unheimlich*, the unsymbolised Real, presses relentlessly.

To adopt a Žižekian frame, Alice is not simply a meek Victorian girl, dreaming that she is a subversive and provocative shape-changing inter- loper; instead we have an interloper playing at being a retiring Victorian girl (and, of course, it is the former that we savour).[15] In fact, the whole curious doubling of the dream, evoked by her sister's repetition, seems to do the very opposite of what it espouses, suggesting that this other realm is not simply a dream: it recurs, it persists and won't go away. Indeed, it insists, as, of course, has Wonderland itself, long ago breaking free of its restrictive frame-story and invading everyday life over the last 150 years. It is 'dehiscent', to use one of Lacan's favourite words. The daylight logic of attempting to delimit signification, to have but one signifier representing a signified, has already been undone: 'the signifier stuffs the signified', as Lacan pithily expresses it (quoted in Fink, 2004: 83). In short, the sounds have been shown to look after themselves – with sense coming a poor second. The attempt to shut down signification in this chapter, then, is an attempt to impose the logic of the future anterior: 'it will have been'.

In contrast, this particular chapter (on the Uncanny) requires a more prescient tense. So let me move towards a conclusion. In this section, I have argued that *Alice* is an uncanny text in many regards, drawing on various aspects that Freud teased out. However, I have not subscribed to Freud's somewhat convoluted, shifting and evasive, and ultimately untenable explanation of this phenomenon (in terms of Oedipal castration anxiety). There is repression but, read in a more Lacanian way, it has been initiated as a result of Alice's uneasy habitation of the Symbolic. She experiences a world where signifiers shift and slide, where 'the symbol manifests itself first of all as the murder of the thing' (Lacan, 1977a: 104), where the subject is a being 'inescapably divided, castrated, split' (Evans, 1996: 196), and where, finally, subjects experience a sense of lack, their sense of existence fluctuating and **fading** as their being becomes hollowed out (the process that Lacan terms *aphanasis).* This experience is particularly apparent in the case of the Cheshire Cat which, as discussed earlier, is really nothing but the realisation of a string of signifiers; and, if Alan Garner (1998) is correct, there is a more macabre way in which this 'symbol manifests itself ... as the murder of the thing', with the phrase 'a grin like a Cheshire Cat' being a Cheshire term for someone that had had their throat cut.[16]

Alice is thrown[17] into this underground world that 'one does not know one's way about in' (as Freud defined the uncanny) and it is a realm where the gaps and fissures of the Symbolic are more apparent: its inability to say all and everything becomes clear. The feeling that this realm is poorly constructed, that the holes show through, persists. Alice comes to realise that not only does she not simply *exist*, but that her being straddles the border between three orders (the Symbolic, the Real and the Imaginary). In Wonderland, in fact, she finds herself in danger of *ex-sisting*, as an extinguished candle flame might. One could see this dislocation as being the result of the pressure of the Real, which continually threatens to tear apart the Symbolic as puns, slips and fractures multiply. Moreover, Alice's imaginary picture of herself is also under attack as she finds not only that her name does not signify, but neither does her body: its exterior is continually being disrupted. Other images that might proffer some support for her ego are also being undermined such that what she thinks of as the 'loveliest garden you ever saw. How she longed to … wander among those beds of bright flowers and those cool fountains' (Carroll, 1970: 30) turns out to be a realm stalked by a murderous mother-figure, a grim-reaper who, perhaps like Snow White's stepmother (in some versions), really lives up to her name as a Queen of Hearts.

In summary, then, *Alice* evokes that more disturbing sense of the uncanny, disrupting the standard divisions between self and other, sameness and difference, presence and absence. The very coordinates of our existence in the realms of the Imaginary and the Symbolic are undermined, with the Real threatening to overwhelm and undercut us, pulling the very ground from beneath our feet – literally (the earlier title, in fact, featuring the word 'underground', more readily captures this mortifying aspect).

Conclusion

Let me return, finally, to the issue of the child being seen as an uncanny presence in children's literature, as advanced by Nodelman:

> the childhood of children's literature is so clearly an adult fantasy, an attempted imposition of adult views of childhood on children – adult views that see childhood as a safe place but also see children themselves as inherently and dangerously *unheimlich*. (Nodelman, 2008: 225)

Though it is not clear from this quotation, from what Nodelman writes elsewhere it is apparent that he means both the child as depicted in children's literature and in society at large. He does refer explicitly to Max in Sendak's *Where the Wild Things Are* (1967), along with the protagonists of three of his other chosen texts, 'Alice, Dr. Doolittle [*sic*] and Buhlaire',[18] but makes the more general statement that 'the protagonists of children's literature already have unhomely desires while at home that precede and cause their leaving' (ibid.: 224).

However, as I suggested at the outset, I think that Nodelman (like Zipes) has redefined the uncanny rather too literally in terms of its etymology, as being concerned with 'ways in which children lack safe homes or question the values of homes or have the safety of their homes disrupted'. Thus at the end of these stories,

> home finally becomes the safe place it was always supposed to be, a place for innocent childhood, with whatever was *unheimlich* – or childish –

about it at the start expelled at least temporarily by the journey away, the unhoming the unfortunate presence of the *unheimlich* led to. (Ibid.: 225)

Having 'childish' as an alternative to *unheimlich* does not seem to clarify matters sufficiently. There might be a desire to escape home on the part of the protagonist, but there is no notion that the child is her or himself disrupted by uncanny experiences (unlike those Alice suffers in relation to her identity). In fact, the move into the unhomely space is actively initiated by these other characters, whereas Alice's is described as a 'fall'. Moreover, in relation to Dolittle and Max, at least, the away space is generally enjoyed (a notion that Nodelman's phrase, 'unhomely desires', seems to capture). As with Zipes, then, associations of the uncanny with the frightening seem to have been relegated in favour of a more domesticated conception. For Zipes, the *Unheimliche* simply becomes a device that 'liberates readers', allowing them to return to 'familiar (*heimlich*)' moments in early life from which a utopian, non-alienating space can be conceived (celebrating the Imaginary). In Nodelman's terms, its etymological roots in 'home' are even more faithfully mined, allowing him to fit this into his model of children's literature as enacting journeys (often initiated as a result of 'unhomely desires') from Home to Away, thence back again, as a result of which the unhomely element is 'expelled'.

A related attempt to appropriate the uncanny for children's literature occurs in the work of Mitzi Myers, whose contribution I have not had time to discuss in this chapter. But she too seems to lose the specificity of the term, reinterpreting it in ways reminiscent of Jentsch's 'intellectual uncertainty':

> I've located children's literature (like the criticism addressing it) as a generic site for the uncanny, as epitomizing in its cross-writing of genders, genres, generations, and socio-psychic themes those 'moments of breakdown that occur when an interpretive scheme encounters a particular object or events that it cannot satisfactorily interpret' …. (Myers, 1999: 71)

Rather than water down this concept, in order to make it fit children's literature, I am therefore in agreement with Coats, who sees the uncanny as 'precisely what is excluded from children's literature' (1997: 495). We have other terms for these more general notions of the unhomely, whereas the *Unheimliche* is a fitting term to reserve for the more troubling and disturbing shifts out of familiarity that we witness in what, so far, are a few exceptional texts of children's literature (e.g. *Struwwelpeter*, by that other Hoffmann (Heinrich), 'The New Mother' by Lucy Clifford, and, of course, Carroll's *Alice*) – without, of course, wishing to deny individual child readers their own, idiosyncratic examples. And we might also argue that the uncanny is an area becoming less excluded from children's literature, as we see in works like Gaiman's *Coraline*, several of Sonya Hartnett's novels (e.g. *Thursday's Child* (2000), *What the Birds See* (2003) or Sally Gardner's *The Double Shadow* (2011)), as well as in some of the darker works often termed 'magic realist' (e.g. David Almond's *Clay* (2005)). There is no time here to explore this development, though we might see it as connected with a growing crisis over childhood, as we come to see children as beings that are not only less able to represent an unfettered innocence in our modern world, but also as themselves less definable according to traditional sociological templates. In this chapter, then, I hope to have restored some of this edginess to the concept, to recruit it for a more energetic textual exegesis.

Earlier I quoted Freud's increasing sense of indeterminacy towards the end of his meandering and circling essay, reminding us of his peregrinations round that 'red light' district in Italy that he confesses to have been trapped in. Hélène Cixous makes a similar confession in her essay on the uncanny (as, of course, have I, and so too will others):

> the text ... pushes forth and repels until it reaches an arbitrary end. (The Unheimliche has no end, but it is necessary for the text to stop somewhere.) And this 'conclusion' returns and passes as a recurrence and as a reserve. Will there be a terminus for theoretical hesitation? (Cixous, 1976: 545)

The terminus, of course, is to be found along the Möbius Strip, everywhere and nowhere, to which we shall now 'turn'.

Part IV

Real, Symbolic, Imaginary

6 Fantasy and Realism Contained: From Fortunatus Cap to the Möbius Strip

Having framed earlier chapters in terms of Lacan's three orders, this one draws them together to reconsider how we discuss 'fantasy' and 'realism' as competing trends in children's literature texts, as captured, for instance, in Geoffrey Summerfield's *Fantasy and Reason* (1984). Though the lines of difference are now seen to have been rather artificially contrived, I want to suggest a more radical way of rethinking the divide between fantasy and realism. First, though, it is worth rehearsing the background, in which that 'cursed Barbauld crew' of Mrs Trimmer, Maria Edgeworth and others were seen to be waging a war against stories that were not rooted in the everyday world. The champions of imagination and fantasy were, of course, the Romantics, predominantly male authors who, like Wordsworth, wanted to hold on to the old, more fantastic tales:

> *Oh! give us once again the Wishing-Cap*
> *Of Fortunatus, and the invisible Coat*
> *Of Jack the Giant-killer, Robin Hood,*
> *And Sabra in the forest with St. George!*
> *The child, whose love is here, at least, doth reap*
> *One precious gain, that he forgets himself.*
> (Wordsworth, 'The Prelude',
> Book 5, lines 364–9)

The more didactic and sombre tales were seen to hold sway well into the nineteenth century, backed by a utilitarian attitude towards education (made most famous by Gradgrind in Dickens's *Hard Times*), until

Carroll's *Alice* came on the scene. The standard history of children's literature, about Carroll's book initiating a 'liberty of thought in children's
books' (Darton, 1982: 260) was quoted earlier. However, this view has
since come in for criticism from a number of directions.

There are those who have looked more closely at the tales of
Edgeworth and others, Myers being a key player, showing how we have
swallowed uncritically the patriarchal view of the Romantic poets with
their figuration of the 'proper' child. Re-readings have shown that
these stories are far richer if viewed with New Historicist insights into
contemporary discourses. Other writers have shown the extent to which
fantasy continued to be available in these utilitarian years, in the rather
frowned upon chapbook literature and in oral culture. More specifically,
it has been convincingly shown that Carroll was himself part of a longer
tradition of fantasy/nonsense literature, rather than his work emerging
ex nihilo (Susina, 2010).

Regardless of this, the basic paradigm that juxtaposes realism and
fantasy has been remarkably resilient. Taking the metaphor of the
Möbius strip, which has appealed to writers from Carroll to Lacan (and
beyond), in this chapter I will argue, adopting the same broadly Lacanian
approach used elsewhere in this volume, that reality and fantasy, outer
and inner, are more irrevocably conjoined.

Primary and secondary worlds

My starting point for thinking about this issue grew out of a basic
discontent with Nikolajeva's early work, *The Magic Code*, in which she
defines 'fantasy [... as] a canonical genre' (1988: 118).[1] For me, this
is as unacceptable as seeing children's literature in generic terms (see
Chapter 5). She then excludes the fairy tale (thus running counter to
Zipes's position):

> fairy tales take place in *one* world where, within the frames of the genre,
> everything is possible: animals can talk, wishes come true by magic, people
> can fly etc. All these supernatural elements are taken for granted, and never
> does the protagonist wonder at them.
>
> In fantasy two worlds, a real one (*primary*) and a magic one (*secondary*),
> are involved. (Ibid.: 13)

In the first paragraph we can almost see a rerun of the position taking by Freud
in relation to the uncanny: because 'the world of ... reality is left behind' in

fairy tales, we do not experience any anomalous shifts in what is possible as we read them. Whereas, for Nikolajeva, when it comes to fantasy, there is always a real world that is in some senses departed from. Nikolajeva adopts Tolkien's term, 'Secondary World', for this, regarding it as 'the most important narrative element in fantasy' (ibid.: 35, 43). However, restricting this term to works of fantasy is itself problematic, for Tolkien's usage is more inclusive, encompassing both realistic and fantastic creations. The only difference he notes is that '"the inner consistency of reality" is more difficult to produce' when there is more deviation from the Primary World (ibid.: 45). In other words, the world of *Treasure Island* is easier to fashion than that of say Earthsea; or, as Tolkien rewords it in his next sentence, a sense of 'reality' is easier to produce 'with more "sober" material' (ibid.). As Catherine Butler elaborates, '[t]he world Thackeray conjures in *Vanity Fair*, for example, is as legitimate an example of sub-creation as Middle-earth, despite its more "realistic" setting' (Butler, 2013: 107). To make it a fairy-story (to use Tolkien's terminology again – which, of course, is not Nikolajeva's), the added 'quality of strangeness and wonder' is then needed (Tolkien, 1964: 44).[2]

Serious though this misreading is, it is nonetheless a common one, and it does play favourably into my revised conception of the division between fantasy and realism. For the moment, then, let me go on to examine how Nikolajeva deploys Tolkien's term. She divides secondary worlds into 'open' and 'closed' types. The latter are often known as 'high fantasy' works, wherein the secondary world is independent, unconnected with our material world. Tolkien himself wrote extensively about such a closed world, Middle-earth, in *The Hobbit* (1937) and *The Lord of the Rings* (1954–6). Other well-known instances, cited by Nikolajeva, would be Le Guin's Earthsea, mentioned above (1968–2001) and the books about the Moomin family by Tove Jansson ('with some reservations', Nikolajeva adds (1988: 36)). Open worlds, as she says, are ones where 'both primary and secondary worlds are present in the text' (ibid.), citing Michael Ende's *The Neverending Story* (*Die unendliche Geschichte*, 1979). Lewis's 'Chronicles of Narnia' would, of course, be another famous example, though, as Nikolajeva points out, *The Horse and His Boy*, on its own, depicts a closed secondary world. These categories are fairly straightforward (with reservations, we also might add). The real problems arise in fantasies where there seems to be no secondary world. So Nikolajeva suggests we invoke an 'implied' secondary world.

As an example, she draws on the work of Nesbit, and *Five Children and It* (1902) in particular. Although 'there is no tangible presence of the secondary world', since 'the whole narrative takes place in the primary world ... , most researchers would claim that this novel belongs to the fantasy genre' (ibid.: 39), therefore a secondary world must be implied (de facto, given that Nikolajeva's definition of fantasy hinges on this). The magical 'It' creature, then, the Psammead or 'Sand-Fairy', is a 'magical agent' that must come from a secondary world 'not portrayed in the text'; this 'world is extratextual, but it cannot be ignored' (ibid.). I don't think this comment is strictly true, for the Psammead does talk about the olden days when its kind was more plentiful, in the age of megatheriums, and even explains how the species came to be almost extinct as a result of coming into contact with water. I am not seeking to deny the Psammead's magical status, but merely asking why such magical motifs need worlds building round them in order to be, if you'll forgive the wording, taken seriously as fantasy. Such creatures seem to be there precisely because they are anomalous. They do not need a convincing backstory, a valid passport stating place of origin.

In taking this stance, I am suggesting that Nikolajeva – like many other critics – makes the everyday physical world the bedrock from which fantasy departs, hence, of course, the term 'primary world'. Alan Garner (1970), whom she also quotes, takes just this position: 'If you are going to use fantasy ... then you must relate this to known facts, that is to the material world' (Nikolajeva, 1988: 25). Fantasy, in short, must be 'realistic'. However, we might want to argue against this default position and suggest that the psychological world is equally real or, even more significantly, is responsible for our construction of *what* is real. If we were to take this alternative seriously, then there would be no need to insist that all fantasy depends on physically realisable secondary worlds. What I am really suggesting, then, is that the Psammead's origins are, indeed, sufficiently 'implied' by the text, requiring no further justification. Here is a key passage:

> It was at the gravel-pits. Father had to go away suddenly on business, and mother had gone away to stay with Granny, who was not very well. They both went in a great hurry, and when they were gone the house seemed dreadfully quiet and empty, and the children wandered from one room to another and looked at the bits of paper and string on the floors left over from the packing, and not yet cleared up, and wished they had something to do. (Nesbit, 1959a: 22–3)

The children find 'It' precisely when the mother departs, and It leaves shortly after her return; moreover, as I've pointed out elsewhere, the Sand-Fairy and the five children are seen to have a number of characteristics in common (Rudd, 2006a). In short, It exists in the primary world, but not as we know it: It's reality is of a psychological nature.

So, rather than see fantasy as being concerned with *"the presence of magic ... in an otherwise realistic world"* (Nikolajeva, 1988: 12), I suggest that we think of fantasy as intrinsic to the structuring of *our* world. Attempts to shut out these elements are as fruitless as Gradgrind trying to delimit the world to a place of 'facts'. Indeed, if one thinks of most realistic novels, the fantastic elements are never far away, the most common one being the omniscient narrator: the person who has the ability to peer into everyone's heads and tell us what they are thinking. But even in novels that do not feature such a godlike presence, there is still the ability to shift time and space for the purposes of the story: moving on or going back through the generations, across cities and continents. Even in first-person novels, we are still required to see our narrator as someone who either has a photographic memory, recalling scenes and conversations accurately, or we allow for 'poetic licence'. The current vogue for present-tense, first-person narration might thereby be seen to be more credible in terms of the narrator's memory, but in other ways such novels stretch our credibility even further. In Carrie Jones's *Need* (2010: 185–6), for instance, the first person narrator writes about her feelings – indeed, her needs:

> My heart pings in my chest, hope making it beat fast, too fast. His hand reaches out and touches the back of my head. His fingers entwine with my hair. It happens again, that melting feeling, the longing feeling. I want to gesture my body against his body, to explain things like need. ... His lips warm against mine. My arms wrap around his shoulders and he presses me to him.

When will he shout at her, 'For God's sake – close your laptop!', we might wonder. Or, more helpfully for the reader, perhaps, plead with her to consider a second draft when she has more of her faculties about her. Of course, this present-centred fiction, one could argue, exactly reflects our contemporary world: one where palm-held devices *do* record people's ongoing thoughts, which, along with pictorial backup, are then shared (a world more dystopically realised in Suzanne Collins's similarly narrated 'Hunger Games' trilogy (2008–10), in fact).

It should go without saying, of course, that the above narratorial techniques are simply conventions of realistic writing that we have come to accept, but here I want to foreground these effects of the real, as Barthes termed them (1986: 141–2), to point up their artificiality.

To begin with, let us note that the tendency to see realism as the bedrock from which certain works deviate is itself a modern phenomenon. In many respects one could argue that it is not the fantastic that is the aberration, but realism. Before the latter's emergence, the fantastic was everywhere in literature, in myths, legends, epics, Romances, and so on. However, I also realise how anachronistic it is to try to impose any sort of realistic/ fantastic dichotomy on earlier periods. We need to appreciate that, up until the Enlightenment, most people lived in a world far more imbued with a sense of the religious and the supernatural, such that, in many of these works, the fantastic trappings that we now see as obtrusive, would nevertheless be very much part of the everyday world.

A genre like the fable, for instance, despite its fantastic surface (anthro- pomorphic animals), is unthinkingly accepted as depicting 'real' human concerns. *Aesop's Fables*, in fact, is seen as one of the earliest examples of literature suitable for children. But though fables might be most overt in carrying more realistic, often didactic messages, the same would be true of other works that we would now categorise as fantasy. Spenser's *The Faerie Queene* (1590/96) is a key example, celebrating the reign of Queen Elizabeth I and the importance of various virtues, yet conceived in an Arthurian, allegorical setting, and obviously having a particular cultural significance for an Elizabethan audience. Fairy tales also, it is too easy to forget, would almost always have reflected the concerns of the period in which they were told, besides being more fine-tuned to specific audiences. Thus the early and earthy oral version of 'Little Red Riding Hood', entitled 'The Grandmother's Tale' (Orenstein, 2002), which features a werewolf, was (apparently) far more popular in areas where werewolf trials were prevalent. Later, as Zipes (1993) and Orenstein (2002) have detailed, we find these tales including more Christian and patriarchal elements as middle-class mores become more established – a shift most explicitly noted in the version told by the Brothers Grimm, with its clear instruc- tions as to how women and children should deport themselves.

In short, in many creative works from earlier periods, what we now separate out as fantastic as opposed to realistic elements were far more organically interlinked.

Modernity, rationality and the child

Realism, as a literary movement, has its beginnings in the eighteenth century (Watt, 1957); that is, in the wake of Enlightenment thinking, facilitating both the growth of capitalism and the beginnings of the Industrial Revolution. Following Descartes' lead, British empiricist philosophers (Locke, Berkeley, Hume) were emphasising the importance of the known, observable world (albeit recognising difficulties about how exactly it might be known), while explorers were beginning to chart the detail of this 'brave new world', bringing back both material artefacts (including the 'natives' themselves) and factual accounts of their travels, undertaking the groundwork for the subsequent building of empire (most successfully, of course, in Britain's case). Out of all this emphasis on the material world, on industry and developing notions of property, the novel emerged as a form that could capture these narratives concerned with travel, possessions and social position.[3] Early novels are accordingly full of journeys and detailed accounts of the property acquired, *Robinson Crusoe* (1719) being not only a key example but also itself the template for hundreds of other works (the Robinsonnade; cf. Horne, 2011; O'Malley, 2012), perhaps most famously emulated in Johann Wyss's *The Swiss Family Robinson* (1812). But the key thing about these novels is that, for all their emphasis on travel, property and family relationships, such external elements are there mainly to show us the development of character: how material things both form, test and reflect the characters at their centre (Crusoe himself, Tom Jones, Moll Flanders and, we might note, Margery Meanwell, alias 'Little Goody Two-Shoes').

With the emergence of a literature seen to be specifically for (and by) the new 'middling classes' also comes a denigration of upper and lower-class literature (Romances – in both cases – and, more specifically for the lower orders, the refraction of these in chapbook form, where they are intermixed with folk and fairy tales, Bible tales, sermons, accounts of criminals, and so forth). For the middling classes, it was the realistic mode that was championed. Moreover, this new class – with its emphasis not only on material wealth but also on the family as the vehicle for consumption and display – gives increased attention to its progeny: its lines of inheritance, its genealogical successors; in other words, to the child and its development (indeed, the whole notion of 'development' is being developed here). There was a need for the child to learn the distinct ways that its class deported itself.

Hence the modern child comes into being with its discrete material goods (toys, books, clothes), spaces to inhabit (schools, nurseries), games and distinct codes of behaviour. Books in particular, were not just 'material goods', either. They were also a key means of teaching a child what exactly childhood was and how it might be more appropriately inhabited. Children's literature, then, has not simply been developed to cater for this new form of being, the child, but is itself responsible for the construction of this being (here we are back with Rose).

The one other thing that needs noting, though, before moving on to consider realism in more depth, is the fact that this new emphasis on reason, on realism, brought alongside it, as its shadow, a fascination with the irrational, with the dark and the unknown. These aspects had always been there, but the increasing stress on rationality crystallised the boundary. It is not surprising, then, that, as noted in the previous chapter, this was the time when the uncanny also came into its own. In a similar way, magical realism would later be a product of colonising powers seeking to impose their 'enlightened' ways on the colonised (especially in Latin America, often seen as the home of magical realism; cf. Faris, 2004).

To sum up, then: capitalism, the middling class, consumerism, the novel, notions of rational behaviour and an emphasis on realism emerge and interfuse. And, as also noted, the modern child is a product of this age, a great deal of energy being expended on making this fledgling being both biddable and rational; and yet, as a result, the child (like the adult woman) is seen to stand in opposition to the *proper* adult: as someone, in short [*sic*], who does not yet possess these qualities; indeed, as someone associated with the 'wrong' end of many of these now more clearly delineated binaries: natural rather than cultural, feminine rather than masculine, emotional as opposed to reasonable, impulsive instead of reflective; and, as was often said, in many regards bestial rather than human. The notion of the child as an uncanny presence can therefore all too easily be conceptualised; and with it, the attempts by many in the field of children's literature to seek to eliminate its less rational, more fantastic elements (most famously, perhaps, in the writings of Mrs Trimmer).

The paradox is clearly captured early on in the development of the novel, in the eighteenth-century vogue for what have been termed 'It' or 'Thing' narratives, written both for adults – such as Charles Johnstone's *Chrysal, or the Adventures of a Guinea* (1760–5) or *The Adventures of a Hackney Coach* (1781) – and for children (for instance, the anonymous *The Story of a Pin* (1798)[4] or Mary Ann Kilner's *Adventures of a Pincushion*). These stories only became significant with the Industrial Revolution and the growth of capitalism, many of them being about the sorts of commodities that were then becoming popular, and quite a few of them also being concerned with money (the guinea, above, for example). Indeed, these stories were also known as 'circulating' narratives, stressing the way that goods and capital changed hands. Such works modelled the 'proper' child – a being that other classes might seek to emulate. However, this would be a hard act for poor labouring children to follow, for the 'proper' child was also the 'propertied' child, and many of the manufactured goods of the new world were there to show the child how it should behave, play and conduct itself, books being key items (as noted above), especially when accompanied – as, famously, was John Newbery's *Little Pretty Pocket Book* (1744) – with its offer of free, gendered playthings: pincushions for girl readers (to record good and bad deeds, note) and balls for boys.

It hardly needs saying that these narratives could not possibly be thought realistic, though this is the veneer they display. What is especially of note is that they were composed at a time when fantasy was frowned upon by many (again as noted earlier): it was associated with the imagination, which could lead to challenges to the social order, as, of course, was subsequently to be witnessed in France. Consequently, for all their fantastic basis, these It narratives tend to be quite moralistic and didactic. But, as I have remarked elsewhere, there is always a double-edge to this:

> Not only do these objects suggest a more pagan universe, raising problems for orthodox religion, but, by having objects and animals talk, they also seem to undermine the very rationality of the Enlightenment. And while seeking to establish the sovereignty of the individual (objects being separated out and given voices), these works simultaneously undermine it; for not only is individualism parodied (it is seen as excessive if *everything* has it: 'It thinks, therefore it is'), but, in the process, the owners of the objects also become more replaceable, expendable and, as 'propertied classes', dependent on property for their being. Commodity fetishism rules, in Karl Marx's terms, with objects concealing human labour and agency within them. Interestingly Marx sometimes uses fairy tale terms in *Das Kapital* to depict this very process: 'Mister Capital and Mistress Land carry on their goblin tricks as social characters and at the same time as mere things', creating 'an *enchanted*, perverted, topsy-turvy world'. And it is precisely these topsy-turvy novels, where the objects write back, that often 'spill the beans' about their origins. If people are defined by their possessions, small wonder that these objects seem possessed. (Rudd, 2009: 248–9)

I also mentioned animals in the piece above, for stories about them were also popular at this time, with Dorothy Kilner (sister-in-law of Mary Ann, above), producing – for instance – the popular *The Life and Perambulation of a Mouse* (*c*.1785).[5] Sarah Trimmer was then to contribute her *Fabulous Histories: Designed for the Instruction of Children Respecting their Treatment of Animals* (1786), later to be published as *The History of the Robins*. Trimmer's deep-seated concerns about fantasy are explicit in her Introduction, where she makes it clear that the stories told about this family of robins are not 'the real conversations of birds (for that it is impossible we should ever understand), but … a series of FABLES, intended to convey moral instruction applicable to themselves' (Trimmer, 1798: viii). She also forbade her original text being illustrated (i.e. to be made more sensory) for the same reason.

The double-edge that always accompanies such attempts to socialise the child – to make it a law-abiding creature of reason – are here evident, as the text seeks to produce a monological reading. But, as I speculated in relation to Trimmer's work,

> the ambivalent nature of anthropomorphism … is ineluctably present: hearing the conversations of Robin, Dicky, Flapsy and Pecksy might help readers understand and identify with the little birds, but it thereby compromises their difference, their otherness; moreover, in suggesting affinities, we thereby query our own species' (or specious) claim to distinction. So while Trimmer's book clearly underwrites the class and gender inequalities of her time, she cannot help but destabilise that very order in her natural history. On the one hand, then, the robins' behaviour celebrates family values, but on the other, we learn that each parent had a previous mate and earlier broods of children, effectively undermining the nuclear family. (Rudd, 2009: 245)

As the first part of this quotation suggests, if there are too many affinities with animals, we could not possibly consider eating them. Trimmer's work thus has the character Mrs Benson state that certain beasts 'have been expressly destined by the *Supreme Governor* as food for mankind', albeit we should still make 'their short lives … comfortable' (Trimmer, 1798: 165). However, an unnamed (and proto-Marxist) farmer goes further, suggesting that animals should be 'entitled to wages' (ibid.: 137), which rather undermines Mrs Benson's claim about their being divinely ordained to be food: it's just a job! This farmer's sentiment is certainly progressive, predating that of Dr Dolittle (who tries to establish banks for animals) or, indeed, of the inhabitants of *Animal Farm*.

A brief history of realisms

Before coming back to these issues, let me chart the way that a sense of realism has become central to considerations of the novel and at how literary criticism has supported this position.

First, as the above suggests, to speak about 'realism' in the singular does not help; we should instead talk of the different 'realisms', that is, ways of representing everyday reality in what is considered a mimetic way. Thus, in the early novel we witness a gradual shift away from the idealised types of the romance to focus on more mundane, individual characters (often speaking to us in the first person). From here we see the development of the omniscient narrator, so common in the Victorian novels of Dickens, Eliot and others. But the false sense of a fixed order of things, ordained and overseen by some almighty presence, then gave way to what was termed 'naturalism', a more anthropological examination of society such as we see in the works of Émile Zola and George Gissing, where there is an attempt to discern the 'laws' of society, often drawing on Darwinian ideas about the 'survival of the fittest'. In contrast, other writers saw realism in more subjective, relativistic terms, consisting precisely of the thoughts and feelings of characters. This version was practised most eminently by Henry James, later to be taken up by modernists like Woolf and Joyce, pursuing the streams of consciousness of characters as we observe them, likewise, meandering through life. With this shift, of course, the modernists also tended to ditch the rather contrived plots of earlier writers in favour of more open-ended narratives, with characters' lives not necessarily resolved at the end (and they all meandered passably thereafter).

In terms of contemporary writing, it would be modernism that came to dominate the new departments of literature as they were established in England and America, and which led to the neglect of many 'middlebrow' popular writers (as noted in Chapter 1)[6] and, alongside them, writers for more specialised audiences: genre and children's fiction. The association of 'good' writing with a modernist aesthetic had quite a hold over scholarship until relatively recently. Here, for instance, is Philip Pullman (1996) voicing his concerns:

> There are some themes, some subjects, too large for adult fiction; they can only be dealt with adequately in a children's book.
> The reason for that is that in adult literary fiction, stories are there on sufferance. Other things are felt to be more important: technique, style, literary knowingness. Adult writers who deal in straightforward stories find themselves sidelined into a genre such as crime or science fiction, where no one expects literary craftsmanship.

Of course, his claim is a vast oversimplification: good literary storytellers have always been there, despite the superior cultural capital of a more elitist and consciously aesthetic modernism (cf. Carey, 1992). The following 'storytellers', for example, come immediately to mind: Stan Barstow, Grahame Greene, Patricia Highsmith, Winifred Holtby, Olivia Manning, John Steinbeck, Iris Murdoch and Henry Williamson. Some of these – indeed, like the modernists – also drew on generic fiction (Greene and Highsmith, especially), but were by no means restricted by it.

However, regardless of their storytelling ability, a realistic mode of representation was certainly in the ascendant, as celebrated in Leavis's (1962) suggested 'Great Tradition' (comprising four exemplary authors: Austen, Eliot, James and Conrad). Fantasy only made its resurgence in the 1960s, again as a result of the counter-culture and explorations of alternative realities, turning Tolkien's *Lord of the Rings* into a cult work, along with stories by rediscovered writers like Jorge Luis Borges, Lord Dunsany and David Lindsay. Courses on 'The Fantastic in Literature' then began to filter into some of the newer university syllabuses.

More recently we have witnessed a crisis over notions of realism (and of reality itself) as the Enlightenment project has come to be seen as increasingly myopic, especially in the wake of colonialism (with postcolonial voices making themselves heard), the oppression of women and other minorities, the experience of two world wars (followed by the polarisation of the Cold War), and increasing criticism of the way that Western powers have sought to impose their ways of thinking on other nations. It has led to a general questioning of grand narratives, the omnipotence of reason and, indeed, the whole belief in a knowable reality. In short, modernity has given way to a postmodern sensibility; as Zygmunt Bauman (1991: x) puts it:

> postmodernity can be seen as restoring to the world what modernity, presumptuously, had taken away; as a *re-enchantment* of the world that modernity tried hard to *dis-enchant*. [... For] the declaration of reason's independence [... meant that] the world had to be *de-spiritualized*, de-animated: denied the capacity of the *subject*.

Now the angels are back (appearing in Pullman's own award-winning trilogy, of course, and David Almond's *Skellig* (1998), among many other works), their popularity, according to Brian McHale (2012: 202), a result of their being 'realized metaphors of the violation of ontological boundaries'; in other words, that division between fantasy and reality.

Fantasy: a subversion of reality?

The above might make it sound as though fantasy is a particularly postmodern phenomenon, though the longer history that I have traced shows that this is precisely not the case: fantasy has been there from the outset, though forced into the margins since the Enlightenment; and, in this process, it came to be opposed to notions of reality. Moreover, it is as a result of this opposition between two modes of representing the world – the mimetic and the fantastic – that so much of our current confusion arises. But, as the above brief history also suggests, it is as a result of a more postmodern sensibility that former notions of realism are no longer seen as adequate, with magic realism and other variations (e.g. fantastic realism, Waller, 2011) seeking to supplement its inadequacies; moreover, writers featuring angels and the like still feel themselves able to claim that what they write is 'stark realism' (Pullman, n.d.).

Rosemary Jackson's (1981) highly influential monograph is a case in point. She certainly sees 'the emergence of fantastic literature in its strictest sense' (Louis Vax, quoted in ibid.: 18) resulting from the development of what she terms 'a secular economy' (i.e. capitalism), though there is an older form, more to do with the marvellous, that persists:

> In what we could call a supernatural economy, otherness is transcendent, marvellously different from the human: the results are religious fantasies of angels, devils, heavens, hells, promised lands, and pagan fantasies of elves, dwarves, fairies, fairyland or 'faery'. In a natural, or secular economy, otherness is not located elsewhere: it is read as a projection of merely human fears and desires transforming the world through subjective perception. (Ibid.: 23–4)

This latter type of fantasy is a product of nineteenth-century realism, which 'the fantastic began to hollow out' (ibid.: 25):

> [It] points to or suggests the basis upon which cultural order rests, for it opens up, for a brief moment, on to disorder, on to illegality, on to that which lies outside the law, that which is outside dominant value systems. The fantastic traces the unsaid and the unseen of culture: that which has been silenced, made invisible, covered over and made 'absent'. (Ibid.: 4)

It exists as the 'inside, or underside' of the realist novel, 'opposing the novel's closed, monological forms with open, dialogical structures, as if the novel had given rise to its own opposite, its unrecognizable reflection' (ibid.: 25). Thus fantasy 'seemed to become a genre in its own right because of its extremely close relation to the form of the novel, a genre which it undermined' (ibid.: 35). To call the novel 'a genre' is an unfortunate slip, but then Jackson is also inconsistent in her use of the terms 'fantasy' and the 'fantastic', which are often treated synonymously. In this instance, though, she does seem to be talking about 'fantasy' as a distinct genre, for she has just spoken about how the fantastic 'assumes different generic forms', one of them being '[f]antasy as it emerged in the nineteenth century' (ibid.).[7] Generally, however, she insists (in contradistinction to Todorov) that the fantastic is not a genre but a mode.

But this is then contradicted in her title – *Fantasy: The Literature of Subversion* – which has another flaw, for the idea of a mode (or even a genre) being inherently subversive makes little sense;[8] no more, in fact, than it would to call realism the literature of conservatism, thereby dismissing any number of writers who have challenged the status quo – Dickens, Zola, Orwell, Steinbeck, Wharton, Eliot, Hesba Stretton, and so on – let alone those 'realistic' books that have incontrovertibly resulted in social change, such as *Nicholas Nickleby* (1839), *Uncle Tom's Cabin* (1851) or *The Jungle* (1906). Form or mode, then, has no inherent ability to either subvert or stabilise;[9] this only occurs when form is yoked to specific content; and even then, a work is still dependent on the context of its consumption in order to have particular effects.

However, the notion of the fantastic being 'subversive' is central to Jackson's book: 'Structurally and semantically, the fantastic aims at dissolution of an order experienced as oppressive and insufficient' (Jackson, 1981: 180), albeit, in order to do this, she has to marginalise those 'transcendent' fantasies, mentioned above, which concern themselves with 'elves, dwarves, fairies, fairyland or "faery"' (ibid.: 24). Whereas the 'original impulse' of all fantasy might have a common root, she argues, the 'transcendentalist' proponents end up 'expelling their desire and frequently displacing it into religious longing and nostalgia. Thus they defuse potentially disturbing, anti-social drives and retreat from any profound confrontation with existential dis-ease' (ibid.: 9); in contrast, the 'modern fantastic', as she sees it, is 'transgressive' rather than 'transcendental' (ibid.: 173). It is perhaps worth noting here that writers like Tolkien are also seen as *initially* having 'disturbing, anti-social drives', which are only then displaced (some might say sublimated) into a religious longing, rather than – as Tolkien himself saw it – that he was simply expressing his sense of joy in creation (in what he termed a 'Eucatastrophe' (1964: 60)).

But this claim about Tolkien and others is necessary, of course, for Jackson to establish some sense of consistency, a 'common root'. Having achieved this, as she sees it, the 'modern fantastic' (itself a rather loaded term, given Tolkien's historical location) can then be elevated: '*The fantastic, in becoming humanized, approaches the ideal purity of its essence, becomes what it had been*' (Jackson, 1981: 18). There is some special pleading at work here, and a sudden loss of any notion of historicity, as this version of fantasy – that is, the modern fantastic – is somehow seen to encapsulate its essence, its subversive heart.

Here we are closer to Todorov's asocial, structuralist theorisation of fantasy, which Jackson has drawn upon in order to hive off the 'transcendent' fantasists. For Todorov (1975), the fantastic constitutes that point at which the reader of a text experiences uncertainty, hovering between a supernatural explanation of an event and a psychological one. Very few works maintain this hesitancy on the part of the reader till the end, thus making it very restricted as a 'pure' category (Henry James's 'The Turn of the Screw' is, in fact, one of very few, eligible texts). Most others settle down ultimately either to be read in supernatural terms (the marvellous) or to have a psychological explanation (the uncanny). So, for Jackson, the 'classic fantasy' writers (Tolkien, Lewis and T. H. White) are consigned to the category of the marvellous, which is – again, somewhat contentiously – aligned with the status quo. Such writers, she argues, take 'a transcendentalist approach', having 'a nostalgic, humanistic vision'; they 'look back to a lost moral and social hierarchy, which their fantasies attempt to recapture and revivify' (ibid.: 2).

Jackson has one further problem, though, for Todorov's model, as she notes, lacks 'social and political implications' (ibid.: 6) – albeit, as I have suggested above, Jackson's own claim about the fantastic approaching 'the ideal purity of its essence' effectively casts it adrift from any specific socio-historical mooring. However, it is clearly quite a leap to bridge the divide between a Todorovian notion of the fantastic – which involves hesitancy – and some form of activity, let alone activity of a political nature. One can certainly see how the fantastic might trouble order, indeed subvert it, but there is no reason why this should lead to action rather than, say, to its opposite: inaction, quiescence, stasis – states that many of Samuel Beckett's protagonists find themselves in (or, indeed, his equivalent in children's literature, the existential philosopher, C. Serpentina, author of that absurdist drama performed by the 'Caws of Art Experimental Theatre Group'; Hoban, 2005: 51).[10] But, ironically, it is the latter – states of inertia, death, entropy and the unreal – that predominate in Jackson's own discussion of the modern fantastic; and it is because of this that her occasional attempts to give subversion a more political edge seem so out of place: 'De-mystifying the process of reading fantasies will, hopefully, point to the possibility of undoing many texts which work, unconsciously, upon us. In the end this may lead to real social transformation' (Jackson, 1981: 10); and slightly later, she approvingly quotes Sartre's notion of fantasy's 'proper function: to transform this world' (ibid.: 18).[11]

Though coming from very different theoretical backgrounds, this ability of certain areas of fantasy to lead to social transformation is what

Zipes also argued, as discussed previously. He too speaks of how certain tales can 'provide a social and political basis for the fantastic projection so that it is instilled with a liberating potential' (1983: 190); and, like Jackson, seeks to divide fantasy literature (fairy tales mainly) into the reactionary and the more progressive.

In concluding this discussion of Jackson's work, it is worth setting it alongside a similar position taken by a champion of realist writing, the Hungarian Marxist, Georg Lukács (1969 [1937]; 2001 [1938]), who also divides writers on a progressive–reactionary spectrum. Whereas for Jackson it is realism that is, by its nature, more conservative, for Lukács it is precisely the opposite: he criticises those writers who do not confront 'objective reality'. Thus Scott, Balzac, Tolstoy and Mann are progressive, with revolutionary potential, whereas Flaubert, Kafka, Joyce and Beckett – writers more celebrated by Jackson – are not. For Lukács, the latter have protagonists that, ironically, seem to hesitate too long, resulting in inaction, stasis, and ennui.

Or fantasy: a version of reality?

It seems to me, then, that Jackson and Lukács each deal with only half the equation, the former criticising realism (for maintaining the status quo), the latter (Lukács) being critical of the very area that Jackson finds subversive, 'the modern fantastic'. But the two positions, as I've suggested, are ineluctably entwined. This is where, after so many one-sided discussions of particular modes in isolation, Kathryn Hume's more 'inclusive definition' (1984: 21) comes as a tonic: 'fantasy is not a separate or indeed a separable strain, but rather an impulse as significant as the mimetic impulse, and to recognize that both are involved in the creation of most literature' (ibid.: xii). As she elaborates elsewhere:

> *mimesis*, felt as the desire to imitate, to describe events, people, situations, and objects with such verisimilitude that others can share your experience; and *fantasy*, the desire to change givens and alter reality – out of boredom, play, vision, longing, for something lacking, or need for metaphoric images that will bypass the audience's verbal defences. (Ibid.: 20)

Hume's clarification is certainly a step in the right direction, but she still tends to see the terms as oppositional. Moreover, mimesis remains the bedrock from which fantasy can 'change givens and alter reality', fantasy thereby being the mode with the subversive potential, again favouring

Jackson's reading. Finally, to speak of a mimetic or fantasy 'impulse' suggests that its use is far more incidental in the production of a literary work. Instead, drawing on Lacan's work, I want to suggest that fantasy and realism (or *mimesis*) are intertwined at a deeper level – while recognising that much of what Hume and others write has undoubted heuristic value.

In order to introduce this area I shall look at Anthony Browne's picturebook, *Zoo* (1992). The prolific Browne, a fairly recent UK Children's Laureate, is an artist/author who has frequently problematised and played around with this inner–outer divide, using surrealist techniques to query our standard notions of reality. Although some of his works more overtly project a child's feelings onto an external environment (such as *Gorilla* (1983) or *Willy the Wimp* (1984)), others do not restrict themselves to a single character's unconscious wishes. In *Zoo*, for instance, Browne queries the whole inner–outer divide that the concept of a zoo demarcates, and various categories around it: animal/ human, wild/domestic, entertainment/education and, ultimately, nature/culture. The book might initially suggest, with its black and white cover, that such binary opposites are indeed distinctly separable (see Figure 6.1).However, we soon learn otherwise; indeed, the book might be renamed *Who's Who?* or, even better, *Whose Zoo?* Things are not nearly so black and white (to gesture towards another famous picturebook, by David Macaulay (1990)). In fact, the very curve of the lines on the cover might convey the idea that reality is itself wavering – as in that technique so frequently used in old films to indicate a shift between one realm and another (inner and outer, for example). More concretely, the lines on the front cover – especially considering the title – suggest the bars of a cage; however, once again, their slight contouring also invokes something more animate; it is an animal, of course: the flank of a zebra. From the outset, then, figure and ground, animal and cage, are interlinked, such that we might find it difficult to separate the two, especially in a purpose-built realm like a zoo; that is, in a place where animals are held captive in order to captivate, as is also demonstrated in the way the family is placed on the front cover. There's the feeling that, though it is there in black and white, they don't see it. They are the elephant in the room, one might say.

The inattention of the male members of the family, shown throughout, becomes most explicit when they are asked about their favourite parts of the day, and not one of them mentions the animals. As the mother says, 'I don't think the zoo really is for animals ... I think it's for people' – and in this picture, as in an earlier one, the family are themselves represented

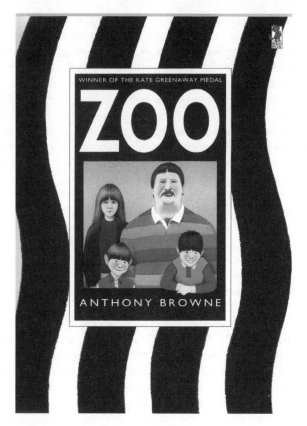

Figure 6.1   Anthony Browne's *Zoo* (1994)

behind bars, as is the narrator in his subsequent dream (if one wanted to
make a Lacanian reading more explicit, at this point one could proclaim:
see, they are all barred subjects!). However, the narrator does not make
the obvious leap overt, though he has helped to nail an inference that
is visually explicit elsewhere in the book: that humans are themselves
animals, except that they are less self-aware in that they presume to
stand outside the animal kingdom, outside the cages; indeed, outside the
prison-house of language (as though unbarred subjects). In fact, they see
themselves as altogether superior; whereas, as Derrida might almost have
said, there is no non-animal human outside the text. Browne, though,
makes quite explicit the falsity of restricting the signifier 'zoo' to this inner

space. It is there on the cover, encompassing all, and perhaps especially the only fully visible creatures below this sign: a human family, peering out of their cage. Again, in Lacanian terms, despite its blatancy, it might be a signified that has slipped out of conscious sight.

Throughout, in Browne's surreal representations of humans, their bestiality is paraded before us, sometimes shown in their physical appearance, but often by way of their behaviour. The fact that Browne has chosen to represent the family using a more primary palette, and in more of a cartoon style, in contrast to the greater care and attention devoted to his depiction of the animals, is indicative, suggesting that the former are more trapped in a fantasy space than the animals. The contrast in representation is especially poignant in the case of our close relative, the gorilla, with its oh-so-human eyes looking to the family on its right (see Figure 6.2). We are embarrassed at the father's 'aping' behaviour, and will perhaps pick up on the irony of the narrator's comment that 'luckily we were the only ones there', once again showing the way language, like bars, frames us (the gorilla's gaze is 'there' and unrelenting, from a perspective that we can never inhabit).[12]

The gorilla, though, does not just *see* him: it looks at him metatextually, from another plane, whereas the family, if anything, is gazing at *us* (making the mother's comment more direct and involving). The gorilla is an impossible onlooker in this context, unnerving and unexpected (especially given that all the other animals in the book are presented in long-shot). And, given the iconic pose of the father, mimicking King Kong, the gorilla seems to be playing into this fantasy construction, being about the right size to play King Kong, especially given the way that he is framed as though through a window – as Kong gazes in on Fay Wray and Bruce Cabot in the original film (Cooper and Schoedsack, 1933). However, the black edges of the frames quartering the animal behind bars also have a darker meaning, suggesting, from their positioning, a crucifixion, as though the silent gorilla were thinking, 'forgive them, for they know not what they do' (Luke 23:34). His trapped status might also suggest another cry from the cross, though: 'My God … why hast thou forsaken me?' (Matthew 27:46). We are used to Browne merging inner and outer, showing us how our classification of reality is itself a fantasy construction, and how, through fantasy, we attempt to suture the obvious flaws and inconsistencies of our symbolic reality. We are also shown, finally, how contingent is this ordering of society and, therefore, how it might be otherwise.

Once again, to frame this in Lacanian terms, and make the more general point, we could say that the gorilla looks out at us from the Real, standing

Figure 6.2   'Aping' King Kong in Anthony Browne's *Zoo* (1994)

outside signification, outside the Symbolic – and, indeed, the impact of this huge face, noted above, is disturbing in this manner: there is too much of him and in too much detail, the frame thereby suggesting that he can hardly be contained or encompassed by our symbolic categories: we experience an *aphanasis* (a fading) under his gaze, feeling 'rather out of place in the picture', like a mere 'stain' (Lacan, 1977b: 96–7).[13] Though we also are creatures of the Real, we cannot recognise ourselves in this way: we are barred from the Real, trapped in the two other orders that do not trouble the gorilla (or only indirectly, as a result of humans). And both of these orders are fantastic constructions, characterised by idealised images or 'empty speech'.[14] There is the hint, of course, in the image on the reverse of the picture of the gorilla (see Figure 6.3), that the narrator's imaginary, ideal ego has been temporarily shattered, that he is moving towards a position of meaningful speech beyond the usual social conventions (hence the *aphanasis*). But this gap is left for the reader to fill. Moreover, there is also a hint that, as this picture is on the reverse of the gorilla's head (verso to recto), it just might represent the animal's fantasy: that for a moment we are inhabiting the gorilla's dream – and, furthermore, that the boy has an inkling of this.

The merging of inner and outer, of fantasy and reality, in Browne's *Zoo* has demonstrated this more complex figuration of how subjects see

Figure 6.3   Whose Dream – an ape's or a boy's? (from Anthony Browne's *Zoo*, 1994)

the world, which always involves a combination of these two aspects. As Žižek (1989: 44) expresses it, 'in the opposition between dream and reality, fantasy is on the side of reality: it is … the support that gives consistency to what we call "reality"' (as Lacan's work develops, fantasy comes to assume ever greater importance, too).

Fantasy, then, fills us out. It prevents us from collapsing into the emptiness of a symbolic universe. It is fantasy that helps keep our desire circulating by staging scenarios in which we are seen as moving ever-closer to achieving some sense of full-being. Fantasy helps provide us with the solace of being meaningful. However, fantasy also prevents us (ultimately) from attaining such an end-point – the term 'end-point' being used quite deliberately here, suggesting our obliteration; in other words, if we were to come too close to our desires, we would effectively be annihilated in our condition as subjects. We would end up as psychotics stranded in the Real.

Let me now develop these ideas, beginning with a work that draws on Lacan's use of topological figures, and the Möbius strip in particular; a work, in fact, that seems almost custom-made.[15]

The *objet a*, or, how to keep the missing piece in circulation

Shel Silverstein's *The Missing Piece* (1976) furnishes an excellent example of our human condition, existing on the edge of the three orders of the RSI. In Silverstein's book, the protagonist is a two-dimensional, round shape with a slice cut out of it (resembling a mouth). It goes in search of what it sees as a missing piece that would render it complete, making it a perfect circle; for currently 'it is not happy'. We witness it on this quest, engaging with the sensual world of worms, beetles and flowers, and, as it goes, it sings itself a song about 'lookin' for my missin' piece'. Eventually it does indeed find a piece that seems the perfect fit. However, as a result of this infill, it discovers that it can do nothing but roll past everything that had previously engaged it (i.e. the very things that made it an inter-subjective being – interacting with others); more significantly, 'now that it was complete it could not sing at all'. In short, it has nothing to sing about and no one to talk to, having foregone its place in the Symbolic (as a desiring being); in fact, no longer experiencing lack, it ceases to exist as a subject, since it is this very gap between us and the world – the fact that we are slightly out of kilter – that gives us a space, without which we would effectively 'implode'.

Consequently, in order for the thing to re-establish its desire, lack (i.e. its missing piece) must be re-introduced (i.e. the piece removed), so that fantasies of attaining some sort of coherence can once more circulate – which is what is neatly captured in the thing's cyclic movement. It can then resume its song, which is also its *raison d'être*: 'Oh I'm lookin' for my missin' piece'.[16] Indeed, we could interpret that first word, 'Oh', as encapsulating its dilemma, constituting a punning *mise en abyme* of its condition, hovering between 'O', suggesting a gestalt, a whole, and 'Oh', emphasising a lack. The missing piece must forever come to terms with the fact that for its fantasy of coherence to continue, it has to *remain* a fantasy; revising the words of the popular folksong, the circle must not be unbroken.[17]

The cover of this book, bearing the work's title, is therefore of particular interest: *The Missing Piece*, it declares, below which we see this ungendered creature, suggesting that the title does indeed name it ('it' stands beneath the signifier). And, in a way, the title does name it, in that labels exist within the Symbolic only (the Real cannot be signified). Thus a name always points to someone or thing that has chosen *meaning* over *being*: a signifier for other signifiers. Names, therefore, like all signifiers, are relational, and cannot help but point to our lack. That is, while names seem to capture a person in a label that we try to 'live up to' in our imaginary figurations (as individual, unique, quirky), most of our being is eclipsed, caught in the signifying chain but fleetingly (the *aphanasis*). With Silverstein's creature, this fact is particularly evident, its very name metonymically capturing this slippage, the 'missing piece' being a synecdoche, the part representing the whole (and, likewise, the hole!).[18] In more Žižekian terms, we could argue that this missing piece has, in the course of the story, effectively 'traversed the fantasy', coming to realise that it itself is the missing piece. More precisely, the piece has come to realise that the only way forward is to continually 'miss' – as of a target one might aim at – its missing piece. So, although outwardly things might appear no different, it has learned to 'enjoy the symptom' of its existence.[19]

Silverstein's tale, then, beautifully encapsulates 'our' existential plight. We don't know that the thing ever experienced the complete state it thinks it now lacks, but this is irrelevant; the important point is that this very lack is what fuels its desire. In this way, the missing piece functions as what Lacan terms the thing's ***objet a***: its object cause of desire. The *objet a* is one of Lacan's most complex ideas, but also one that he saw as a major contribution (and it is crucial to our understanding of fantasy). It is both the thing that we think we once had but lost (hence its ability to instigate our perpetual 'desire' to get it back), and, in our attempt to retrieve it, the thing that also seems to represent the goal of our desire (the thing we most want).

I will return to explicate the *objet a* later, but first, let me suggest a more everyday example of the way our desire keeps circulating, which many of us involved in the book world are likely to have experienced. When I was researching Blyton and trying to obtain cheap, second-hand copies of the hundreds of titles she wrote, I encountered many collectors whose goal was to obtain pristine first editions of all the works she'd ever written (many of these collectors were not interested in the contents; indeed, the books were all the more valuable if unread). I was surprised to note that a number of these collectors had former lives acquiring the *oeuvres* of other authors, only to have their obsession wane when completion came within sight, whence they moved on (or branched out into spin-offs: merchandising, film versions, and so forth).[20] In other words, once again, it is the process of keeping desire circulating, with the *fantasy* of having a full set at some future date ('it will have been'), being the crucial element; thus, simultaneously, many had pre-empted the anxiety of attaining their goal (attaining their missing piece) by opening up other areas (a new quest!), where lack could persist.

Fantasy reconfigured: loosening the Borromean Knot

The Borromean Knot is another topological figure that Lacan used, in this case to conceptualise the relationship of the three orders of existence: the heresy of the RSI (see Figure 6.4). It is worth tracing one's fingers round this knot, for one can then see that any two of its three rings are *not* inter-linked. Two (any two) always depend on the third to hold them together, such that, as Bowie (1991: 194) puts it, 'if any one of the links is severed the whole thing falls apart' (a Borromean Not!). So, as the human, 'speaking-being' exists on the edge of these three, very different, but ultimately inter-linked, orders, the way that fantasy operates within each likewise shifts.

For most people, fantasy is conceived as a compensatory, escapist enter-prise – which is how Freud sometimes envisaged it. But this is just fantasy in its imaginary guise, wherein we find what Freud termed 'His Majesty the Ego' always seeking to enhance his status. Hence we try at all times to protect and bolster our self-image, our ideal ego, and identify with various attractive images and scenarios proffered by society which might assist us in this enterprise, be it a flashy car or a new pair of shoes; or, indeed, notions of being Harry Potter, or the love object of Edward Cullen (*Twilight*, Meyer, 2005), or, more actively, perhaps, Katniss Everdeen (*The Hunger Games*, Collins, 2008). This is why, as Lacan puts it, development proceeds in a fictional direction; there is, moreover, no factual alternative we might take (though we might pretend otherwise). We will forever be captivated by images of wholeness, of utopia. This, then, is the version of fantasy that is most regularly juxtaposed with reality.

However, fantasy takes on a different configuration in the two other orders. In the Symbolic, fantasy is more of a central prop, a support for our existence, filling out and covering over the porosity of this order. As noted elsewhere, the Symbolic is not-all: it slices up existence, dicing the world to fit predetermined categories: of gender, ethnicity, age, abled-ness and the like. It can thereby always undermine imaginary identifications (but never replace them). However, the Symbolic is itself only a realm of empty signifiers, sundered from the Real. In this, the final order, fantasy is closely

Figure 6.4   Lacan's Borromean Knot

connected with the *objet a*, introduced above. From this perspective, we have the notion that a small piece of the Real, associated with the lost mother, lingers somewhere, and we endlessly strive to regain it.

While psychoanalysis is renowned for its theorisations of loss (of the womb, the umbilical cord, the breast, of a pre-specular being), the final loss, we might say, is seen as the unkindest cut of all: the Oedipal, which is not for nothing (a telling phrase!) associated with the castration complex. Lacan, as noted elsewhere, conceives this in symbolic terms, wherein language comes to replace a world of things. However, it is still fruitful to conceptualise it metaphorically, as something that cuts into our existence, barring or dividing us from the immediacy of the signified.

This disappearance is experienced in negative terms only, as an absence, a hole in our existence, which initiates our sense of yearning. Moreover, it itself is experienced only post hoc (i.e. after the event). Entry into the Symbolic thus marks the birth of our desire, being granted a recognised place, and thence being able to share the process of signification with other, likewise barred subjects. These are our gains, but as a result of this process, we now have the ability to hark back to something lost, to the memory of something more. As noted elsewhere, it is this feeling that prevents us from becoming mere symbolic functionaries; namely, we have a lingering sense of the Real that has escaped us. In Lacanian terms, this feeling is not simply a reminder that *persists* but a trace that inflects all our utterances within the Symbolic; it does not thereby merely *persist*: it *insists*. It is a rem(a)inder, as Lacan puts it, his representation attempting to indicate how the too-straightforward lexis of the Symbolic is punctured by the *a* (standing for *l'autre*, or the (m)other), a disruptive force. But only in such indirect ways can it be glimpsed: it has no straightforward signification or specular dimension. Hence Lacan's untranslatable term *objet a*, which he formerly referred to as the *objet petit a*, which spells out the elements more fully: a small part (or part object) of the (m)other. The rem(a)inder, then, signifies the way in which the mother is buried at the heart of this fantastic object that acts as a tear in the Symbolic, reminding us that there is something more, something that drives us ever on.[21]

Lacan is fairly enigmatic about how we experience these rem(a)-inders, but they are frequently related to edges, to those things that divide inner from outer. Lips are a good example, as they both connect and disconnect, parting and coming together as we speak, and as they do in physical contact for a kiss. The softness of lips, as they part, also reveals the hardness of teeth (or a thimble), with their myriad associations. Peter Pan, for example, might uncannily disturb when we hear that he still has his milk teeth, yet wears a skeletal gown. Or we might think of the strange attraction of ventriloquists' dolls with their moving mouths, often out of synch with the sounds that emerge; or, finally, the attraction of moveable books, like Jan Pieńkowski's *Dinner Time* (1981), which plays on just this fascination with mouths opening and closing, with presence and absence.

Like the lips, other marginal zones also tend to be things that were once part of the body, but can subsequently be experienced as separate from it – and, in returns of the Real, can be disturbing precisely because of their uncanny detachment. The breast and excrement are therefore key contenders (going back to Freud's oral and anal stages), both being associated with early development and seen as pleasurable erogenous zones in their own right. They are also key parts of that more fluid sense of a boundary between self and other that the young child not only experiences but is required to focus on: the child taking sustenance and pleasure from the breast, but also experiencing pleasure in the process of excretion (a gift exchange, where that which has been taken from the mother, through the breast, is returned, transformed, in the form of something that attracts attention and praise). Next there is the voice, which can also be experienced as detached from the body, perhaps especially in song; in, say, a lullaby that emerges out of the darkness or in an unattributed voice intoning 'goodnight' (Brown, 1975).

Finally, Lacan mentions the gaze, which is what we experience in the look of significant others, like the mother. Once again, though, this is a complex process; for in coming into existence through the (m)other's look, we also become the object of an external gaze and, throughout life, will continue to have this sense of being observed (by the Big Other). In many ways this is rewarding ('look at me'): our existence is confirmed. However, Lacan also notes its more disturbing aspects, in that we have the feeling of being seen from a perspective that we, as the recipients of this gaze, can never inhabit, suggesting an otherness which, once again, contributes to a sense of lack at the heart of our being (paranoia is clearly a pathological development of this feeling).[22]

In sum, then, these inklings of the Real are what drive us throughout life, as we strive to re-attain this lost object, this lost sense of plenitude, and so we organise fantasies that stage its reappearance. But as I have also noted, these returns of the Real can be disturbing, traumatic, and need the screen of fantasy in order to keep them in check (something that has been explored in Chapter 5, on the uncanny). Horror fiction has certainly learned how to both fascinate and terrify its audiences by recourse to such rem(a)inders – and we, in turn, have learned how much of this horror we ourselves can be comfortable with.

Let me reiterate, then, that fantasy can be escapist, but it also functions at a far deeper level, shaping how we desire (how we exist as subjects) by helping us fill out the gap that signifiers themselves create. Fantasy is thus not a luxury, but an essential support. And it works in two ways: as just noted, it helps us structure our dealings with the Symbolic, fleshing them out; but it also stops us coming too close to the Real, to the terrifying prospect of realising our desires – and being thereby immobilised.

Finally, in this section, it is worth noting that, as we still live in a largely patriarchal world, the Symbolic is least visible to those at its centre, who are most easily interpellated by its calling; who are its ideal 'implied readers', in fact; for whom being an adult, white, middle-class, able-bodied, heterosexual male is the default, requiring least processing and, thereby, in need of fewest coping strategies. This space of acronymically caricatured beings (WASPs, DWEMs, Yuppies, etc.) is something that troubles others, however: women, non-white ethnic groups, those with disabilities, different sexualities, different value systems – and, of course, most children. Such groups are more likely to experience the flaws, the porosity of this everyday reality. To quote the American novelist, John Barth (Enck, 1965: 8), 'reality is a nice place to visit, but you wouldn't want to live there' – not, once again, without the fantasmatic support that keeps our desire circulating, that keeps us moving through life with a sense of purpose (looking for our missing piece). Fantasy, in effect, to reformulate Barth, is where you are more likely to find yourself living, supplementing a threadbare reality by recourse to the surplus that our desires construct. In the more familiar (and readable) work of the British psychoanalyst, D. W. Winnicott, we find a similar notion (from a humanist perspective): that we are creatures of a fantasised reality, a realm that is neither inner nor outer, but part of each. As he puts it, this is '[t]he place where we live', continuing, 'where we most of the time are when we are experiencing life' (1974: 122).

Once upon a time is forever: the Möbius strip rides again

'How does this have anything to do with the Möbius strip?' I might hear you asking (although disembodied voices, dear reader, are a sign of psychosis, to say nothing of that habit of apostrophising absent beings). Like the Borromean Knot, this topological figure attracted Lacan, as it had previously attracted Lewis Carroll (who we'll come to later). Lacan saw it as a useful device for representing what we have just been discussing – what it means to be a subject in the Symbolic – especially as, like other topological figures, let alone those intimidating Lacanian graphs and algebraic symbols, it resists easy signification, confounding any simple appropriation by the Symbolic (or, indeed, the Imaginary).

The Möbius strip, then, is a useful way of representing Lacan's model of the subject, which, unlike Freud's older, humanist version, avoids ideas of surface and hidden depth; that is, there is no notion of a conscious self visible to all while, down below, our repressed desires and dreams are locked in an unconscious cellar (attractive and productive though this is, metaphorically). In Lacan's model, the conscious and the unconscious exist on the same plane. The notion of a binary opposition is therefore disrupted, as are other, similar divisions, such as that between self and other, inner and outer; and, as I am suggesting here, that between fantasy and reality: all are conjoined. Of course, as the Symbolic works only in terms of a binary logic (yes/no, on/off, male/female), it will always separate things in this manner, working precisely according to a 'divide and rule' policy where negation (the 'No' of the father) is the norm. Prefixes like *non-*, *dis-* and *un-* can therefore always *un*hinge (*non*plus or *dis*establish) what might otherwise be connected; except, of course, such a notion is true within the Symbolic only. In those more semiotic aspects of language (mentioned earlier) such logic (that which Bauman depicted in his sketch of modernity) never fully obtains, and a word like the *uncanny*, the *Unheimliche*, can all too readily twist into its opposite regardless of its prefix.

Seen in these terms, the Möbius strip, metaphorically, is more closely aligned with the semiotic and, thereby, with the young child, for whom inner and outer, self and other, sense and nonsense, have yet to be *un*yoked. Rather, everything is there on the unifying surface: polymorphously perverse, instantly to be gratified, with no notion of a heterosexual default or conceit about phallic superiority. In this model (which is Freud's, of course), it is only with the development of the ego and the subsequent assumption of a place in the Symbolic that these ideas will come to seem 'perverse' (in what is the '*père version*', to use Lacan's playful term, derived from the *nom-du-père*).

I am suggesting, then, that we can most usefully picture the Möbius strip as representing our pre-Oedipal state, a time when the above divisions did not obtain, when language is more closely linked to the body and its rhythms. It is the Oedipal cut, that threat of castration, which turns this formerly cyclic strip into something linear, into something that now has an underside, as we are henceforth launched on a gendered and, we might also say, 'straight' trajectory. We thereby become part of history, too, in that we now have a sense of mortality, having both a beginning and an end. Locked into what Lacan called 'the defile of the signifier', we become the 'barred' or split subjects I have discussed before, caught in a place where the signified always slips, slightly unfocused, beneath the signifier, and we consequently feel that some of our 'being' is now lost to us, fading beneath us.

John Barth, whom I quoted earlier,[23] also uses the Möbius strip. With instructions for its assembly, it features as the 'Frame-Tale' of his short story collection *Lost in the Funhouse* (1969): 'Cut on dotted lines', we are told, in order to remove a vertical strip of the page, the ends of which we then attach, having given the strip a single twist. On one side is written

'ONCE UPON A TIME THERE' and, on the other, 'WAS A STORY THAT BEGAN', which is what the tale will continue to do, once hooked up, for as long as we want to play. Indeed, its jokiness is reminiscent of many circular oral tales: 'It was a dark and stormy night, and the captain asked the mate to tell a tale, and this was the tale he told. It was a dark and stormy night ... '. The story thereby subverts the linearity of most tales, denying any sense of an ending.[24] Beyond this, the very creation of Barth's tale has involved an attack on the Symbolic, desecrating the book in order to liberate part of its content. Though with far more brevity, Barth's frame-tale works in a manner similar to Joyce's *Finnegans Wake*, whose very title combines an ending (*fin*) with a beginning (*egan*/again), which it effects by starting and ending mid-sentence. Released from its moorings, then, the tale becomes a fount of variants and versions, able to signify across time and culture, regardless of artificial borders, let alone that more insistent one that seeks to proclaim 'The End'.

But the Möbius strip does not just have significance for postmodernist texts; rather, it is a metaphor for the intertextuality of all stories – though most are not as radically overt in their borrowings as is Joyce's work. But all narratives inescapably draw on earlier texts and change them in the process, shedding and accreting meaning as they do so (creating what Stephens and McCallum (1998) term 'reversions'). Thus Red Riding Hood escapes thanks to her own wiles ('The Grandmother's Tale' in Orenstein, 2002); or Red Riding Hood is devoured (Perrault); or she is rescued by a woodcutter (Grimms); or she (and her grandmother) kill the wolf themselves (Grimms; Merseyside Fairy Tale Collective, in Zipes, 1993); or perhaps Red Riding Hood finishes off Wolfie single-handed (Dahl, 1982); or maybe Red Riding Hood makes love to the wolf (Angela Carter, 1981); or, indeed, runs away with him (in another version that also involves some cutting), escaping the story entirely (Jon Sciezska and Lane Smith, 1992).

This dialogism is another dimension of the Möbius strip, which matches the way that Lacan conceives the whole signifying process: as a far more open and tenuous affair than the imposition of punctuation marks and signs like 'The End' might suggest. They are necessary for meaning to coalesce, to register the fact that we need to reflect on the sense of a particular lump of text (functioning as a quilting point, in fact). It is, indeed, as the Queen of Hearts avers in *Alice*, 'Sentence first – verdict afterwards' (Carroll, 1970: 161), which is why Lacan always stressed the importance of the future anterior tense: it will have been. As Peter Brooks (1984: 22–3) expresses it, 'we read in a spirit of confidence, and also a state of dependence, that what remains to be read will restructure the provisional meanings of the already read'. And, one might argue, for many stories it is a long time after that last full stop that we pin down what we feel is a satisfactory sense of a story's meaning – something that will have shifted and shunted in the course of our literary journey.

What is depicted above (and suggested by the Möbius strip) is Lacan's notion of 'signifying chains', which work in a circular as well as in a linear way. He poetically describes them as comprising 'rings of a necklace that is a ring in another necklace made of rings' (Lacan, 1977a: 153). In other words, though sentences undoubtedly move from beginning to end, as we move along them we experience a range of things: different connotations suggest themselves and alternative paths are opened up, each leading to possible destinations (see note 21 on p. 207). And, whatever the narrated tense of a work (even the narrative past of 'she went'), we will always initially experience these things in the present, as ongoing, as the signifiers flow by eye and brain.

As narrative accumulates, though, the recurrence of particular juxtapositions of character and event, or the repetition of certain phrases, allows us to discern motifs, larger patterns emerging, which can swell into thematic concerns. And lastly, as noted above, the text itself is always read in the context of prior texts, which have their own reverberations, whether these come from complete intertexts (as with the Red Riding Hood corpus, above) or from more chance phrases, likenesses of character, similarities of landscape, familiarities of plot device, story-type, or whatever. In these and other ways, the circular wheels of story turn alongside the linear flow, as we experience the delights of being caught up in something resembling an airborne fairground ride. As suggested in the course of this book, then, the notion of a textual energetics implies that the signifying never stops: at some point we simply disembark.

To round off this section, before we come to a more extensive analysis of Sendak's *Where the Wild Things Are*, let me just re-emphasise the key point. Namely that, in the very process of signifying (whether in language or through pictures), alternative possibilities are always being created (through metaphor, association, puns, slips-of-the-tongue and so on) which simultaneously do two things. They make the Symbolic bearable; make it – for all its raggedness and inconsistency in representing the world – hold together, by supplementing it (fantasy's work). But in this process, the artificiality, the conventionality of the Symbolic, also has attention drawn to it: to the way things might be otherwise (and especially for those who do not feel themselves so centrally represented within the symbolic mandate). It is for this reason that it makes no sense to see a particular form or mode as, by definition, subversive or reactionary in the manner of which Jackson speaks – although that potentiality is ever present: *Speaking Desires Can Be Dangerous*, as Elizabeth Wright (1999) expresses it in her punning title. This is where context is all-important, not simply in a work's original articulation, but in how the work is taken up by readers in different social locations, both in cultural and historical terms. Thus a quietly received Hollywood film like *The Wizard of Oz* (Fleming, 1939) would later become a more subversive text for gay and queer communities in the 1950s (Bronski, 1984), let alone a key expression of escape for young and old readers worldwide. Likewise, Sendak's *Wild Things*, in common with Rowling's 'Harry Potter' series, holds a special meaningfulness for homosocial communities.[25] However, only the future anterior will decide.

Where the Wild Things ... will have been

> 'Everything is oedipal ... edible.'
> (Mel Stuart, 1971)

Maurice Sendak's *Where the Wild Things Are*, though it has been interpreted in many different ways over the years, always seems to have something new and important to say, and here I suggest how it might productively be approached from a more Lacanian perspective. As others have noted, it is in many respects quite a didactic tale, rehearsing Dorothy's *cri de coeur* that there's no place like home. Max could thus be seen coming to terms with his id, as a result of which his outlandish behaviour and his attempts at 'instant gratification' are curbed. Max's anger is then turned inwards, where it is worked through in sublimated form (in the wild rumpus), allowing a more socially adjusted Max – now human rather than bestial in appearance (as he removes that 'hoody' part of his costume) – to enjoy his supper, previously withheld. Both he and the reader then come to realise that words (not pictures) have the last word.[26] Proper behaviour – the realm of the Law, of the Symbolic – rules!

Before moving on to a more explicitly Lacanian reading, though, let me pause to consider an earlier 'Freudian' reading of this work by the once revered authority on fairy tales, Bruno Bettelheim, for he unwittingly offers some sound advice that any close reader of a text should heed (which I'll come to later). But first, let us remember that it was Bettelheim who argued that fairy stories – unlike many modern children's stories which 'exposed only ... the sunny side of things' – were invaluable in that they captured the fact that 'real life is not all sunny ... a struggle against severe difficulties in life is unavoidable, is an intrinsic part of human existence' (Bettelheim, 1991: 7–8). Thus monsters, witches and ogres have their place. However, when it comes to Sendak's tale, he remains unconvinced

> that the child *really* believes that the monsters are his invention and that he therefore controls them. It's entirely possible that some children believe this; on the other hand (like the sorcerer's apprentice), when you've got a monster by the tail you can't know for sure that it won't turn against you. (Bettelheim, 1969)

This concern might seem strange from someone who reads the more 'realistic' and less predictable wolf in the Grimms' 'Little Red Cap' as morphing between father, villain and hunter (cf. Darnton, 1984).[27] But Bettelheim is less concerned with the monsters than with the monstrous behaviour of Max's mother: 'To be sent to bed alone is one desertion, and without food is the second desertion. The combination is the worst desertion that can threaten a child'. One might begin to wonder whether Bettelheim ever reached the end of this story (the quilting point), to discover that this desertion actually involves some real dessert ('still hot'). And one would be right to wonder. For, we learn, Sendak's story has actually been related to Bettelheim in conversation with some mothers. We are never told how many, but four are designated – sounding very much like members of a Shakespearean chorus: 'First Mother', 'Second Mother' and so on. He, however, as the master presumed to know, remains 'Dr. Bettelheim' throughout. Despite Sendak's classic being six years old by this time, Bettelheim confesses, 'I don't know the book ... but I've seen others ... '.[28] This limited perspective does not prevent him offering Sendak a few tips, however: 'If I were writing the book ... I'd first let the mother explain why children want to eat up their mothers and not have her send them to bed without supper'. Again, one is tempted to rehearse the advice Bettelheim gives elsewhere, to the effect that explaining a tale's allure 'destroys ... the story's enchantment, which depends to a considerable degree on the child's not quite knowing why he is delighted by it' (Bettelheim, 1991: 18).

Bettelheim, though, has reality and fantasy in very distinctly labelled boxes, and seems keen that the child keep them so, with monsters sealed firmly in the latter space – though he elsewhere confounds this division, and, of course, the infusion of the one by the other, one might argue, is central to psychoanalysis (albeit not that version influenced by ego psychology, deriving from another Freud: Anna, Sigmund's daughter). Nevertheless, reading the text from a more Lacanian stance allows us to see the two modes – fantasy and reality – as irrevocably intertwined. From my perspective, then, Sendak's work can be seen to trace the way that fantasy operates across all three orders of our existence: the Imaginary, the Symbolic and the Real.

Let me begin by mentioning the Lacanian psychotherapist Éric Laurent, who quotes from a case study involving a child who was labelled a 'bad boy' by his mother, the boy being thereby 'identified as such and behaving as such'. Laurent comments, '[a]t the very moment at which the subject identifies with such a signifier, he is petrified'; in other words, he is fixated by this signifier (bad boy), although it does provide the child with a 'fantasy that brings him some jouissance' (Laurent, 1995: 25). Laurent's reasoning is that one's initial signifiers are not themselves part of the signifying chain; thus desire cannot move freely along its links but is trapped, all subsequent signifiers being thereby connected to and supporting this initial conception. Being a 'bad boy', then, just like being a 'wild thing', becomes a **'master signifier'** (or quilting point), which thereby structures the boy's entire existence.

Thus, at the beginning of Max's story, we might see him functioning at the imaginary level where, although separated from his mother (whom we never see, of course), he still hopes to complete her in some way (to be her missing part).[29] And this, precisely, is to be her 'Wild Thing', something that his given name, Max, also suggests: a sense of potency, aligning him with something monstrous and libidinal. On the second spread, therefore, we see that he has signed a picture of a monster with his own name, 'Max'; alternatively, this might be a self-portrait. However, given the largesse of the psychic economy, it can as readily be both. Of course, we presume that it was Max's mother who initially gave him the wolf suit in which he now cavorts. With his pointy features and extrava- gantly hirsute tail, Max certainly provides an energetic and impressive display of cock-sureness (belying an underlying recognition of the fact that this image does not fully represent him). He also displays the typical signs of aggression that Lacan says are associated with the Imaginary, where an individual develops a certain rivalry and jealousy around his own 'image', in that it is seen as not quite identical with him, threatening, perhaps, to usurp him. But he is not prepared for his mother's reaction when he responds to her cry of 'WILD THING!' with what he presumes is the natural response of an adjacency pair: 'I'LL EAT YOU UP!'

She disappoints him by failing to reciprocate his oral desires (which Freud certainly saw as 'cannibalistic' but, equally, as a form of love, connected ultimately to that primary object, the breast – something that Willy Wonka's Freudian slip, quoted in the epigraph above, captures). Instead, his mother responds as though Max's desire that they be united – be as one in this fantasy scenario – is actually a threat of disobedience. Accordingly, he is sent to bed 'without eating anything'. There are several points to note in the picture that accompanies this verbal text. First, we might observe that the crescent moon shows clear signs of being eclipsed, which is exactly how Lacan describes the process of moving into the Symbolic; that is, our sense of full-being becomes eclipsed by a signifier. Max might well signify a Wild Thing but, without supper, he is, more literally, an empty one! If we are to see intimations of a castration scene at this point, though, perhaps most obvious is that closed door, coupled with the mother's negation, her refusal to accede to his demand that she provide his fulfilment ('filling' him in both senses of the word: with love and supper).

It is also worth noting here the distinction that Lacan draws between a need, a demand and a desire. A need exists in the Real; that is, as something biological that food can satisfy. But when the child moves into the Symbolic, needs are no longer automatically satisfied (with breast or bottle) in response to cries of hunger. Needs are now expressed in language, addressed to another. Yet language can never articulate exactly what the *individual* wants; it can only cater for subjects in general, having socially acceptable forms of expression. So these 'demands', as Lacan terms them, might express the need for food, but they also express the wish for more; namely, for things that were formerly intrinsic to the mother-breast reciprocation. What the child really wants is the undivided attention of this other. Language, then, always carries this trace of desire flowing through it. Language always encodes a surplus that can never be openly and fully articulated.[30] Clearly, Max has attempted to express his desire through his cry, 'I'LL EAT YOU UP!', where the signified that this is meant to represent ('I love you so') should have been implicit.

Max's behaviour at this point warrants close attention: he turns away from the door that once linked them, but which now seems to indicate that he is a barred or split subject. He is, one might say, a shadow of his former self (as the crescent moon also intimates). The Lacanian formula for fantasy – $\$ \lozenge a$ – is also worth considering here, as it not only illuminates Sendak's text but also the way that Lacan conceives fantasy. The $, as already mentioned, is the barred subject, whereas *a* symbolises the cause of his newly found desire; that is, the *objet a* discussed earlier; in other words, at this point Max faces an eternal division from the real mother, with whom he once felt himself at one. It is the felt loss of her that drives his desire, which is to re-access this sense of oneness he thinks he once experienced. So the *a* acts as both a reminder of this primordial loss and also – in that there is always felt to be a certain something left behind – a 'remainder' of it (a rem(a)inder, as discussed earlier). The eclipsed moon, emphasising edges and margins, can also be seen to signify this remainder.[31]

I have dealt with both ends of Lacan's formula of fantasy, but in-between there is what Lacan terms 'this something which is presented as a lozenge shape, which I earlier called the diamond (*le poinçon*), and which, in truth, is a sign that was forged expressly to join together in itself what can be isolated from it' (Lacan, 1966/67: I 2). It is a symbol that Lacan uses to show how things are simultaneously linked yet held apart. As André Nusselder (2013: 26–7) glosses it:

> Fantasy … is in the intricate connection of subject and object of desire. It is their *interface*, the surface where subject and object meets [*sic*]. Lacan expresses this in his formula of fantasy $ ◊ *a* (which can be read as: subject / window / object). Fantasy is like a window both *connecting and separating* inside and outside.

Or, in Pierre Skriabine's terms, 'in the fantasy, "a window on the real is constituted for each of us" – a real that this fantasy comes precisely to veil; according to *The Four Fundamental Concepts*, "the real supports the fantasy, the fantasy protects the real"' (Skriabine, 1997: 41).

In other words, fantasy is not merely a compensatory device but an essential part of our subjectivity. At this point in the story, then, Max finds himself situated precisely at the intersection of reality and fantasy, struggling to determine the nature of his desire. Like Peter Pan, he hovers between alienation and separation, currently refusing to take the next step. In the following four-page sequence, starting with the illustration of Max initially shut in his room, this small protagonist seems to evoke Lacan's formula for fantasy quite explicitly, as we see Max ($) in the room, eyes closed, with the moon (*a*) standing above and beyond him, the open window (◊) aligning them, the lozenge itself acting as 'a window both *connecting and separating* inside and outside', as Nusselder expressed it. The window frame stands over Max like a speech or thought bubble, voicing his desire for the moon, as he begins to enter a space where he hopes to demonstrate more fully his prowess as a Wild Thing. And so we marvel at how the 'forest grew', along with the picture space itself, more clearly to show how fantasy helps fill out Max's precarious 'reality', helping him stage his desire. Over three page turns we witness how the inside becomes the outside as the more primal space of the forest opens out.[32] And, in the process, the two points of the crescent moon seem to have rotated in a slightly anti-clockwise direction, such that they now point upwards – evoking both the horns of monsters and, indeed, his own, pointed, horn-like ears – as he turns to do obeisance to the moon. The moon, of course, as noted earlier, is clearly associated with his mother and, in line with her 'symbolic' closing of the door, with his inchoate unconscious, too.

At this point, Max is 'stuck', as also noted earlier; he realises that he cannot be 'all' for the mother: she has denied him this role. He is thus alienated from any former imaginary relationship with her. However, he has yet to find his own place in the symbolic order. He thus cleaves to the notion of being a Wild Thing (his master signifier), exploring his options, one might say, on this existential journey undertaken in his very own 'private boat', metonymically linked to him by name (a name that we never hear his mother use). He sets out to chart the coordinates of his desire.

Though I use the word 'options' above, Lacan points out that this 'vel of alienation' (see p. 28) is a Hobson's choice: an either/or that is really no option at all. This said, although *some* decision is necessary (the vel), there are different ways in which one's subjectivity might be structured. Briefly, these are the neurotic, psychotic and perverse positions (which, to some extent, we all inhabit; so, unlike the Freudian scheme, they are not pathological, outside of which some normality is possible). Thus, the neurotic is one who comes to accept the Oedipal situation, though remaining resentful; the pervert, in contrast, only partially accepts this situation, still thinking that access to the mother might be possible; whereas the psychotic refuses to accept the symbolic mandate in any form.

Going back to the beginning of this analysis, then, I suggested that Max had become fixated on the master signifier of being a Wild Thing. In imaginary terms, therefore, he is trying to prove his capability to his mother, to complement her in his attempted role as imaginary phallus; or, to put it in more traditionally Freudian terms, he is trying to enact the role of 'His Majesty the Ego, the hero alike of every day-dream and of every story' (Freud, 1985a: 138). In other words, the (male!) ego always desires to win honour, power, wealth, fame and the love of women; but he lacks the means for achieving these satisfactions. Consequently, like any other unsatisfied man, he turns away from reality and transfers all his interest, and his libido too, to the wishful constructions of his life of phantasy, whence the path might lead to neurosis. (Freud, 1973: 423)[33]

There are certainly other parts of the text that support this notion of Max engaging in an imaginary fantasy. On the title page, for example, we see 'Wild Thing' Max linked to two parental monsters, clearly gendered male and female, who fill the left-hand spread, the aptly named home space. We are in the territory of what Freud (1977a) terms the 'family romance', where a child imagines its own parents to be imposters, seeing itself, rather, as the progeny of more illustrious parentage, often fantasised in terms of royalty. In this scenario, Max has redesigned his family in line with his imaginary ideal (as 'pureblood' Wild Things), with the respective stances suggesting that it is on Max's own terms: there is no Law of the Father here; rather, the parents defer to the Law of the Child! (of course, this scenario suggests a Freudian 'displacement' of the real seat of power).

It is significant that this paratext occurs on the title page, hinting that Max is, indeed, 'stuck' in this position. He can fantasise about being His Majesty and experience a buzz of *jouissance* that is not obtainable within the Symbolic (where it is rationed). However, he is ultimately trapped by this master signifier – which, for him, is related to the fact that he has not accepted his mother as merely (mère-ly?) a 'maternal' signifier. It certainly seems of note that the earlier, eclipsed moon is full during the rumpus sequence. There is a suggestion that Max is performing for his mother; that, indeed, the spotlight (her gaze) is upon him, such that he imagines her entirely captivated by his performance, just as he saw himself in the mirror phase, framed by her desire. Max's attempt to recreate this scenario in his dealings with the Wild Things relays this exhibitionistic ploy: to fix them and, in turn, to be fixed within their gaze, precisely as the 'Wild Thing' his mother called him.

The three pages of the Wild Rumpus stress this cyclic, repetitive position: being King of all Wild Things might start out fun but it eventually starts to pall. In more psychoanalytic terms, Max is trapped in a world where signification is stuck. It is certainly *his* fantasy – it is his master signifier, after all – but only in a world of boringly repetitive Wild Things, who can do little else but 'rumpus' (i.e. do Max's narcissistic bidding).[34] In other words, he is not yet in a fully intersubjective realm. In holding fast to this delimiting master signifier, his desire is not yet able to move freely along the signifying chain (he is still trying to be all for the mother: to fill her gaze). He must therefore 'dialectize' the signifier, as Lacan terms it (Fink, 1995: 77), letting go of this repetitive world where everything can be only another rehearsal of the Wild Thing. Language, of course, can only mean through difference, which means that Max will have to give up his dream of an ultimate, static notion of being, fixed like his self-portrait tacked to the wall (or indeed, as he is frozen in characteristic pose on the title page).

This point arrives as Max sits, ultimately 'lonely', following the exhausting, dilatory space of the rumpus. The moon, that bright spotlight, has now disappeared and the Wild Things are themselves no longer supporting the narcissistic gaze of his exhibitionism. It is of note that, for Lacan, desire does not simply manifest itself in the signifying chain of language but also in what he calls the 'scopic drive'; that is, Lacan argues that our whole view of the world is coloured by our desire. As he puts it, the disappointment with a loved one arises from that which is 'always missing'; namely, the fact that '*You never look at me from the place from which I see you*' (Lacan, 1977b: 103). In Max's terms, then, in his fantasy he has tried to hold on to the idea that his mother views his exhibitionistic Wild Thing scenario in its three-dimensional entirety (from her moonlike position of plenitude). But this is a fantasy of the Imaginary; from the perspective of the Symbolic (itself a realm of incompletion, of signifiers), there is no such place: our look, precisely because it is distorted (coloured) by desire (through fantasy), will always give us a partial (and thus inadequate, lacking) view. Max realises this in what we might term 'the cool light of day'. He must enter the intersubjective realm and, with it, come to accept the constraints of linear time (which is simultaneously an acceptance of mortality, no longer freely able to sail in and out of weeks and almost over a year).

Max also realises that it is only in this realm that he can make demands that are met: 'BE STILL! ... let the wild rumpus start! ... Now stop!' Max is 'His Majesty', after all, but, as noted earlier, what he really wants is the very thing that fulfilment of these demands cannot express. He wants 'to be where someone loved him best of all'. The state of oral oneness proffered by the Wild Things ('we'll eat you up – we love you so!'), in contrast, will continue only to trap him in this more solipsistic state.[35] Hence Max responds with his own 'No!', recognising that his notion of full being, as a Wild Thing, must give way to its lack. Of particular note here is the fact that he seems to have relinquished the idea of being all to the mother ('I'LL EAT YOU UP'). What replaces it is a more distanced, metonymic relation with her, captured in the smell of 'good things to eat'. He can now return home and take up his place in the Symbolic, his fixation overcome, the signifying chain established. Removing his wolf hood also suggests that he recognises that he is not now this imaginary object of desire for his mother. It would be too strong to call this picture an image of castration, but his formerly perky outfit is certainly somewhat saggy now, if not flaccid!

In these terms, the ending of Sendak's text has more poignancy, as we leave Max in a space without pictures or conversation: in a space devoid of sensuality, in fact. There are only stark, black signifiers remaining, set against a white background, seeming to belie the very thing they signify: 'and it was still hot' (there is an irony here: the intersubjective realm of the Symbolic can be a very lonely place ...). And in case this 'it' might already have faded from the minds of readers – we have no images to satisfy us – we will have to turn back to look at that supper: a slice of cake, together with a tumbler of what appears to be milk, both of which (and certainly the former) are more likely to be cold rather than hot; the one remaining item, a bowl of something (perhaps 'mush', referencing Brown's *Goodnight Moon* (1975)), could well be 'hot', although there is no tell-tale steam rising from it. Is there a slight mismatch here – a sardonic undercutting, perhaps? Even if the supper is metonymic of his mother's love, that phrase 'still hot' seems to lack conviction, especially in the absence of any supporting visual representation. It is as though we are explicitly having it demonstrated to us that Max is now irretrievably in the world of the Symbolic, where signifiers are all there is; that one needs to turn the page (to go back to an earlier time, in fact) in order to fill out these empty signifiers.[36] Moreover, the narrative past, used throughout the tale, here takes on a particular poignancy ('it *was* still hot' – my emphasis). And even, his name, Max, can be seen to have ironic overtones now that he is within the Symbolic: indicating that he has a limiter, or governor, controlling his access to enjoyment.

Wild Things can certainly be read as a compensatory fantasy, in terms of the Imaginary, with Max striving to be all for his mother (already conspicuous by her absence – see note 34 on p. 209); but it can also be read in Symbolic terms, showing how crucial fantasy is in the constitution of one's subjectivity, helping the subject come to terms with his or her position. Lastly, though I have not concentrated on these aspects, there is a sense of the Real evoked, too, where Max is seen sailing rather too close to the wind of his fantasy scenario. This is especially evident in a page that escapes most people's interpretations (and, as I have found, children's retellings); it occurs just before Max arrives at the place where the Wild Things are. Here, while still 'at sea', Max is confronted by a creature that is less anthropomorphic (or egomorphic – see note 34 on p. 209) than the others. Max's relatively smooth journey is disrupted, the wind has changed direction (according to the pennant) and his boat is upended as it runs aground. None of this, however, is mentioned in the text. It is as though this creature from the deep is a less biddable monster – not necessarily an imaginary Wild Thing at all (they appear to live round the next bay). It thus sticks out in the way that **anamorphic** spots emerge suddenly and disturbingly from otherwise orderly paintings (e.g. Holbein's *The Ambassadors*, cf. Lacan, 1977b; Rudd, 2006b). In short, this monster appears like an eruption of the Real, marking the point, as mentioned above, at which Max comes too close to his desires (to a more disturbing representation of the mother figure). He adjusts the cut of his fantasy jib accordingly, as we witness on the following page, where he reaches a far safer, more satisfyingly egomorphic and welcoming haven.

One might speculate that this earlier monster is a more phallic representation of the castrating mother: the figure who shut the door on him; indeed, this monster occupies a similar space to that of the mother, if we imagine her behind that closed door. Certainly, this monster is the only creature in the story that manages to sneak up on Max and usurp his position in the home space. If it is, indeed, the mother, we might also note that this monster is the only one to exhale smoke or steam, again suggesting something more fiery and, perhaps, rather too hot (unlike his meal, later). In fact, we might speculate that, in his everyday world, it would have been at this point that his mother brought in his supper, temporarily disrupting his fantasy.

In many ways, this reading is little different from many others, apart from the fact that it gives serious attention to the way that fantasy is central to our construction of reality. Hence the ending of the book marks not Max's coming to terms with socialisation – a triumph in ego-psychology terms – but, instead, it shows how civilisation creates, indeed instantiates, its own discontents, such that Max now needs a fantasy dimension in order to make life in the Symbolic sustainable.[37] A mirror image, shadow, doppelgänger, underground domain – call it what you will – will haunt Max hereafter, as ontology becomes hauntology (to borrow Derrida's (1994a) witty pun on 'ontology' – a pun that also sounds more convincing delivered with a French accent). Its title needs reiterating at this point, for it is not (as ego psychology might suggest)

'Where the Wild Things Were': they are very much ongoing accompaniments and will need continual revisiting, although their function and form might shift.

It is interesting to contrast *Where the Wild Things Are* with *Peter Pan*, for I argued that Barrie's figure, as a betwixt-and-between character, never accepted the symbolic mandate, refusing ultimately to give up the mother and take his place in the symbolic order. In his perverse position, he maintains his cockiness as the imaginary phallus, forever crowing about his abilities, his perfection ('I'm joy' etc.), as does Sendak's next protagonist, Mickey, who also likes to crow 'Cock-a-Doodle Doo!' (*In the Night Kitchen*, (1970 [1970]). Of course, when Peter did try to return, so he tells us, he found the window barred: he had been replaced by another child. Peter Pan is therefore tied to his master signifier, the eternal boy, recycling this myth down the generations (and every Christmas, come to that, in an untimely and ungodly parody of some future place of resurrection). Max, on the other hand, has come to accept the symbolic mandate, accepting this metonymy of love, his supper, and therefore his own necessary separation from his mother.

But this won't stop the fantasising. We know that the full stop (following 'hot') is a necessary quilting point, but it will mark only the temporary cessation of desire, which Sendak was to open up, metonymically, in the two other works of what he saw as a trilogy. However, this official reading (and overall quilting) need not be the case. The work is free to be appropriated and reworked by the reader, with further *jouissance* perhaps being squeezed out of the story as a child listener insists that, say, her father read it differently, as we saw earlier: '"No, Dada," she admonished. "Not like that. It's: 'and Max stepped onto their private parts and waved good-bye.' Like that'" (Wolf and Heath, 1992: 44). In other words, all these young avatars of Max will have to strut their stuff on their own Oedipal stage – or something similar – at a theatre somewhere near you.

Conclusion

Lewis Carroll was also fascinated by the Möbius strip, which had been discovered in his lifetime (1858), independently, by two other mathematicians. Though August Möbius would go down in history, Johann Listing has been largely forgotten – although the Listing strip does have a nice ring to it (but then that goes with the topology!). In Carroll's *Sylvie and Bruno Concluded* (1893), it features under another name, as 'the puzzle of the Paper Ring', where we also find the closely related topological form, 'Fortunatus' Purse ... a very twisted, uncomfortable, uncanny-looking bag'. It, too, undoes the division between inner and outer, hence its value, for '[w]hatever is inside that Purse, is outside it; and whatever is outside it, is inside it'. Thus, as Carroll wittily puts it, it contains 'all the wealth of the world' (Carroll, 1893). Just so, the place where the Wild Things are will always provide a portal for the needy reader, and we will always find ourselves on both sides of that impossible border that seeks to demarcate the human zoo.

7 The Children's Book – Not Suitable for Children?

In this final chapter, as at the end of the last, we find ourselves returning to Peter Pan, a text that, as Rose also found, it is hard to escape when discussing children's literature. Even if we do not fully accept Rose's thesis, it is undoubtedly the case that the books categorised as children's fiction almost always have children at their centre. In some ways this might seem obvious, tautological even: the books are for children, after all. But without rehearsing Rose yet again, this seeming obviousness is just what she queries; that is, the extent to which these children are constructed in particular ways by adults, who thereby try to ensure that the former are shown their rightful place.

A. S. Byatt's novel, explicitly entitled *The Children's Book* (2010 [2009]), approaches this topic in a more unusual way. Despite its title, and despite the fact that it charts the development of a number of child characters, it is precisely *not* for children. In fact, judging by the number of colleagues who confess to have failed to finish it, it is a book that defeats many adult readers too. Perhaps it is a work that fits that enigmatic category to which Woolf assigned *Middlemarch*: 'one of the few English novels written for grown-up people' (Woolf, 1938: 167). To my mind, what Byatt's book does do is fill out many of the issues that Rose addresses: exploring how childhood is conceptualised by a society, and what adult preoccupations and motivations inform the writing of children's books. Like the initial tales of Peter Pan, too, which were contained within the adult novel *Little White Bird*, Byatt's novel also includes several stories for children, written by the book's main character, Olive Wellwood.

But beyond this, Byatt's novel returns us more explicitly to *Peter Pan* and the notion of a boy who would not grow up, a *puer aeternus*. We follow Tom, Olive's eldest son, from pre-puberty into his twenties. At age 12, asked about his future, he responds: 'I don't ever want to leave here. I want to go on being in the woods ... '. An adult onlooker responds, 'And to be boy eternal' (Byatt, 2010: 52), referencing Shakespeare's *The Winter's Tale*.[1] Worryingly, though, this desire of Tom's persists long past its sell-by date. In his mid-twenties, we are told that he 'wanted, but he did not know he wanted, to be like Ann, to stay in a world, in a time, where every day was an age' (ibid.: 399). As a toddler, though, Ann's claim is more legitimate.

One might initially consider the representation of Tom to be a deliberate response to Rose's famous thesis:

> Suppose ... that Peter Pan is a little boy who does not grow up, not because he doesn't want to, but because someone else prefers that he shouldn't. Suppose, therefore, that what is at stake in Peter Pan is the adult's desire for the child ... a form of investment by the adult in the child ... which fixes the child and then holds it in place. (1984: 2)

For Tom really *does* seem to be someone who – as his sister Dorothy reflects – 'didn't want to be a grown-up' (Byatt, 2010: 364). But, contrary to Rose, this desire does not seem to be because of any specifically adult pressure. In fact, even his mother would like him to do something and stop '*lurking* in the bushes' (ibid.: 467). Ironically Olive's breakthrough children's story was entitled *The Shrubbery, or the Boy who Vanished* (ibid.: 34), which foreshadows Tom's fate in certain respects.

Byatt, in fact, is not really concerned so much with the impossibility of children's fiction as with the impossible position that the offspring of children's writers are placed in:

> I noticed that the children of the great writers for children often came to unhappy ends – even suicide – and this interested me dramatically. Kenneth Grahame's son [Alastair], for whom *The Wind in the Willows* was ostensibly written, lay down on a railway line when he was at Oxford. Two of the Llewellyn-Davies boys, for whom Barrie wrote *Peter Pan*, ended in suicide .... And Alison Uttley ... lost both her husband and her only son to suicide. My initial thesis was that the writers wanted to prolong their own childhoods and that the children thus had no place to be themselves. (Byatt, 2009)

But, though *The Children's Book* might have begun with this thesis, it is quickly rejected in favour of a more general examination of the cultural shift from Victorian into Edwardian, then Georgian England, organised around three ages: of Gold, Silver and Lead.

The Silver Age is the most central, but also the most intangible, as one might expect from an age named after a metal associated with mirroring, with reflection and, we might add, with superficiality and narcissism. And this is how it is painted. There's a lack of contact with larger political issues; an ignorance of colonial and imperialist annexation and exploitation, of the build-up of arms; moreover, there's a growing jingoism. These issues remain amorphous, although all the characters are animated by worthy causes: with building a better society, with improving the lot of the poor (through the Arts and Crafts movement, inspired by Ruskin and Morris, and via the Fabians and Anarchists), with the position of women (the Suffragists), and, of course, with the quality of life itself (self-improvement, sexual liberation, artistic endeavour). The child, too, is part of this shift, besides being a symbol of a new age. Thus people realised,

> in a way earlier generations had not, that children were people, with identities and desires and intelligences. They saw that they were neither dolls, nor toys, nor miniature adults. They saw ... that children needed freedom, needed not only to learn, and be good, but to play and be wild. (Byatt, 2010: 394)

However, as Byatt goes on to note, they realised this only because of their own desire for a 'perpetual childhood, a Silver Age' (ibid.). This is cleverly contrasted with what Byatt terms an 'imagined Golden Age' (ibid.: 391) – that is, a construct invented by the Silver Age, to which Grahame's eponymous volume, *The Golden Age* (1895) – a longing, nostalgic look back at childhood by an adult – is central. Whereas the Golden Age section begins straightforwardly with the plot, the Silver Age opens with seven pages of historical reflection (and the pun, evoking the looking-glass, is deliberate). Tom certainly sees through this facade, but only because he really *does* believe in a Golden Age: 'the Garden of England was a garden through a looking-glass, and [Tom] had resolutely stepped through the glass and refused to return' (ibid.: 364).

But, as with all Golden Ages, it was never thus – and certainly not for Olive and her sister, Violet, whose hometown of Goldthorpe, a mining village in Yorkshire, is cruelly misnamed. Here is the darker side of Victorian England: its industry, poverty, disease and death; however, there is also the notion that Olive's best fiction is fuelled by this darker past, acting as a fantasy screen that allows her to avoid confronting it.

She lost her mother and a sibling at 12; later, the mines claimed her older brother, Petey, who was terrified of the dark, then her father, also a storyteller, and also named Peter. It was he who had spoken not only of invisible beings underground, but also of former forests and creatures compacted in the mud and coal. The stories of these personal deaths travel with Olive, occasionally giving her nightmares, but generally being metaphorically contained within a securely knotted package, carried by a woman whom she observes endlessly walking 'across the moor, in the wind, with the closed, calm parcel, containing the obscene things' (ibid.: 87).

If Grahame hovers behind this text, E. Nesbit is at its forefront, with Olive sharing many of that novelist's qualities. Nesbit had also lost a parent, her father, when a child, and, from then on, had no secure home, attending a series of boarding schools in Britain and Europe. The young Nesbit also suffered nightmares, one in particular after being taken down into a crypt containing decaying, mummified bodies. Beyond this, Nesbit also brought up two children, Rosamund and John, who were not her own but those of her companion and help, Alice Hoatson, only belatedly discovering that her husband, Hubert Bland, was their father (Rosamund, in fact, would later be seduced by H. G. Wells, who shares not just the first name but many of the beliefs of the fictional espouser of free love in Byatt's text, Herbert Methley). Nesbit's children only discovered the secret of their origins in adolescence, as do two of the Wellwood progeny. To draw one last parallel, just as Olive is shattered by her beloved Tom's fate, so Nesbit was devastated by the death of her favourite child, Fabian, following a routine tonsillectomy. (Of course, Byatt herself had lost a son, aged 11.)

Apart from the biographical parallels, there are literary ones too. The magic of trains, central to Nesbit's *The Railway Children* (1960 [1906]), recurs here. Then there are Olive's thoughts after witnessing a production of Hoffmann's *The Sandman*: 'Suppose a puppet managed to free itself and come to life [... and then] walked into a nursery and was attacked by a flannelly array of simulacra' (Byatt, 2010: 82–3), raising memories of Nesbit's Ugly-Wuglies in *The Enchanted Castle* (1979). There's also the recursive story of Olive's *The People in the House in the House*, which nods towards Nesbit's 'The Town in the Library in the Town in the Library', and, of course, at the novel's opening, Olive visits a museum friend, seeking advice for a story involving 'an ancient treasure with magical properties' (Byatt, 2010: 10), referencing Nesbit's *The Story of the Amulet* (1959b).

However, as I have already indicated, Byatt seems to have quickly rejected the idea that Olive's children could not grow because she had prolonged her own childhood: far from it. Olive grew up all too quickly, stories, as Olive informs us, being the sisters' salvation:

> 'stories are the inner life of this house. ... I am Mother Goose quacking away what sounds like comforting chatter but is really ... what holds it all together. ... Well, it makes money, it does hold it all together.' (Byatt, 2010: 358)

Like a number of women writers (Nesbit included), economic necessity was the key driver, their independence hard won. She is certainly driven, and preoccupied, but no more than other families we meet in the novel, the most immediate being that of Benedict Fludd, a tormented artist. Whereas Olive contains her past in a 'parcel, containing … obscene things' (ibid.: 87), Fludd has a 'dark pantry full of obscene … jars' (ibid.: 299) – though his are undoubtedly more sinister, with hints of filial incest (Fludd's daughters being, initially, as shadowy as Tom).[2] But the point is made that few are innocent, childlike. Tom's sister, Dorothy, for instance, also has to fend off sexual advances from her father (though, as she later discovers, he is not her father).

Likewise, the suicide count for the offspring of children's writers seems no higher than that for, say, adult writers (e.g. Nicholas Hughes, son of Ted Hughes and Sylvia Plath; Klaus and Michael, sons of Thomas Mann; or Carol, Robert Frost's daughter). It simply seems expected that, somehow, children's writers should sire Polyanna-like, Edenic beings: 'Sunny Stories', as Enid Blyton would like to have it (but, likewise, in her fiction only – cf. Rudd, 2000).

What Byatt more brilliantly does, though, is show how intricately children's literature, and the fairy tale especially, was woven into the fabric of this age (as Caroline Sumpter (2012) has recently detailed). It is this infatuation with a more desirable world that makes the Age of Lead – of the First World War – the more shocking in the book's devastating, telegrammatic finale, mocking the tidy closures of Victorian novels. All that can be said here is that 'some of them lived … hereafter'. As Olive had earlier put it, in considering Tom's death, which is shortly followed by her own sister's:

> … this is a story, there is a story in this.
>   And then she saw that there was not. There would be no more stories, she thought, dramatically, uncertain whether this too was a story, or a full stop. (Byatt, 2010: 536)

The 'Age of Lead' is particularly well named, dominated by munitions and armaments, but also with notions of being leaden, mired in mud, as opposed to the aerial antics witnessed earlier, in theatrical machinations (often executed by Germans, ironically); 'lead' and 'dead', in fact, rhyme too easily – something that the Silver Age had hidden away, just as Olive had transmuted Goldthorpe's

> pinched life of ash pits, cinders, rumbling subterranean horrors and black dust settling everywhere. The woods, the Downs, the lawn, the hearth, the stables were a *real* reality, kept in being by continuous inventive willpower.

In weak moments she thought of her garden as the fairytale palace the prince, or princess, must not leave on pain of bleak disaster. They were inside a firewall, outside which grim goblins mopped and mowed. She had made, had *written*, this world with the inventive power with which she told her stories. (Ibid.: 301)

As we saw in the last chapter, fantasy and reality are mutually dependent, but there's also the unnerving threat of the Real, as Olive realises that 'she had to ignore a great deal, in order to persist in her calm, and listen steadily to the quick scratch of the nib' (ibid.). Here Byatt seems to approach the uncanny aporia from which children's literature usually retreats. *The Children's Book* encapsulates this paradox: Olive's 'securely knotted package' seemingly as innocuous as one of Mary Poppins's favourite things, but within, 'obscene things' lurk (ibid.: 87) – things that Rose, together with Anne Higonnet (1998), James Kincaid (1992) and others, has helped us unwrap. The paradox is even encoded in the Wellwood home's name, Todefright, which, despite a journalist's claim that it merely combines the amphibian's name with a word for meadow – 'No death or spectres!' (Byatt, 2010: 527) – does not fool its inhabitants: 'in, through, and under' its solid presence is an 'imagined, interpenetrating world, with its secret doors into tunnels, and caverns, ... her home standing on terrifying strata of underground rocks and ores ... through which snaked rivers ... ' (ibid.: 141–2).

Olive's doubled existence harks back to her childhood, when she first storied herself, as Cinders in the ashes, or as Peter Piper, escaping to the sea from an orphanage (ibid.: 89). And she continues to story the world to survive, such that each of her children has, aside from its real existence, a fantasised one that she explores in personalised books that shadow (and sometimes foreshadow) their lives – sometimes, indeed, seeming to take them over, as, once again, is most fully realised in the case of Tom. Accompanying the incessant scratch of Olive's nib, then, is the scratch of underground rats, like the one that steals Tom's shadow in his 'own' story, proleptically entitled *Tom Underground*. He then has to retrieve this shadow, undergoing a traditional *katabasis*. Tom's story also has its own intertextual revenants: of Chamisso's *Peter Schlemihl* (1861 [1814]), who sells his shadow to the devil and ends up aimlessly wandering the earth; or Andersen's 'The Shadow' (2011 [1847]), in which its owner is eventually replaced, his shadow taking over his life. Just so, Tom finds the shadowy realm becoming more solid as reality pales into a facade, turning Todefright into 'a whited, plaster-cast sort of a place, a model of a home merely, which propped up the constant shape-shifting of the otherworld.... What he feared was that everything might turn out to be cardboard and plaster of Paris, though he feared this in the depth of his gut and behind his eyes' (Byatt, 2010: 149–50).

Which brings me to Tom's end, after he has run away. He comes to a railway where, hearing a train approaching, he hovers 'between the shining tracks', thinking 'he could simply stand there, and let it' (ibid.: 530). Alastair Grahame's suicide, at a similar age, naturally comes to mind. Byatt, though, is teasing here, for in the next sentence Tom 'found himself on the other side', watching the train's 'steam, and fiery grit and busy, clattering piston' (ibid.). Alastair's shade is still there, but only as refracted through the character that he supposedly inspired, the unpredictable and impetuous Toad, also mesmerised by trains: it's a Toad fright only!

But there are closer intertextual threads pulling at Tom – in fact, too many, suggesting that he is trapped, like a puppet, within this constructed realm. And for those who don't know the book, who perhaps abandoned it before approaching the ending that is anything but a eucatastrophe, it is time to avert your eyes. Tom walks into the sea at Dungeness, with the sun going down over Beachy Head, and then slips – as does another Tom in Charles Kingsley's tale – and is drowned, or transformed (Olive earlier spoke of him as one of the 'sealfolk' (ibid.: 187)). Tom is overdetermined, driven and riven by texts: two, in particular, that he runs from, and two that are old friends. The former are what he associates with this new, superficial age of 'fairy electricity'. One is *Peter Pan*, which he detests for being 'cardboard' and 'make-believe', unlike *Alice in Wonderland*, 'a real other place' (ibid.: 465–6). He also finds fakery in his mother's play, *Tom Underground*, which is his personalised story gone public (like Andersen's Shadow). Effectively, this turns Tom into a spectral presence (his fictional double, too, has his shadow stolen). The play's theatrical success seems to be at Tom's expense, stealing his essence, and he takes flight. (In some ways his mother has precipitated this action, and is culpable, but she had also realised – if only subconsciously – that if a son won't abject his mother, the mother must abject the fledgling.)

Two other texts comfort Tom, though: *The Pilgrim's Progress*, which he 'had read ... over and over, as a little boy ... linking the walking to heaven' (ibid.: 531). This imagery of purification (as with his Water-Baby forebear) is deftly tied to Tom's increasing sense of etiolation: he conceives himself 'in shades of cream, and white, and silver, a bleached, leached, blanched story, the colour of the skeletons of seaweeds, or indeed, of humans and beasts. … In his head, the white pilgrim sat down on a creamy couch of pebbles' (ibid.). He incarnates the England of the chalky cliffs and Downs. Poor Tom of King Lear comes to mind as well – 'Fathom and half, fathom and half: Poor Tom!' (*King Lear*, III, iv, 37–8). Tom o'Bedlam, of course, also loses his identity, becoming split as 'a poor, bare, forked animal' (ibid.: 110), and, moreover, sought 'to course his own shadow for a traitor' (ibid.: 57).

Tom's other *vade mecum* is Kipling's *Puck of Pook's Hill* (1906/8), which opens with two children unwittingly summoning Puck by enacting a piece from *A Midsummer Night's Dream* three times on Midsummer Eve. Tom always played Puck in the Wellwood family productions (and, in Olive's story, the boy that flees into the shrubbery, into the world of faery, is renamed 'Pucan' (Byatt, 2010: 100)). 'Dymchurch Flit' (a chapter of *Puck*), which is narrated by Puck disguised as the dead Tom Shoesmith, fills Tom Wellwood's mind at this moment. Like the fairies of Kipling's tale, Shoesmith realises that he 'must flit out o' this, for Merry England's done with, an' we're reckoned among the Images' (Kipling, 1906/8: 267). Thus, in Tom's words, they 'streamed over the midnight beach to leave the country which no longer believed in them' (Byatt, 2010: 531). Not only does Tom align himself with these mere 'Images', but also with the Bee-Boy of Kipling's tale, who 'slipped in like a shadow'. He is a Wordsworthian wise-fool who 'could see further into a millstone than most' (Kipling, 1906/8: 258); likewise, Olive's fictional Tom has always treasured a stone with a hole in it – known as an adder or hag stone – during his underground adventures. It is at this point, on the pebble beach, that Tom, too, finds one: 'these were, or once were, magic, you could see the unseen world through the hole' (Byatt, 2010: 532). It is a stone that Olive will later ask to be placed under her pillow (ibid.: 537).[3]

But there is one more literary reference that needs mentioning: 'Dover Beach' (Arnold, 1867), with its 'moon-blanch'd land', its 'flung pebbles' bringing an 'eternal note of sadness in', and, most explicitly, the 'melancholy, long, withdrawing roar' of 'The Sea of Faith', ending with the famous lines:

> And we are here as on a darkling plain
> Swept with confused alarms of struggle and flight,
> Where ignorant armies clash by night.

Clearly, neither Arnold nor Tom foresaw war on the horizon, but the insecurities of the Silver Age are keenly felt. Tom symbolises this age and is a casualty of it, but he is by no means alone: there is also Grahame with his Open Road, George Borrow with his gypsy caravan, plus the wistful escapism of Edward Carpenter, Richard Jefferies, W. H. Hudson and others.[4]

Children's books, the very warp and weft of this novel, are also carried into the Age of Lead, but transmuted once again. Julian Cain, a contemporary of Tom's (they are the characters we meet on the opening page), finds many of the trenches with names like Walrus, Gimble, Peter Pan and so on, and manages to write a poem out of this pity. But more powerful, after he suffers a shell-induced amnesia, is Julian's work, 'The Woods', inspired by the wood in *Through the Looking-Glass*, 'where things have no names' (Byatt, 2010: 589); as Julian comments: 'Names are getting away from things. They don't hold together' (ibid.: 590).

Tom is the fullest realisation of this split self – shadow from substance, puppet from master, signifier from signified – but he is by no means unique (except that his vision of the fairies' exodus to Flanders fields encodes a cruel irony) – and he is certainly not merely the victim of having a children's writer for a mother, any more than the many other casualties of this devastation could blame Henty, Herbert Strang, Percy Westerman or P. C. Wren. This said, these boys' writers are, perhaps, the most obvious omissions from a work that is otherwise so rich in its cultural re-creation.

Conclusion

There is so much more to say about Byatt's work, of which I have merely skimmed the surface. But I now want to link it to the concerns of *Reading the Child*, drawing out the wider implications. I have concentrated on how Byatt shows us that 'children were people' (ibid.: 394) in this society, such that its various discourses could not help but impact on them. Moreover, Byatt's work also shows us that this was a reciprocal process: 'adult' material found its way into children's texts, certainly (it could not be otherwise, language being what it is), but children's texts were themselves widely discussed and disseminated. In fact, though I think Byatt abandons her initial thesis about children's writers being particularly dangerous as parents, there is an abiding concern that this whole age was overly focused on childish things, thereby not seeing the European (and world) disaster that lay ahead.[5]

Thus the narrator writes of how '[p]eople talked, and thought, earnestly and frivolously, about sex', while '[a]t the same time they showed a paradoxical propensity to retreat into childhood, to read and write adventure stories, tales about furry animals, dramas about pre-pubertal children' (ibid.: 300). Of course, this is not really paradoxical, especially given Freud's contemporary work on infantile sexuality (1905), which Byatt herself references elsewhere in the novel (ibid.: 396). Regardless of this, I detect a disparaging tone, which is implicit in her periodisation, wherein the Golden Age is seen as an Edenic time of eternal youth, whereas, in the Silver Age, 'the people lived for 100 years as children, without growing up, and then quite suddenly aged and died' (ibid.: 394). Given the ensuing War, this might seem prescient. But the notion that the Silver Age had a 'backwards stare', with an 'intense interest in, and nostalgia for, childhood' (ibid.), such that '[i]t was seriously suggested that the great writing of the time was writing for children, which was also read by grown-ups' (ibid.: 395), deserves more critical scrutiny.[6]

It was not that the culture became somehow 'infantilised' (though Byatt might consider the situation, a century later, rather differently, as her critique, 'Harry Potter and the Childish Adult' (2003), suggests); rather, a culture that previously had had a more amorphous notion of children and adults coexisting, now began to carve out a far more distinct place for childhood (with its own games and spaces – like the nursery, complete with children's books). As I noted in Chapter 1, the Modernists, in particular, sought a more exclusively adult culture (Woolf praising *Middlemarch* as being, unusually, for adults, whereas Dickens was seen as suitable merely for 'parents and children', as Leavis (1962: 30) would later declare). So, rather than seeing these Victorians and Edwardians as benighted, they were actually central in formulating a new version of childhood; moreover, in line with Lévi-Strauss's mantra about myths being 'good to think' with, this age used myth, together with the fairy tale, to scaffold a great deal of its thought. I would therefore take the following comment by Byatt's narrator as an oversimplification:

> In 1889 Andrew Lang's *Blue Fairy Book* appeared. Tales for children suddenly included real magic, myths, invented worlds and creatures. Olive's early tales had been grimly sweet and unassuming. The coming – or return – of the fairytale opened some trapdoor in her imagination. (2010: 34)

The fairy tale, however, had been growing in popularity since the Grimms' tales first appeared in English in the 1820s. By the 1840s, original tales like those of Andersen were being devoured, with three separate English editions of his work appearing in 1846 (Sumpter, 2012: 6), the same year that the term 'folklore' was coined. In the *Athenaeum*, where this neologism first appeared, an article argued that, '[c]oincident with the world of Fact, in nearly all ages and among all nations, and lying by the side of that world like a fantastic shadow, has been the world of fairy Fiction' (1853). As Sumpter comments, it was 'more than merely "coincident"', as Fact and Fiction 'could be mutually transformative. The fairy tale was never simply fact's fantastic shadow' (2012: 178).

This is what I argued in Chapter 6, of course, that fantasy and reality are intertwined, and it is certainly the case that discourses about politics, evolution, race, religion, the working class, women's rights, homosexuality and so on, fastened on the fairy tale as a form that was good to think with. Thus, when Byatt has Olive reflect on her own stories, being wary 'not to overstep some limit of the bearable' (Byatt, 2010: 83), we need to recognise that this boundary was, like childhood itself, then as now, being continually redefined and redrawn, by adults and children alike. It is a debate where it is easy to take a rose-tinted perspective and forget that tales like Christina Rossetti's 'Goblin Market', Lucy Clifford's 'The New Mother' (1994 [1882]), Wilde's and Andersen's tales, Stevenson's *Treasure Island* and, of course, Barrie's *Peter Pan* (let alone the Henty-style imperialistic tales – and those of the more subversive new comics) were being published for children.

As Olive realises, the power of her tales grew precisely out of their dark roots, and we hear from Phyllis, Tom's sister, that 'Our dead ones' include Tom's brother, another doomed Peter, 'who died just before Tom was born' (Byatt, 2010: 25), following in the footsteps of Olive's father, and brother Petey (the sound of his name immediately conjures up its morbid homophone, 'peaty'), both killed in the mines (Petey, like Tom, also drowning). Such events 'shadow' many of Olive's stories (as they do so much of children's literature). At one point Olive openly speaks about the inevitability of this: '[s]he kept trying to write a story with the title "Safe as Houses", which would be ironic, because houses were not safe' (ibid.: 141). However, unlike Nodelman, I would not thereby want to point to a shadow text or a hidden adult. This gives adults too much power when they too (as Olive intimates) are caught up within the vagaries of life and language (the Symbolic), being tantalised on the one hand by prevailing idealisations of childhood and home (the Imaginary, as we've seen), yet, on the other, experiencing the unconscious pressures of the Real. Byatt's novel, then, more than most, explores these conflicting anxieties, showing – in effect – how children's literature can never be pure, but neither can it be impossible: it is always a hybrid, negotiated space. Just so, it is less that there are hidden adults in these texts than that these texts will never be able to rid themselves of their contestatory discourses – any more than they can escape the three registers of existence, the Real, the Symbolic and the Imaginary, the RSI, the heresy of our being.

Conclusion

Though Byatt's *The Children's Book* is one of the few 'adult' works to feature a children's writer so prominently, another memorable creation appears in Russell Hoban's *Turtle Diary* (1975): the spinster author, Neaera H., who is known for her 'Gillian Vole' stories. However, as she is contemplating her vocation, she threatens to move away from cuddly to more predatory creatures:

> Each new generation of children has to be told: 'This is a world, this is what one does, one lives like this.' Maybe our constant fear is that a generation of children will come along and say, 'This is not a world, this is nothing, there's no way to live at all.' (Ibid.: 100)

Zipes, in an essay written far later, seems to intimate something similar: 'Children see and recognize very early how we are indoctrinating them ... [they] recognize the cultural homogenisation with which they are confronted' (Zipes, 2001: 22). The way the child is seen to stand outside ideology here, like the Romantic child of Rousseau, is reminiscent of Zornado: 'The child understands this process intuitively. Ideology inflected through adult pedagogy interrupts the child's intuitive understanding' (2001: 215).

Unfortunately, Zipes is less sanguine about children's ability to reject this grave new world: 'The difficulty is that they will not be able to resist the constant pressure to conform to market demands and to retain their critical and creative perspectives' (Zipes, 2001: 22). He mentions the 'Goosebumps' series as an example, which might 'lead to an addiction whereby the young, curious reader is transformed into a homogenized reader, dependent on certain expectations and codes that make it appear the world is manageable and comforting' (ibid.: 8). Zipes sustains such language throughout his volume, with 'authors and publishers' being seen to 'prey upon young readers' dispositions and desires ... to sell them a menu that turns out to be junk food' (ibid.: 47), reaching a climax in his critique of the phenomenon of Harry Potter, 'making children all alike' (ibid.: 188).[1]

Zipes, though, as we saw earlier, has a more humanist notion of our being, deriving from Marx, wherein it is possible to discern the real conditions of our existence and be liberated from our alienated state; whereas, from a Lacanian stance, alienation is our inalienable state.[2] We might feel the constraints of the Symbolic and seek to *adjust* our position, but we can never *escape* it. We will also never be immune from those powerful, idealised images that feed our egos, which influence how we dress, whom we emulate, admire, detest, and so on.

But, for me, this imaginary figuration of the child is little different from other utopian images that circle around a wish for *Heimat*, or home, and Harry Potter seems to deliver exactly this feeling for many children. It is, moreover, precisely a 'utopianism ... contained in the feelings it embodies' (Dyer, 1992: 18), as depicted by a number of cultural commentators, and especially those who have conducted empirical work with readers of popular works (e.g. Radway, 1987; Modleski, 1988; Geraghty, 1991) – work that I certainly drew on in my own, earlier study of Blyton's equally 'phenomenal' appeal (Rudd, 2000). These 'feelings' include notions of *abundance* ('the enjoyment of sensuous material reality') and *community* ('togetherness, sense of belonging' – Dyer, 1992: 20–1) rather than a homogenisation. Furthermore, as Ien Ang (1985: 135–6) makes plain, such feelings are often evoked irrespective of 'the "progressiveness" of a fantasy'. As the feminists Pearce and Walkderine noted, such pleasures are frequently 'off duty' ones that can seem quite reactionary to an outsider.

'Harry Potter', then, has been the most successful imaginary figure of recent times, but there are many others, from the virginal, admired Bella Swan to the more streetwise Katniss Everdeen; or indeed from Hello Kitty (formerly the Japanese Harō Kiti) to Ben 10, or even a Teletubby. Such figures can all too readily be criticised – and most are usually passé within a generation – but what they offer should be recognised in its own terms: aside from the accessories (merchandising aplenty!), they proffer images of plenitude, ways of deporting oneself, acting and framing one's fantasies. Zipes recognises some of this, but contends that 'the pleasure and meaning ... will often be prescripted [*sic*] or dictated by convention' (2001: 172). Certainly, conventions are what we all must work with, but they are amazingly versatile, as the fan and slash fiction sites suggest (e.g. Jenkins, 1992), taking Potter, for example, in very different directions in terms of gender, ethnicity, sexual orientation and, more generally, power relations (e.g. Drouillard, 2008; Tosenberger, 2008). Once again, children's books and other media can never escape adult discourses, rework them how they will.

Throughout this book, therefore, I have argued that not only are there three orders of our being to consider, but I've also indicated how closely interlinked they are, such that their separation is artificial. In the first two chapters, then, not only was a particularly powerful, imaginary being considered – Peter Pan – but it was also shown how this joyous, eternally young child could work only as an idealised image. He is, indeed, an *impossibility*, but, it was argued, this did not thereby make children's fiction *impossible*. Children's fiction is, itself, a construction of the Symbolic, which is partial, flawed, holey; but then, within this order, all of us are: porosity is par for the course. This said, and as Rose so powerfully argued, a great deal of children's fiction is written in order to try to suture these holes – with imaginary beings like Peter Pan – though never, ultimately, successfully.

The next two chapters examined the Symbolic in similar terms. It was suggested that attempts to read children's fiction solely through such grids (of nationalism, empire, gender, class and race) inevitably lost some of the magic of the texts (the energetic 'linguistricks' of signification, the gaps, the imaginary satisfactions). Nodelman's impressive contribution, *The Hidden Adult*, was given particular attention here. It was argued, however, that his binary, of adult vs child, could only end up displacing the child – something that, in Nodelman's terms, was determined from the outset, since he conceptualises children's literature as a genre, thus pre-empting the views of actual child readers. In contrast, I have argued that adults, hidden or manifest, do not have such control: even the most Humpty Dumpty-like, seated on high, will come a cropper if they aspire to regulate signification: look after the sense (cents, scents, saints, sans, Zen's ...) and the sounds will still unseat you (from upstanding *homme* to culinary *hommelette*).

Chapter 5 discussed the Real – a difficult business given that this register confounds symbolisation. However, it was argued that the effects of the Real were indubitably felt, often at that very place where the Symbolic gave way, stuttered and stalled (sense into sans, again, ego into egg). Freud's increasingly popular concept of the uncanny was examined at this point, noting how it too fell prey to being domesticated and thereby incorporated within children's literature studies, but often at the expense of the term's edginess (or energetics); that is, the way it gestured towards the Real, as evidenced in more recent Lacanian approaches.

Chapter 6 then drew on the entire heresy of the RSI in order to rethink seriously the relation between fantasy and realism in children's fiction, arguing that a Lacanian approach had much to recommend it, recognising the more playful and energetic, dialogical nature of texts. Finally, Chapter 7 brought this volume full circle: it began with Rose's argument for the children's book being an impossibility and ended by showing that childhood and adulthood are both fictions impossible to realise and dangerous to try to compartmentalise. Byatt's work shows how all cultural products cannot help but engage with the discourses of their time, however much they might disavow and disguise them. Children's books, fashioned out of a common language, have nowhere else to go. Writers might try to control this but, as Carroll realised, the process of signification, even under the *nom-du-père*, is always liable to slide into the *non-du-père*, linguistics into linguistricks. Byatt's book makes the overlap more overt, and shows us how profitable it is to situate any critical analysis within a wider cultural context. Finally, it also cleverly confounded stereotypical ways of trying to pair adult characteristics with adult characters, and, likewise, childlike qualities with the younger characters.

In Chapter 7 (note 6 on p. 210), I quoted Peter Coveney's comment that there was a new sensitivity towards childhood at the end of the nineteenth century, but that it was not met 'with a truly adult response', being ultimately 'a regressive escape into ... self-indulgent nostalgia' (1957: 193). More significantly, this sensitivity did not entail any attempt to take account of the child's perspective. Now, more than a century later, we have the chance to dismantle this binary – always artificial, always obstructive – more satisfactorily. That is, instead of claiming that we can only *text*, or *page*, or, indeed, simply *read* the child in a self-indulgent, nostalgic way, there is now the opportunity – especially given the new social media – to take cognizance of the child who might text back.

Glossary

This is a 'simple guide' to some of the terms, mainly Lacan's, used in this volume. However, these have shifted in signification over the years, often acquiring contradictory meanings within each order of the RSI. Added to this, other writers have taken his concepts in different directions (e.g. Kristeva, Žižek). Accordingly, I have defined the terms as they are used in this volume, with key pages indicated (see Evans, 1996, for a comprehensive explication).

Alienation – see *Vel of alienation.*

Anamorphosis – an art term used to indicate a transformed shape, which usually depends on the viewer taking a particular perspective. Lacan uses Holbein's *The Ambassadors* (1533), where, viewed from a particular point, an elongated stain on the canvas resolves itself into a skull (a memento mori), thus indicating a disturbing intrusion of the Real: 'too much information', in short (see ch. 6).

Aphanasis – or 'fading'. Lacan uses the word to indicate how our sense of being becomes more evanescent in the Symbolic. In the Imaginary, we have holistic and satisfying images of ourselves; in the Symbolic we are reduced to signifiers. Hence our shared, first-person pronoun, 'I', which I might self-importantly savour in my mouth, is then taken up by someone else. Moreover, the further from the patriarchal centre of a culture we are, the more likely we are to feel this sense of transience (see chs 5, 6).

Desire – a key term in Lacan's work. It is almost synonymous with 'lack' (*manque à être*), in that our desire emerges as a result of a feeling of incompletion once we have separated from the mother. We continually try to plug this perceived gap – fulfilling our desires – but never successfully. In this sense, desire is metonymic, always restless, moving on (something that stories emulate – as indeed does all language, given its dialogical nature). It is the circulation of desire that prevents us from being mere functionaries of the Symbolic. There is always a tension between trying to articulate our desires and their ultimate unattainability. However, it is also the case that the very process of attempting this articulation turns it into a reality, making fiction such a powerful vehicle. Lastly, desire for Lacan is never an internal, biological 'drive'; rather, it is something shared, arising out of our relationship with others, but initially the mother, who initiates the process (see also *objet a*; ch. 6).

Dialogical – a term adapted from Bakhtin, referring to the fact that all words carry a history of earlier meanings, associations and contexts, which are to varying degrees evoked by a speaker; likewise, words are used by a speaker to shape or anticipate particular responses. Though this applies to all language, Bakhtin thought the novel particularly dialogical. Kristeva's later term, 'intertextuality', draws on Bakhtin's ideas (see Introduction, chs 1, 4, 5, 6, Conclusion).

Empty Speech – a term indicating the idle chatter of egos (taking place in the Imaginary), as opposed to 'full speech', which is the nearest that a subject comes to articulating her or his desires, when signification seems meaning-full.

Ex-sist – we exist in language (it creates our reality, gives things names), but we ex-sist in the Real, beyond symbolisation, as bodies. However, from our perspective within language, we can only gesture towards this realm beyond, outside signification, which is thereby often characterised as ineffable. Lacan also uses this and other terms (as does Žižek) to emphasise that, as subjects, we are ex-centric, off-centre. Rather than intimacy, we experience 'extimacy', which queries the opposition between inner and outer, fantasy and reality (see chs 2, 3, 5, 6).

Fading – see *aphanasis.*

Gaze – a term frequently misunderstood in Lacan. It is not used in the sense in which feminists speak about the male gaze (a way that a woman is turned into an object by the power of a man to look at her, rendering her passive). In Lacan's sense, we all have the feeling of being looked at from a perspective that we cannot inhabit. This is initiated by the mother. It is thus initially reassuring, but can later become unnerving, undermining our sense of agency (see ch. 6).

Ideal ego – this is a creation of the imaginary order; it is our idealised image: how we imagine or wish ourselves to be; how we wish others might see us (see chs 2, 3, 5, 6).

Imaginary – one of Lacan's three orders of existence, preceding the Symbolic in emergence. It arises during the Mirror stage, when the child comes to identify with something outside itself: its reflection. Lacan therefore can claim that we are, from the off, alienated from ourselves in that this external image is internalised as 'I'. Development, as Lacan famously expressed it, thereby proceeds in a 'fictional direction' and we become attached to this 'ego', this idealised version of our selfhood. Therefore, we will be attracted by other images that seem to offer us this sense of plenitude, of completion: partners, celebrities, clothes, cars, etc.

Imaginary phallus – before the father's prohibition (the *non-du-père* – see *nom-du-père*), the child tries to complete the mother by being that which he thinks she lacks (see chs 2, 6).

Jouissance – a term generally not translated, though it approximates to 'bliss'. Žižek (1989: 44), however, uses the term 'enjoyment', keeping in place the pun on *jouis-sens* (the 'sense of joy': 'enjoy-meant'). *Jouissance* is usually juxtaposed with 'pleasure', the latter being a limited, tolerated form of enjoyment; *jouissance* goes beyond this, breaking down prohibitions (it is heretical) and is thus very close to being painful, unbearable. My use of the terms 'energetics' and 'erotics' gestures in this direction (see chs 2, 3, 6). I use the term to refer to that which exceeds the Symbolic's attempt to delimit our enjoyment, in what is sometimes called 'surplus enjoyment'. It is therefore linked to the Real.

Lack – see *Desire*.

Manque à être – 'lack of being'; see *Desire*.

Master signifier – a signifier that is seen to make sense of the world (in principle), though in itself it does not designate any one thing. It simply helps a subject quilt meaning, as with notions of speaking as a feminist as opposed to a Marxist, either of which will shift the coordinates of one's understanding accordingly (see chs 3, 6).

Mirror stage/phase – probably the most well-known of Lacan's concepts, marking that moment when the child first comes to see itself, either in an actual image (a mirror) or through a parent's representation of it, as a whole; when, in actuality, it might lack much sense of coordination or self-definition. It marks one's entry into the Imaginary.

Monological – a term from Bakhtin, used in contrast to dialogical, to indicate the attempt to impose one, fixed meaning on discourse (Humpty Dumpty's goal). It might be argued that books of law, instruction manuals and the like are monological, though most thinkers argue that homophones, associations, connotations, etc. will always undo this fixity of purpose (see chs 1, 3, 6).

Nom-du-Père – the 'name of the father', a phrase emphasising the connection of the paternal function with the Law, with the Symbolic – with, in our society, the patriarchal order. However, the phrase also puns on the word *non*, stressing that the father's authority is based on a prohibition: forbidding the child's closeness to the mother. Hence access to the Symbolic always comes with conditions, about who one is, what position one has, and how one should speak.

Objet a – a very complex term, which underwent much revision. It is not usually translated, which helps it maintain its paradoxical status. Basically, it refers to a remainder of the *Real* (a part-object, usually linked to the mother), which we feel we have lost and which thereby precipitates our desire. It is, therefore, also closely associated with Fantasy (see ch. 6). The part-object is a bit of the *Real* to which we are attracted precisely because it is something that cannot be rendered whole (i.e. in the Imaginary); such objects thus oscillate between presence and absence and can be simultaneously disturbing and alluring. Lacan particularly mentions the voice/lips, the breast, faeces and the gaze (see ch. 6).

Phallus – one of Lacan's most contentious terms. Initially it seems helpful in distinguishing the biological 'penis' from a cultural object which 'stands for' power in our society. In this sense, for Lacan, we are all 'castrated' as we work through the Oedipal phase; that is, we come to accept that we cannot be all to the mother (i.e. complete her by being the imaginary phallus). In compensation, we are assigned a place in the Symbolic (a name, an identity). The phallus in this order, then, is an empty thing: a symbol (of one's station, of power; e.g. a wig, crown, sceptre), behind which there is nothing; hence it is always veiled (think of the Wizard of Oz). It thus separates ('cuts') signifier from signified, allowing endless signification (it is 'potent') but, in itself, lacks any, one, precise and final meaning.

Quilting point – or *point de capiton* (sometimes translated as 'anchoring point'). Lacan refers to the way that the stuffing in a mattress is held in place by 'anchoring' it at various points. Just so, argues Lacan, the process of signification would endlessly slide without being halted at certain points. One could argue that James Joyce's *Finnegans Wake* shows a lack of such quilting, as does much poetic language (Kristeva), whereas punctuation helps tie things down (with 'full stops' and so on). Lacan argues that it is only at such halting points that we 'take stock' of the words presented to us, and thus make sense (of a sentence or, indeed, larger units of discourse).

Real – the hardest of Lacan's three orders to conceptualise, as it resolutely resists symbolisation. It is the universe as it exists outside signification, continuous, without differentiation. Animals live in it but we do not, although we undertake activities in the Real (eat, sleep, defecate, etc.). It can therefore only be experienced at moments of crisis, or perhaps of ecstasy, trance.

RSI – the initials are pronounced 'heresy' in French. It is a term Lacan jokingly used for his 'unholy trinity' of orders of existence: Real, Symbolic, Imaginary.

Semiotic – a term used by Kristeva to designate that early period in life prior to the advent of the Symbolic when the child's language is not bound by patriarchy and the rules of grammar; for Kristeva, semiotic language is more influenced by the mother (usually), by somatic elements like rhythm (cradling and rocking), stress (heartbeat), tone, vibration, melody, and associated emotions and smells (all of which might reach back to the womb). Though we move into the Symbolic, the semiotic elements of language remain influential, especially in literary works (from nursery rhyme to avant-garde poetry).

Separation – see *Vel of alienation.*

Symbolic – the most pervasive and powerful of Lacan's three orders from a subject's point of view. Basically, it is the order of language (though language is not unique to this order); it is an order predicated not on things but the way that they are organised/structured: where they stand within the system and how they differ from other things (man against woman, child against adult, and so on). It is therefore a realm of signifiers, where nothing has a positive value (it is always based on negation: of *this* not *that*). It is also the realm of the Law, of our culture, and, in accepting it, we are allocated a place (under particular signifiers, such as girl, black, Catholic and so on). As with the mirror image of the Imaginary, we come to identify with something essentially outside ourselves, which grants us meaning ('I am David'), though it can also deny us that (by calling us alien, stateless, unclean – heretical!).

Traversing the fantasy – a term used by Lacan for someone who, at the successful end of analysis, accepts that there is no *objet a* to be attained; that is, accepts that such a search is always a fantasy, a way of coping with the incompleteness of existence. Realising that one doesn't have a fixed place in the scheme of things is thereby seen as liberating, and the very coordinates of one's being can therefore shift. It is often as a result of a seemingly meaningless act (one in the eye for the Symbolic) that this shift in perception occurs (see ch. 3).

Vel of alienation – when the child moves from the Imaginary into the Symbolic (undergoing the Oedipal process) it goes through two stages: of *alienation* then *separation*. In the former, the child realises that its mother's desire lies elsewhere, but still struggles to fulfil her (by completing her, being the imaginary phallus). Most children realise that this is impossible, and come to accept separation (i.e. the law of the father, the prohibition on complementing the mother), and thus enter the Symbolic (Peter Pan does not, Max does). The word 'vel' is Latin for 'either/or', but the choice is really a false one, which Lacan likens to the robber's cry of 'Your money or your Life'. Could you agree to give away your life and hold onto your money?

Notes

Introduction: An Energetics of Children's Literature

1. Using slightly different terminology, Susan Sontag (1994: 14) famously called for 'an erotics of art' instead of 'a hermeneutics'. My choice of 'heretics' retains echoes of such 'erotics'.
2. The article in question is Herbert Kohl's 'Should We Burn Babar?', a title so catchy that it became the title of a collection of related essays (Kohl, 1995).
3. 'Is it possible that a children's literature exists?'
4. As for why it's *an* heretical approach, this could itself be heretical; it's certainly dated! I refer interested readers to H. P. Fowler's *Dictionary of Modern English Usage*, 2nd rev. edn, Sir Ernest Gowers (ed.) (Oxford: Oxford University Press, 1965).

1   Many Happy Returns: To Freud, Rose, the Child and its Literature

1. I am delighted to open this book with a chapter that reworks an article appearing in *Children's Literature Association Quarterly* (Rudd, 2010a), especially as it was awarded best article of that year by the Children's Literature Association, who generally said nice things too embarrassing to repeat here.
2. The complete omission of Rose's work from Hollindale (1997), which takes an essentialist view of childhood (in biological, psychological and emotional terms), is perhaps most indicative.
3. Also, Rose claims that the play in book form 'had nothing to do with children' (ibid.: 6).
4. It might be such remarks that prompted Perry Nodelman's criticism of Rose for her gullibility in accepting some of the 'ridiculous comments that writers and critics make about children's books' (Nodelman, 1985: 99). A later endnote, pertaining to Rose's quotation about the nature of the pun (Rose, 1984: 41), does mention three early psychoanalytical readings of *Alice* (published in the 1930s and 1940s), but schizophrenia is not mentioned. She does, though, criticise these readings for being 'psychobiographically' oriented (ibid.: 146); significantly, only one exception is mentioned, despite the wealth of material that prefers a textual to a biographical approach (e.g. Sewell, 1952; Flescher, 1959; Rackin, 1966; Blake, 1974; Stewart, 1978).

5. Some critics, such as Bakhtin's translator, Michael Holquist, think that Bakhtin authored *Marxism and the Philosophy of Language*, although it appeared under Vološinov's name, whereas others dispute this claim, e.g. Dentith (1995).

6. See Chapter 4 for a detailed discussion of Nodelman's views on this. He sees children's texts as inevitably double in their address, seemingly speaking naively to a child, whilst simultaneously having a 'shadow' of knowingness of which, as Nodelman conceives it, the child is itself aware.

7. This separate 'printing' (which sounds more like a separate publication) is, perhaps also significantly, not mentioned in her otherwise full bibliography of 'Peter Pan' publications.

8. There were, then, comparatively few writers who wrote 'modernist' children's texts, and those that did tended to be pursuing a specifically modernist aesthetic, for example Gertrude Stein, E. E. Cummings and Eugene Ionesco (Reynolds, 2007). However, once again, it needs stating that this state of affairs was not true everywhere; for example in Russian literature we find modernism far more in evidence in the children's work of writers such as Daniil Kharms, Vladimir Lebedev and Samuil Marshak (Pankenier, 2006).

9. MacCabe (1986) himself was later to edit the collection *High Theory/Low Culture*. However, this still did not discuss popular literature, only television and film.

10. I have given examples elsewhere of children's 'dissident' readings of texts, whether by accident or design (Rudd, 2000; 2004).

11. Towards the end of her critique of children's literature criticism, Karín Lesnik-Oberstein (1994: 167) writes: 'We have now left children's literature criticism behind us ... arguing that it cannot be reformulated from its present position into taking account of the varying constructions of the "child". This is bound to raise two important questions: the first will be asked in a practical spirit by those people who now feel lost with respect to (their) children and books, and who will want to know how to deal with giving books to children if children's literary criticism is disposed of....' This said, contributors to her subsequent edited work (Lesnik-Oberstein, 2004) did present more engagement with texts ostensibly for children.

12. He even discusses Adam and Eve. Ironically, of course, these were (supposedly) the only two individuals never to have had a childhood. Despite this, Zornado reads them as children, suffering at the hands of God the father (Zornado, 2001: 6).

13. 'The author's literary text can then be read as a site of unconscious projection – or ideological representation – of his unconscious experiences as a child. From this perspective *Hamlet* can be understood as children's literature in that it dramatises the story of how a culture built on the quest for power, violence, domination, and subjugation produces and reproduces itself first and foremost in the relationship between the parent and the

child' (ibid.: 43). In these terms, most texts could claim to be children's literature.

2   Peter Pan and the Riddle of Existence

1. I have been here before in two different essays (Rudd, 2006b, 2012c) which cover some of the same ground. But the text itself, like the annual play, and indeed like Peter Pan himself, does seem to compel returns.

2. Hook is not only explicitly doubled but is also explicitly phallic, as his cigar holder, 'which enabled him to smoke two cigars at once' (ibid.: 73), demonstrates. One is reminded of a remark Freud was once supposed to have uttered, about how a cigar sometimes represents nothing but a cigar (Freud himself smoked them, of course); but *two* cigars is surely excessive. It is also worth noting that, while Hook's name is an excellent synecdoche for him, metonymically pinning him within the Symbolic, it too is rather overdetermined: he seems to have been fatalistically nominated. Barrie provides us with a logical answer, however: 'Hook was not his true name' (ibid.: 168), which Geraldine McCaughrean, in her official sequel, *Peter Pan in Scarlet*, has picked up on, having Hook declare that he was named 'Crichton' by his mother (McCaughrean, 2007: 89). It is a brilliant intertextual link to Barrie's 1902 play *The Admirable Crichton*, which mostly takes place on a deserted island, where Crichton, the butler, and his aristocratic employers and their friends are shipwrecked. Crichton soon emerges as their natural leader, and is known as 'the Guv.'. However, once rescued, he resumes his role as butler and the class barriers are reinstated (for fans of the British comedy *Red Dwarf*, the eminently capable robot, Kryten, fulfils a similar role).

3. Lacan does not, of course, simply replace the term 'penis' with 'phallus' in order to go on talking about the same thing, as some have accused him of doing, though this is not to deny that there are problems with this nomenclature. In his defence, I would suggest that Lacan was both drawing attention to the centrality of the male organ in our society and also pointing out that it need not be so, for the phallus, were it not for all the cultural hype it receives, is really nothing. I offer more detail below, but it might make more sense after the main text of this chapter has been read. When Lacan refers to the child trying to be the maternal – or imaginary – phallus for the mother, then, it might be more acceptable simply to think of the child as imagining itself completing the mother, making her whole. But in this sense, the phallus also signifies loss, in that the mother is seen as incomplete. In a very basic manner, then, the phallus represents the bar of the signifying process: the moment the father says 'no' and sunders signifier from signified, resulting in a sense of primordial loss (of the mother). There is the feeling that if this object (the mother) could be retrieved, one would have the phallus, but, of

course, it cannot, and no substitutes are ever quite good enough. Thereafter, signifiers will always stand in for signifieds (words for things). But this initial moment only registers the split itself: a distanciation, a parting of word/ thing. This is why Lacan so often speaks of no one actually having the phallus (though some are credited with its possession); why, indeed, it is always veiled, and behind the veil there is nothing.

4. Of course, it perhaps needs emphasising that we always have these three dimensions of existence (at least, once we enter the Symbolic). So Hook also has his idealised image of himself, as someone possessing 'good form' (see p. 43). Peter Pan tries to rob him of this identity, suggesting that he is more of a 'codfish', at which point Hook, we are informed, 'felt his ego slipping from him. "Don't desert me, bully," he whispered hoarsely to it' (Barrie, 1986: 115).

5. One could pursue this further, of course, picking up on the expression 'what your right hand's for', with its (usually male) masturbatory connotations. Hook is certainly a very phallic being, and thereby necessarily flawed. But note below how Geraldine McCaughrean reworks Hook's image in her retelling.

6. The phallus is a pure signifier that cannot be located anywhere; it always hides, or veils that which it adorns (e.g. symbols of power such as a crown, a mace, a wig, an erect posture, a swastika or a crucifix). It is precisely what is opened up in the move into the Symbolic when signifier and signified are sundered: it is, in fact, the gap, which is what makes it so generative of meaning.

7. This is a reworking of Descartes's *Cogito, ergo sum*: I play, therefore I am. With Peter it is almost '*ego sum*', as well.

8. It is notable that Nana is female, just as is the Crocodile that puts an end to Hook. In McCaughrean's reworking of the story, Hook repeats Nana's act: 'In one lithe movement, in one painless motion, with a blade not even visible within the sleeve of his cardigan, Ravello [Hook] sliced away Peter's shadow' (2007: 164). Hook follows this act by immediately discussing the irrelevance of mothers, again seeking to emphasise the attractions of the Symbolic order.

9. I have previously speculated that Peter's disturbing dreams might be concerned with just this (cf. Rudd, 2006b: 273), especially as they are associated 'with the riddle of his existence' (Barrie, 1986: 158).

10. Hook is himself associated with the devil, as Jack (1991) has detailed. Moreover, this satanic association also occurs in earlier stories about losing one's shadow, like *Peter Schlemihl* (1861) by Adelbert von Chamisso. McCaughrean (2007: 185) also has Peter make the association: 'Hook, you are a scoundrel and a villain. Only the Devil steals a man's shadow!' See also p. 181 of this book.

11. Following up this notion of perversion, I elsewhere wrote: 'Peter Pan can be seen to function as a fetish, impossibly embodying that which is not really there (just as the fetish satisfies the viewer by seeming to body forth the very thing that is missing)'. This is in line with Rose's interpretation

of the story, where Peter Pan acts as a fetish, disavowing the idea that children are also split subjects; that is, denying that they exist in a world where there is death, sexuality and the divisions of gender and race. Peter Pan is there to represent the purity and innocence of childhood (an imaginary conception). I also conceived this in terms of Žižek's (1989) terminology, where Peter is '"the sublime object of ideology", that which hides our inadequacies, making reality bearable through its sublime presence: Peter's purity, innocence, eternal youth and optimism. He can encompass "everything" that the rest of us, as socially located beings, cannot' (Rudd, 2012c: 60).

12. Once again, I have explored these associations elsewhere (Rudd, 2006b), suggesting that Peter Pan functions like the primal father of Freud's *Totem and Taboo* (1983): he who stands beyond social law and has all the women for himself; consequently, he is a figure that other males – such as Hook – want to destroy, in order to establish a proper, rule-governed society.

13. Notably, in the novelisation, it is the drum within him that says this (Barrie, 1986: 121), as though imitating the derring-do of Victorian heroes. McCaughrean, in her sequel, does not balk at the implications, though. When war is mentioned in Neverland, John objects and Slightly points out that Michael, John's brother, 'was...Lost' as a result of 'the Big War', giving the phrase 'Lost Boys' an extra, darker resonance. 'Perhaps, in far off Fotheringdene', the narrator comments, 'someone leaned against the war memorial on the village green' (McCaughrean, 2007: 58). Later, Hook outlines his own contribution, when asked about the fate of his pirates:

> 'I sent them off to do their bit in the war,' said Hook. 'As every man should. They sent me postcards first off. From Belgium and France. Then they forgot, I suppose. The postcards stopped. I imagine they were having too good a time. I imagine they were too busy living it up on booty and the spoils of war.' (Ibid.: 216)

14. Christopher Boone, in Mark Haddon's *The Curious Incident of the Dog in the Night-Time* (2003: 20), wants something similarly unique – 'I want my name to mean me' – but realises that it cannot be.

15. Of course, Peter Pan is 'barred' in the opposite way from the rest of us, he espouses to be the phallus, the signified; it is the signifiers outside of which he stands, hence he can 'neither write nor spell; not the smallest word' (ibid.: 102).

16. In some ways this is similar to what Lyra does in Pullman's *His Dark Materials* (1995–2000), thus leading the 'lost' out of a place of limbo.

17. 'The Ravelling Man gave a snort of disdain. "Call yourself what you please, mayfly. Your summer is ended, and winter is come"' (McCaughrean, 2001: 184).

18. One of the closest links between the texts, though, comes when Curly, also accepting his grown-up status as a doctor, exits Neverland with Slightly:

'And cutting his own door in the air with his surgeon's lancet, he stepped through it and into banishment' (McCaughrean, 2007: 221).

19. The only thing that seems to ring a false note here is that it is sad thoughts that make the shadows regrow (ibid.: 274). In terms of imagery, this works well, but it is at odds with the idea that it has been their removal that has made them less happy.

3   Holes and Pores: Slipping Between the Cracks of Social Criticism

1. Although elsewhere Stephens has indicated that the self is a construction: 'the subject exists as an individual, but that existence is within a dialectical relationship with sociality' (Stephens, 1992: 47).

2. Stephens (1992: 137) contrasts Nesbit's approach with Maurice Sendak's more subtle handling of 'power in parent–child relations'. Stephens's reading of each text is very different from my own; see Chapter 6 for my interpretation of Sendak and Rudd (2006a) for a more detailed reading of Nesbit's work.

3. For example, Mary Winn (1983: 61), coming from a very different perspective, claims an equal right to speak on behalf of children: 'In the Golden Age of Innocence, children read books about fairies and animals, or about other children engaged in the carefree pleasures of childhood', and argues that we should equally 'fight for their rights' to occupy this space. However, from her perspective this means avoiding many modern 'issue' books which discuss sex and broken families.

4. In Chapter 6, I shall argue that the whole division between fantastic and realistic literature wants rethinking, which is not to deny that people will champion one mode over the other.

5. This is in line with Karín Lesnik-Oberstein's view, that 'children, in culture and history, have no ... voice' (1994: 26). See Rudd (2004) for a critique of this notion.

6. For those that like more overt theoretical reference points, I'd mention Deleuzean notions of 'lines of flight' once again, and Derrida's more obvious concept of 'parasitology', being that which 'introduces disorder into communication ... derails a mechanism of the communicational type, its coding and decoding [and] ... is something that is neither living nor nonliving' (Derrida, 1994b: 12).

7. There are also some successful female authors of empire, of course, such as Bessie Marchant.

8. Kutzer recognises that elephants are indigenous to both India and Africa, but asserts that '[t]he Heffalump is emblematic of the fear and mystery and mythology of the Dark Continent' (Kutzer, 2000: 101) with no other evidence forthcoming. Personally, I have always thought that its name is influenced

by the sobriquets Stalky & Co have for their large-footed master, Prout, who is known as 'Heffy', 'Heffles' and 'Hefflinga', among others names (Kipling, 1987 [1906]).

9. Elsewhere, Kutzer discusses how exploration also marked 'British superiority', but misses a trick with the 'Expotition to the North Pole', where she mentions, from Britain's former colony (America), two contenders, Peary and Cook, but not, strangely, the third: Matthew Henson, an African American who some claim deserves credit for the discovery (Counter, 2001; his story also features in E. L. Doctorow's *Ragtime* (1975)).

10. The term 'quilted' I have taken from Lacan; for him, 'quilting points' (*points de capiton*) are the places where meaning is established and secured, just as buttons (in a mattress) hold the stuffing in place. An alternative translation, 'anchoring point' is used by both Sheridan (Lacan 1977a: 303) and Fink (1995), however.

11. An earlier version of material from this section appeared in Rudd (2008b).

12. Lacan speaks of '**master signifiers**' that act as our basic ways of making sense of the world, which individuals can use to explain everything, sometimes very inappropriately (as with literary critics who open with comments like, 'Speaking as a Lacanian/Feminist/Marxist'). See also pp. 166–70.

13. Strictly speaking, Jean Baudrillard (1994) should be credited with originating this image.

14. The question of the racial origins of the Egyptians themselves has been a hotly debated topic since the eighteenth century (Bernasconi, 2007).

4 Hiding in the Light: Perry Nodelman and the Hidden Adult

1. I realise that Stanley Fish (1989), unsurprisingly, would take issue with me on this, just as he did with Iser, arguing that Iser's facts are themselves already within the realm of interpretation.

2. From Edward Purcell's article, 'Of Purple Jars', in the *Pageant* (1897), as quoted in Caroline Sumpter (2012: 147–8).

3. Nodelman's comments elsewhere suggest that he might be aware of issues around consumerism (2008: 43) and, possibly, associations of the purple jar with the heroine's own genitalia (ibid.: 202).

4. In a later sentence (ibid.: 205), Nodelman does gesture towards Iser's conception more explicitly.

5. It seems of note that it is as a result of her mother that Rosamond first comes up with the idea of using the jar for a plant. Clearly, had it been kept purely as an object of desire – as something to be gazed upon – its allure might have been sustained.

6. An edition of this is to be found in Project Gutenberg, though not one featuring 'The Purple Jar', see: www.gutenberg.org/cache/epub/3655/pg3655.html

7. See Nikolajeva (2010) for the introduction of this term, which addresses the way that adulthood is the norm ('aetero' means 'age').

8. Lesnik-Oberstein (2004) might argue that he and, indeed, I are always talking about textual constructions of the child.

5 Home Sweet Home and the Uncanny: Freud, Alice and the Curious Child

1. A certain Rudd (1997) also discusses it at this time, but this is sufficiently obscure as to be missed by most literature searches. However, it is developed more substantially in Rudd (2000).

2. Jeffrey Mehlman's key work, *Revolution and Repetition: Marx/Hugo/Balzac* (1977), was one of the first to link Freud's notion to a Marxist concept of alienation. Anthony Vidler's influential *The Architectural Uncanny* (1994) also pursues the notion of alienation and the unhomely.

3. Zipes (2011: 1) adds the words 'other forms of fantastic literature' to fairy tales.

4. Available online from the Hockliffe Collection: www.cts.dmu.ac.uk/hockliffe/items/0777.html

5. Thus Freud contrasts two stories, declaring of one that 'the severed hand... has no uncanny effect' (1985c: 375).

6. Samuel Weber (1973: 1119) observes that, in a footnote, Freud suggests that he has 'reconstructed' Hoffmann's original tale, as though there were once an 'Urtext', 'fully free of all distortion and repetition, and which antedates the fantasy-work of the writer' [i.e. Hoffmann].

7. As other commentators on this essay of Freud's have noted, death, although frequently elided, remains a key subtext (Cixous, 1976).

8. In fact, Freud almost undoes the difference between *repressed* and *surmounted* anxieties that he had painstakingly established earlier, calling 'the distinction... often a hazy one', and he even contemplates using the former term (*repression*) to cover both areas, before admitting that this move 'extends the term... beyond its legitimate meaning' (ibid.: 372).

9. Or, as Nicolas Royle (2003: 5) more pithily declares: 'The uncanny is (the) unsettling (of itself).'

10. Richard Gooding, for example, seeks to account for the uncanny effects in *Coraline* by building up a developmental case, based on Freud's division between the *surmounted* and *repressed* elements of the uncanny. It is a bravura performance, but ultimately flawed, as Gooding seems aware: 'Young readers' responses are notoriously elusive, perhaps for the very reasons that convincing portrayals of young protagonists pose such challenges for writers. In the same way that Coraline sometimes seems impervious to feelings

of uncanniness and sometimes doesn't, patterns of response among young readers are probably more complex than Gaiman lets on' (2008: 404). This said, Gaiman is not the one that ever advances this opinion of his protagonist.

11. Carroll exploits the ambiguity of their very name, 'playing cards'. They might be cards for playing, but they could as easily be cards that play. As in mathematics, or indeed language, the cards are empty signifiers that can be made to stand for whatever the game requires (let $x = 4$, let aces be high or low, and so on).

12. In Edgar Allan Poe's 'Berenice' the main character suffers this condition of semantic satiation, causing him 'to repeat monotonously some common word, until the sound, by dint of frequent repetition, ceased to convey any idea whatever to the mind' (Poe, 2012: 334).

13. Todorov's (1975) conception of the 'uncanny' also makes it more safe, homely and explicable; it is on the side of mechanics rather than energetics.

14. See Bivona's comment on p. 65.

15. Here I am reworking Žižek's remarks on Fritz Lang's *Woman in the Window* (1992b: 16–17).

16. Mervyn Peake's illustration most closely captures this macabre vision.

17. Martin Heidegger speaks about us being 'thrown' into the world. He also was interested in the uncanny, seeing it as causing feelings of angst, or anxiety: 'one feels ill at ease', as he puts it ('ill at ease' being the translator's term for *unheimlich* here), in experiencing nothingness. However, this nothing is not simply a result of the 'mere disappearance' of things. 'Rather, in this very receding things turn toward us. The receding of beings as a whole that closes in on us in anxiety oppresses us' (Heidegger, 1978: 101). Jan Švankmajer's (1988) film version of *Alice* plays up this aspect most ferociously, where everyday objects exhibit a striking [*sic*] malevolence.

18. Buhlaire is the 12-year-old protagonist of Virginia Hamilton's novel *Plain City* (1993). It is the only text of Nodelman's chosen six not discussed in Chapter 4.

6 Fantasy and Realism Contained: From Fortunatus Cap to the Möbius Strip

1. This is dealt with in more detail in Rudd (2012b).

2. I am grateful to Cathy Butler for pointing out to me this common misunderstanding of Tolkien's 'Secondary World' concept.

3. Though many scholars take this view, there are exceptions; e.g. Doody (1996).

4. There is an 1801 version of this available from The Hockliffe Collection: http://hockliffe.dmu.ac.uk/items/0130.html

5. The Hockliffe Collection has volume 2: http://hockliffe.dmu.ac.uk/items/0159.html

6. Woolf was vigorous in distancing herself from the middlebrows, whom she saw 'in pursuit of no single object, neither art itself nor life itself, but both mixed indistinguishably, and rather nastily, with money, fame, power, or prestige' (1966a: 199; cf. Nicola Humble, 2001).

7. This is also in line with a passage that she quotes from Eric Rabkin: 'The wide range of works which we call ... fantastic is large, much too large to constitute a single genre ... whole conventional genres, such as fairy tale, detective story, Fantasy' (quoted in Jackson, 1981: 13). Of the many who distinguish fantasy from the fantastic, Brian Attebury's (1992: 11) is one of the most clear, using *fantasy* for the genre and *fantastic* to 'designate the mode'.

8. It is reminiscent of slogans like that of the Hungarian painter/photographer László Moholy-Nagy, who polemically proclaimed, 'constructivism is the socialism of vision' (*Experiment in Totality*, 1950: http://archive.org/stream/moholynagyexperi007463mbp/moholynagyexperi007463mbp_djvu.txt).

9. Jackson does seek to clarify this at times, arguing that fantasy is subversive on the structuralist rather than the thematic side (1981: 175), that is, in terms of hesitations, questionings around time, space and character; but elsewhere she states that this structural hesitation 'can be read as a displacement of fantasy's central *thematic* issue: an uncertainty as to the nature of the "real", a problematization of categories of "realism" and "truth", of the "seen" and "known".... Fantasy's ambiguous literary effects, on the level of form, enact its thematic uncertainties and hesitations' (ibid.: 48–9).

10. The play opens at 'The bottom of a pond ... mud, ooze, rubbish, and water plants. Two tin cans, standing upright, half buried in the mud at centre stage. At stage left, a rock. A head rises from one of the tin cans' (Hoban, 2005: 53).

11. Towards the end, a different note is struck: 'Those elements which have been designated "fantastic" – effecting a movement towards undifferentiation and a condition of entropy – have been constantly re-worked, re-written and re-covered to *serve* rather than to *subvert* the dominant ideology' (Jackson, 1981: 175). And Jonathan Culler is quoted: 'For the most part, fantasy in literature testifies to the power of the reality principle to transform its enemies into its own mirror image. In the face of this power, it is all the more important that we assert fantasy's responsibility to resist before we accept Yeats's formula: "In dreams begins responsibility".'

12. One is reminded of Lacan's famous story about a sardine can pointed out to him as a young man by a fisherman. In what could be described as an 'uncanny' moment (and yes, there is an intended pun there), he has the feeling of being looked at by this inanimate object (Lacan, 1977b: 95–7). See p. 159 in this book.

13. It is like the process of *anamorphosis*, described later in this chapter, where the huge gorilla disturbs our perspective and, from his view, makes the humans appear imbecilic.

14. Thus we see the gorilla through such imaginary constructions as the celluloid King Kong or Tarzan films; but this is itself undercut by the bars, which reduce him to a creature bearing a label, housed in a zoo.

15. I must defer to Karen Coats (2004: 81–3), the first children's literature scholar to discuss this gift of a book for Lacan-influenced thinkers. However, I think that largely we cover different issues.

16. The missing piece can never be present: it is either represented as an absence – a gap – or the something that comes to 'fill' this space that cannot be it. In short, the missing piece defines an absence, not a presence.

17. This said, the original lyric, first recorded in 1911, makes much the same point: that in this life we *are* broken; only in the hereafter, where a better life will be waiting, could the circle be unbroken.

18. In literature, 'aptronyms', as they have come to be known (from more obscure terms like *adnominatio*), are quite prevalent (Pip, Bumble, etc. in Dickens). The 'Missing Piece' can be seen to mark the same slippage that we see with 'Frankenstein', the unnamed monster frequently being called by his creator's name, so closely linked is their destiny.

19. The phrase comes from a book title (Žižek, 1992a). At the very end of Silverstein's story, in a wordless final picture, such 'enjoyment' is suggested when a butterfly – not mentioned in the written text (whereas other things, the worm, flower and beetle, are) – settles on it.

20. As new, unknown titles of Blyton's have continued to turn up, even to this day, she is a good author to keep the collector's desire circulating!

21. As an example of how signification insists, typing the word 'tear' suggested a rip in something, like a piece of fabric, but as soon as I wrote it, the homograph 'tear', for that all-too-human moistening of the eye, came to mind. This too, seemed appropriate, but it led me to the homophone 'tare', which is the money deducted in a commercial transaction for some residue; for instance, the weight of the container (bag or cask) in which gold is being weighed. Notions of a container and a remainder also seemed apposite. But then I noted that 'tare' is also an older variant of 'torn', the past tense of the verb 'to tear' – bringing me back to where I started, but adding a sense of 'pastness', which also seemed appropriate. I'll stop here (signification needs to be halted at some quilting point), before the Parable of the Tares (Matthew 13:24–30) surfaces. Once again, as quoted previously, we see how 'the signifier stuffs the signified' (Lacan, quoted in Fink, 2004: 83).

22. See Note 12, above, and the description of the gorilla's look in *Zoo*.

23. He is also one of our most inventive story tellers, despite his postmodern playfulness.

24. As noted elsewhere, Pullman celebrated the fact that 'Once upon a time lasts forever', but he might not have meant it in these literal terms!
25. 'Max goes home reassured that, no matter how much he may feel at odds with his family, there is another family, his family of wild things like him who dance and howl with joy in a land far away but reachable' (Steven Cheslik-DeMeyer, quoted in Kidd, 2011: 126).
26. Though pictures, as I could not help saying in a talk on this very topic, are renowned for having the Last Supper. On a more serious note, Silverstein's *The Missing Piece* has – in contrast – a wordless final image.
27. In principle, I would support Bettelheim's theoretical espousal of a heteroglossic approach (which the comments by actual readers seem to endorse – cf. Bernheimer, 2002). Unfortunately, in practice, he usually closes down a tale's signification.
28. This is the lesson in criticism that Bettelheim offers. It is a good example of what Armstrong (2000: 87) terms a 'distance' rather than a 'close reading' – though not in the way she intended. Regarding the publication date, it is of note that it was not until 1968 that the book was published in England, after Judy Taylor of Bodley Head 'refused to be swayed by the general opinion, among librarians, teachers and other publishers who had seen a copy of the American edition, that the wild things would frighten the life out of little children and not sell' (Chambers, 1995: 243).
29. In more psychoanalytical parlance, he tries to be the imaginary phallus (the wild thing?), completing her by providing what he thinks she lacks.
30. As Lacan puts it, 'desire is neither the appetite for satisfaction, nor the demand for love, but the difference that results from the subtraction of the first from the second, the very phenomenon of their splitting' (1977a: 287).
31. One could argue that the moon similarly represents the mother in Brown's *Goodnight Moon* (1975). The moon's association with the feminine, of course, has a long and distinguished pedigree.
32. I cannot recall whether it has been mentioned before, but this transformation is reminiscent of George MacDonald's *Phantastes* (1858), where the hero, Anodos, wakes in his bedroom to find his carpet sporting actual 'grass-blades and daisies' and the dressing table sprouting ivy and 'tendrils of clematis'. His patterned curtains become real 'branches and leaves' and, as he comments, '[t]he tree under which I seemed to have lain ... was one of the advanced guard of a dense forest, towards which the rivulet ran' – the rivulet, that is, that runs across his carpet (MacDonald, 2008 [1858]: 47–9).
33. Freud is speaking specifically about the artist here, but it applies to all; the artist is just more successful in sublimating 'his' phantasies.
34. '... all the objects of his [narcissistic] world are always structured around the wandering shadow of his own ego. They will all have a fundamentally anthropomorphic character, even egomorphic we could say' (Lacan, 1988: 166).

35. Lacan's statement about the mother's desire (which is simultaneously how the child wants to be seen in the mother's eyes, see p. 45) is also relevant here. The reader might also see parallels with the realm of the Other Mother in Gaiman's *Coraline*.
36. Of course, his mother has been absent throughout, represented by verbal signifiers only, so we could argue that we are not watching the original scene of Max's move into the Symbolic; rather, it is a restaging of this event: something of a repetition compulsion, which would mean that Max is indeed still enslaved by his master signifier. In this fantasy scenario, the Wild Things will always be there – just as the bear on the hill will be for Pooh fans.
37. Hints of his sense of alienation have, of course, been foreshadowed in the pictures of beasts on his walls, suggesting that these represent former imaginary identifications of his as a 'Wild Thing'. The difference, of course, is that these were wish-fulfilling daydreams, occurring in his everyday reality.

7   *The Children's Book* – Not Suitable for Children?

1. '...lads that thought there was no more behind/ But such a day to-morrow as to-day,/ And to be boy eternal' (Shakespeare, *The Winter's Tale*, 1.ii, 63–6).
2. Parallels can be drawn with Eric Gill of the Arts and Crafts Movement, though Gill's illicit relations extended further: to his dog, apparently (MacCarthy, 1989)!
3. Likewise, Pucan in Olive's tale, 'The Shrubbery', has a stone like this, which allows him to see into this other world. Gaiman, far more recently, uses a similar device in *Coraline* (2002) – see Rudd (2008a).
4. As Byatt writes elsewhere in the novel: 'The Downs were full of young, and not so young, men in breeches and tweed or jackets, carrying rods or guns, with linen hats flopping, striding from pub to pub and talking wisely about trout, and weather, and the diseases of trees' (2010: 364).
5. There are other lacunae around more apocalyptic movements of the time, especially in terms of the Futurists: 'We will glorify war – the world's only hygiene', as Marinetti's 'Manifesto of Futurism' has it. See: www.italianfuturism.org/manifestos/foundingmanifesto/. In many ways these apocalyptic movements anticipated world war just as Hollywood, with its catastrophe films, seemed to anticipate 9/11 (Žižek, 2002).
6. Peter Coveney (1957: 193) takes a similar view, that these 'acute feelings for childhood' at this time were not 'integrated with a truly adult response'; that the age's sense of freedom was 'illusory', just 'a regressive escape into the psychic prison of self-indulgent nostalgia'.

Conclusion

1. I should say that Zipes counterbalances this with some shoots of hope, but generally sees it as a question 'narrowly open – as to whether some kind of quality literature will survive' (Zipes, 2001: 48).
2. The only link between these positions is that articulated by Fredric Jameson, for whom history is itself the Real.

Bibliography

Almond, David (1998) *Skellig*. London: Hodder.

Almond, David (2005) *Clay*. London: Hodder.

Althusser, Louis (1971) 'Ideology and Ideological State Apparatuses: Notes towards an Investigation', *Lenin and Philosophy*, trans. Ben Brewster. New York: Monthly Review Press, 127–88.

Andersen, Hans Christian (2011), 'The Shadow', trans. Jean Hersholt. Hans Christian Andersen Center, University of Southern Denmark, 1st edn 1847. Online: www.andersen.sdu.dk/vaerk/hersholt/TheShadow_e.html.

Anderson, Benedict (1991) *Imagined Communities: Reflections on the Origin and Spread of Nationalism*. Rev edn. London & New York: Verso.

Ang, Ien (1985) *Watching Dallas*. London: Methuen.

Armstrong, Isobel (2000) *The Radical Aesthetic*. Oxford: Blackwell.

Arnold, Matthew (1867) 'Dover Beach', *The Victorian Web*. Online: www.victorianweb.org/authors/arnold/writings/doverbeach.html.

Attebery, Brian (1992) *Strategies of Fantasy*. Bloomington and Indianapolis: Indiana University Press.

Auerbach, Nina and Knoepflmacher, U.C. (eds) (1992) *Forbidden Journeys: Fairy Tales and Fantasies by Victorian Women Writers*. Chicago, IL: University of Chicago Press.

Bakhtin, M. M. (1981) *The Dialogic Imagination: Four Essays*, ed. Michael Holquist, trans. Caryl Emerson and Michael Holquist. Austin, TX: University of Texas Press.

Bakhtin, Mikhail M. (1984) *Rabelais and His World*, trans. Hélène Iswolsky. Bloomington, IN: Indiana University Press.

Barker, Martin (1989) *Comics: Ideology, Power and the Critics*. Manchester: Manchester University Press.

Barrie, J. M. (1926) 'The Blot on Peter Pan', *The Treasure Ship: A Book of Prose and Verse*, ed. Cynthia Asquith. London: S.W. Partridge, 82–100.

Barrie, J. M. (1986) *Peter Pan*. London: Penguin, 1st edn 1911.

Barrie, J. M. (1995) 'Peter Pan', *Peter Pan and Other Plays*, ed. Peter Hollindale. Oxford and New York: Oxford University Press, 73–163.

Barrie, J.M. (2007) *Peter Pan & Peter Pan in Kensington Gardens*. London: Wordsworth.

Barth, John (1969) *Lost in the Funhouse: Fiction for Print, Tape, Live Voice*. London: Secker & Warburg.

Barthes, Roland (1977) *Image – Music – Text*, trans. Stephen Heath. London: Fontana.

Barthes, Roland (1986) *The Rustle of Language*, trans. Richard Howard. New York: Hill & Wang.

Baudrillard, Jean (1994) *Simulacrum and Simulation*. University of Michigan Press, 1st edn 1981.

Bauman, Zygmunt (1991) *Intimations of Postmodernity*. London: Routledge.

Bayley, John (1997) 'Reading about Things: Hannibal Goes for the Mail', in Philip Davis (ed.) *Real Voices on Reading*. Basingstoke: Macmillan, 125–36.

Belsey, Catherine (1980) *Critical Practice*. London: Methuen.

Bernasconi, Robert (2007) 'Black Skin, White Skulls: The Nineteenth Century Debate over the Racial Identity of the Ancient Egyptians', *Parallax* 13(2): 6–20.

Bernheimer, Kate (ed.) (2002) *Mirror, Mirror on the Wall: Women Writers Explore their Favorite Fairy Tales*, 2nd edn. New York: Random House.

Bettelheim, Bruno (1969) 'The Care and Feeding of Monsters', *Ladies Home Journal*, March: 48.

Bettelheim, Bruno (1991) *The Uses of Enchantment: The Meaning and Importance of Fairy Tales*. Harmondsworth: Penguin, 1st edn 1976.

Bhabha, Homi K. (1994) *The Location of Culture*. London and New York: Routledge.

Billings, Molly (2005) The Influenza Pandemic of 1918. Online: http://virus.stanford.edu/uda/.

Birkin, Andrew (1979) *J. M. Barrie and the Lost Boys*. London: Constable.

Bivona, Daniel (1990) *Desire and Contradiction: Imperial Visions and Domestic Debates in Victorian Literature*. Manchester: Manchester University Press.

Blake, Kathleen (1974) ''Alice's Adventures in Wonderland'', *Play, Games and Sport: The Literary Works of Lewis Carroll*. Ithaca, NY: Cornell UP, 108–31.

Bleich, David (1986) 'Gendered Interests in Reading and Language', in *Gender and Reading: Essays on Readers, Texts and Contexts*, Elizabeth A. Flynn and Patrocinio P. Schweickart (eds). Baltimore, MA: Johns Hopkins University Press, 234–66.

Bloch, Ernst (1998) *The Utopian Function of Art and Literature: Selected Essays*, trans. Jack Zipes and Frank Mecklenburg. Cambridge, MA: MIT Press.

Bloom, Clive (2002) *Bestsellers: Popular Fiction since 1900*. Basingstoke: Palgrave Macmillan.

Bottigheimer, Ruth M. (1996) *The Bible for Children: From the Age of Gutenberg to the Present*. New Haven, CT: Yale University Press.

Bourdieu, Pierre (1984) *Distinction: A Social Critique of the Judgement of Taste*. London: Routledge.

Bowie, Malcolm (1991) *Lacan*. London: HarperCollins.

Bradford, Clare, Mallan, Kerry, Stephens, John and McCallum, Robyn (2008) *New World Orders in Contemporary Children's Literature: Utopian Transformations*. Basingstoke: Palgrave Macmillan.

Briggs, Raymond (1978) *The Snowman*. London: Hamilton.

Bronski, Murray (1984) *Culture Clash: The Making of Gay Sensibility*. Cambridge, MA: South End Press.

Brooks, Peter (1984) *Reading for the Plot: Design and Intention in Narrative.* Oxford: Clarendon.

Brown, Margaret Wise (1975) *Goodnight Moon*, illus. Clement Hurd. New York: HarperCollins, 1st edn 1947.

Browne, Anthony (1983) *Gorilla*. London: Julia MacRae.

Browne, Anthony (1984) *Willy the Wimp*. London: Julia MacRae.

Browne, Anthony (1994) *Zoo*. London and New York: Random House, 1st edn 1992.

Bruner, Jerome S. (1973) *Beyond the Information Given: Studies in the Psychology of Knowing*. New York: Norton.

Burgess, Melvin (1996) *Junk*. London: Andersen Press.

Butler, Catherine (2013) 'Tolkien and Worldbuilding' in Peter Hunt (ed.) *J. R. R. Tolkien:* The Hobbit *and* The Lord of the Rings. *A New Casebook*. Basingstoke: Palgrave Macmillan, 106–20.

Byatt, A. S. (2003) 'Harry Potter and the Childish Adult', *New York Times*, 7 July. Online: www.nytimes.com/2003/07/07/opinion/harry-potter-and-the-childish-adult.html.

Byatt, A. S. (2009) 'A. S. Byatt on The Children's Book', *The Man Booker Prizes*. Online: http://archive.themanbookerprize.com/perspective/articles/1264.

Byatt, A. S. (2010) *The Children's Book*. London: Vintage; 1st published 2009.

Carey, John (1992) *The Intellectuals and the Masses: Pride and Prejudice amongst the Literary Intelligentsia, 1880–1939*. London: Faber & Faber.

Carpenter, Humphrey (1985) *Secret Gardens: The Golden Age of Children's Literature*. London: Allen & Unwin.

Carroll, Lewis (1893) *Sylvie and Bruno Concluded*. Online: www.hoboes.com/FireBlade/Fiction/Carroll/Sylvie/Concluded/.

Carroll, Lewis (1970) *The Annotated Alice: Alice's Adventures in Wonderland;* and *Through the Looking-Glass...*, rev. edn. Harmondsworth: Penguin, 1st edns 1865, 1871.

Carter, Angela (1981) 'The Company of Wolves', *The Bloody Chamber*, Harondsworth: Penguin, 148–59.

Castle, Terry (1995) *The Female Thermometer: 18th-Century Culture and the Invention of the Uncanny*. New York and Oxford: Oxford University Press.

Chambers, Aidan (1995) 'The Difference of Literature: Writing Now for the Future of Young Readers', *Celebrating Children's Literature in Education*, ed. Geoff Fox. London: Hodder, 243–61.

Chamisso, Adelbert von (1861) *Peter Schlemihl*, 1st edn 1814. Online: www.gutenberg.org/files/21943/21943-h/21943-h.htm.

Chapleau, Sebastien (2004) 'A Theory Without a Centre: Developing Childist Criticism', *Studies in Children's Literature, 1500–2000*, ed. Celia Keenan and Mary Shine Thompson. Dublin: Four Courts Press, 130–7.

Cixous, Hélène (1976) 'Fiction and its Phantoms: A Reading of Freud's *Das Unheimliche* (The "Uncanny")', *New Literary History*, 7(3): 525–48.

Cleary, Beverley (1950) *Henry Huggins*. New York: Dell.

Clifford, Lucy (1994) 'The New Mother', *The Oxford Book of Children's Stories*, ed. Jan Mark. Oxford: Oxford University Press, 193–213. 1st edn 1882.

Coats, Karen (1997) 'Underwriting the Uncanny: The Role of Children's Literature in the Economy of the Subject', *Paradoxa* 3: 489–96.

Coats, Karen (2004) *Looking Glasses and Neverlands: Lacan, Desire and Subjectivity in Children's Literature*. Iowa, IL: University of Iowa Press.

Colebrook, Claire (2002) *Gilles Deleuze*. London and New York: Routledge.

Collins, Jo and Jervis, John (eds) (2008) *Uncanny Modernity: Cultural Theories, Modern Anxieties*. Basingstoke: Palgrave Macmillan.

Collins, Suzanne (2008) *The Hunger Games*. New York: Scholastic.

Cooper, Merian C. and Schoedsack, Ernest B. (1933) *King Kong*. RKO.

Counter, S. Allen (2001) *North Pole Legacy: Black, White, and Eskimo*. Amherst, MA: University of Massachusetts Press.

Coveney, Peter (1957) *Poor Monkey: The Child in Literature*. London: Rockliff.

Cox, Roger (1996) *Shaping Childhood: Themes of Uncertainty in the History of Adult-Child Relationships*. London: Routledge.

Crews, Frederick C. (1964) *The Pooh Perplex: A Student Casebook*. London: Barker.

Dahl, Roald (1974) *The Magic Finger*. Harmondsworth: Penguin.

Dahl, Roald (1982) *Revolting Rhymes*. London: Penguin.

Darton, F. J. Harvey (1982) *Children's Books in England: Five Centuries of Social Life*, 3rd edn. Brian Alderson. Cambridge: Cambridge University Press.

Darnton, Robert (1984) *The Great Cat Massacre, and Other Episodes in French Cultural History*. London: Allen Lane.

Deleuze, Gilles and Guattari, Félix (2004) *A Thousand Plateaus*, trans. Brian Massumi. London: Continuum, 1st edn 1980.

Denisoff, Dennis (2008) *The Nineteenth-Century Child and Consumer Culture*. Farnham and Burlington, VT: Ashgate.

Dentith, Simon (1995) *Bakhtinian Thought: An Introductory Reader*. London: Routledge.

Derrida, Jacques (1994a) *Spectres of Marx: The State of the Debt, The Work of Mourning, and the New International*. London: Routledge.

Derrida, Jacques (1994b) 'The Spatial Arts: An Interview with Jacques Derrida', *Deconstruction and the Visual Arts: Arts, Media, Architecture* ed. Peter Brunette and David Wills. New York: Cambridge University Press, 9–32.

Doctorow, E. L. (1975) *Ragtime*. New York: Random House.

Dolar, Mladen (1991) '"I Shall Be with You on Your Wedding Night": Lacan and the Uncanny', *October*, 58, 5–23.

Donald, James (1992) *Sentimental Education: Schooling, Popular Culture and the Regulation of Liberty*. London: Verso.

Doody, Margaret Anne (1996) *The True History of the Novel*. New Brunswick, NJ: Rutgers University Press.

Drouillard, Colette L. (2008) 'Growing Up with Harry Potter: What Motivated Youth to Read?' Florida State University. Unpublished PhD. Online: http://diginole.lib.fsu.edu/etd.

Dusinberre, Juliet (1987) *Alice to the Lighthouse: Children's Books and Radical Experiments in Art.* Basingstoke: Macmillan.

Dyer, Richard (1992) 'Entertainment and Utopia', *Only Entertainment,* London: Routledge, 17–34.

Eaglestone, Robert (ed.) (2005) *Reading* The Lord of the Rings: *New Writings on Tolkien's Classic.* London and New York: Continuum.

Eagleton, Terry (1984) *Literary Theory: An Introduction.* Oxford: Blackwell

Eco, Umberto (1979) *The Role of the Reader: Explorations in the Semiotics of Texts.* Bloomington: Indiana University Press.

Edgeworth, Maria (1918) *Rosamond: A Series of Tales.* London: George Routledge. Online: http://studentzone.roehampton.ac.uk/library/digital-collection/childrens-literature-collection/rosamond/Rosamond%20complete.pdf.

Edgeworth, Maria (2003) 'The White Pigeon', *The Parent's Assistant.* ... Online: www.gutenberg.org/cache/epub/3655/pg3655.html.

Egan, Michael (1982) 'The Neverland of Id: Barrie, Peter Pan, and Freud', *Children's Literature,* 10: 37–55.

Enck, John J. (1965) 'John Barth: An Interview', *Wisconsin Studies in Contemporary Literature* 6(1): 3–14.

Evans, Dylan (1996) *An Introductory Dictionary of Lacanian Psychoanalysis.* London and New York: Routledge.

Faris, Wendy B. (2004) *Ordinary Enchantments: Magical Realism and the Remystification of Narrative.* Nashville: Vanderbilt University Press.

Fetterley, Judith (1978) *The Resisting Reader: A Feminist Approach to American Fiction.* Bloomington and London: Indiana University Press.

Fine, Anne (1999) *The Chicken Gave It to Me.* London: Egmont.

Fink, Bruce (1995) *The Lacanian Subject: Between Language and Jouissance.* Princeton, NJ: Princeton University Press.

Fink, Bruce (2004) *Lacan to the Letter: Reading* Écrits *Closely.* Minneapolis: University of Minnesota Press.

Fish, Stanley (1989) 'Why No One's Afraid of Wolfgang Iser' in *Doing What Comes Naturally: Change, Rhetoric, and the Practice of Theory in Literary and Legal Studies.* Duke University Press, 68–86.

Fleming, Victor (1939) *The Wizard of Oz.* MGM.

Flescher, Jacqueline (1959) 'The Language of Nonsense in *Alice*', *Yale French Studies,* 43: 128–44.

Fordyce, Rachel and Marello, Carla (eds) (1994) *Semiotics and Linguistics in Alice's Worlds.* Berlin and New York: de Gruyter.

Foucault, Michel (1977) 'Nietzsche, Genealogy, History', *Language, Counter-Memory, Practice: Selected Essays and Interviews,* trans. Donald F. Bouchard and Sherry Simon, ed. D. F. Bouchard. Ithaca, NY: Cornell University Press, 139–64.

Foucault, Michel (1981) *The History of Sexuality: An Introduction.* Harmondsworth: Penguin.

Fowler, H. P. (1965) *Dictionary of Modern English Usage*, 2nd rev. edn, Sir Ernest Gowers. Oxford: Oxford University Press.

Freud, Sigmund (1955) *The Standard Edition of the Complete Psychological Works of Sigmund Freud, Vol. II (1893–1895): Studies on Hysteria*, trans. James Strachey. London: Hogarth Press & Institute of Psycho-Analysis, 1st edn 1895.

Freud, Sigmund (1973) 'Lecture 23: The Paths to the Formation of Symptoms', *Introductory Lectures on Psychoanalysis*, trans. James Strachey. London: Penguin, 404–24.

Freud, Sigmund (1977a) 'Family Romance' in *On Sexuality*, trans. James Strachey. Harmondsworth: Penguin, 217–26, 1st published 1909.

Freud, Sigmund (1977b) 'Remembering, Repeating and Working Through', *The Standard Edition of the Complete Psychological Works of Sigmund Freud*, Vol. XII: 1911–13 ..., trans. James Strachey. London: Hogarth Press & Institute of Psycho-Analysis, 147–56. 1st published 1914.

Freud, Sigmund (1983) *Totem and Taboo: Resemblances between the Mental Lives of Savages and Neurotics.* London: Ark, 1st edn 1918.

Freud, Sigmund (1985a) 'Creative Writers and Daydreaming', *Art and Literature: Jensen's* Gradiva, *Leonardo da Vinci and Other Works*, trans. James Strachey. London: Penguin, 129–42. 1st published 1908.

Freud, Sigmund (1985b) 'Dostoevsky and Parricide', *Art and Literature: Jensen's* Gradiva, *Leonardo da Vinci and Other Works*, trans. James Strachey. London: Penguin, 435–60, 1st published 1928.

Freud, Sigmund (1985c) 'The "Uncanny"', *Art and Literature: Jensen's* Gradiva, *Leonardo da Vinci and Other Works*, trans. James Strachey. London: Penguin, 339–76. 1st published 1919.

Gaiman, Neil (2002) *Coraline.* New York: Scholastic.

Galbraith, Mary (2001) 'Hear My Cry: A Manifesto for an Emancipatory Childhood Studies Approach to Children's Literature', *The Lion and the Unicorn*, 25: 187–205.

Garber, Marjorie (1992) *Vested Interests: Cross-Dressing and Cultural Anxiety.* London: Penguin.

Gardner, Martin (1967) 'Introduction', *The Annotated Snark* ... Lewis Carroll's ... *The Hunting of the Snark*. Harmondsworth: Penguin, 15–31.

Gardner, Sally (2011) *The Double Shadow.* London: Orion.

Garner, Alan (1970) 'Coming to Terms', *Children's Literature in Education*, 2: 15–29.

Garner, Alan (1998) 'The Scoundrel Tail (Language and Myth)'. *Legenda: Reading and Writing Myth.* BLCA Conference, University of Lancaster, 15–18 July.

Geraghty, Christine (1991) *Women and Soap Opera: A Study of Prime Time Soaps.* Cambridge: Polity.

Goffman, Erving (1990) *The Presentation of Self in Everyday Life.* Harmondsworth: Penguin 1st published 1959.

Gooding, Richard (2008) '"Something Very Old and Very Slow": *Coraline*, Uncanniness and Narrative Form', *Children's Literature Association Quarterly*, 33 (4): 390–407.

Grahame, Kenneth (1895) *The Golden Age.* London: Bodley Head.

Grahame-Smith, Seth (2009) *Pride and Prejudice and Zombies.* Philadelphia, PA: Quirk Books.

Greene, Grahame (1969) 'The Lost Childhood', *Collected Essays.* London: Bodley Head, 13–19, 1st published 1947.

Grenby, M.O. (2011) *The Child Reader: 1700–1840.* Cambridge: Cambridge University Press.

Griswold, Jerry (2006) *Feeling Like a Kid: Childhood and Children's Literature.* Baltimore, MA: Johns Hopkins University Press.

Gubar, Marah (2009) *Artful Dodgers: Reconceiving the Golden Age of Children's Literature.* Oxford: Oxford University Press.

Haddon, Mark (2003) *The Curious Incident of the Dog in the Night-Time.* London: Jonathan Cape.

Hartnett, Sonya (2000) *Thursday's Child.* London: Walker.

Hartnett, Sonya (2003) *What the Birds See.* London: Walker.

Hearn, Michael Patrick (1988) 'Introduction to J.M. Barrie's *Peter and Wendy*', *Peter Pan: The Complete Book.* Montreal: Tundra, 1–25.

Hebdidge, Dick (1988) *Hiding in the Light: On Images and Things.* London: Routledge.

Heidegger, Martin (1978) 'What is Metaphysics?' in *Basic Writings: From* Being and Time *(1927) to* The Task of Thinking *(1964)*, rev. edn, trans. David Farrell Krell. London: Routledge, 89–110.

Hendrick, Harry (1990) 'Constructions and Reconstructions of British Childhood: An Interpretive Survey, 1800 to the Present' in Allison Prout and Alan James (eds), *Constructing and Reconstructing Childhood: Contemporary Issues in the Sociological Study of Childhood.* London: Falmer, 35–59.

Higonnet, Anne (1998) *Pictures of Innocence: The History and Crisis of Ideal Childhood.* New York and London: Thames and Hudson.

Hilton, Mary, Styles, Morgon and Watson, Victor (eds) (1997) *Opening the Nursery Door: Reading, Writing and Childhood, 1600–1900.* London: Routledge.

Hoban, Russell (1975) *Turtle Diary.* London: Jonathan Cape.

Hoban, Russell (2005) *The Mouse and His Child.* London: Penguin, 1st edn 1967.

Hogan, P. J. (2003) *Peter Pan.* Universal/Columbia.

Hollindale, Peter (1991) 'Introduction', J.M. Barrie, *Peter Pan in Kensington Gardens; Peter and Wendy*, ed. Peter Hollindale. Oxford: Oxford University Press, vii–xxviii.

Hollindale, Peter (1995) 'Select Bibliography', J.M. Barrie. *Peter Pan and Other Plays*, ed. Peter Hollindale. Oxford: Oxford University Press, xxx–xxxiv.

Hollindale, Peter (1997) *Signs of Childness in Children's Books*. Stroud: Thimble Press.

Holzwarth, Werner and Erlbruch, Wolf (2002) *The Story of the Little Mole Who Knew it was None of His Business*. London: Chrysalis.

Homer, Sean (2005) *Jacques Lacan*. London: Routledge.

Horne, Jackie C. (2011) *History and the Construction of the Child in Early British Children's Literature*. Farnham and Burlington, VT: Ashgate.

Hughes, Felicity A. (1978) 'Children's literature: Theory and Practice', *ELH* 45(3): 542–61.

Humble, Nicola (2001) *The Feminine Middlebrow Novel, 1920s to 1950s: Class, Domesticity, and Bohemianism*. Oxford: Oxford University Press.

Hume, Kathryn (1984) *Fantasy and Mimesis: Responses to Reality in Western Literature*. New York and London: Methuen.

Hunt, Peter (1994) *An Introduction to Children's Literature*. Oxford: Oxford University Press.

Hutchins, Pat (1968) *Rosie's Walk*. London: Bodley Head.

Irwin, William and Davis, Richard Brian (2009) *Alice in Wonderland and Philosophy: Curiouser and Curiouser*. London and New York: Wiley.

Iser, Wolfgang (1974) *The Implied Reader: Patterns of Communication in Prose Fiction from Bunyan to Beckett*. Baltimore, MA: Johns Hopkins University Press.

Iser, Wolfgang (1978) *The Act of Reading: A Theory of Aesthetic Response*. London: Routledge.

Jack, R.D.S. (1991) *The Road to Never Land: A Reassessment of J.M. Barrie's Dramatic Art*. Aberdeen: Aberdeen University Press.

Jackson, Rosemary (1981) *Fantasy: The Literature of Subversion*. London: Methuen.

James, Henry (1979) 'The Art of Fiction', *Selected Literary Criticism*, ed. Morris Shapira. London: Heinemann, 49–67. 1st published 1884.

Jameson, Fredric (1979) 'Reification and Utopia in Mass Culture', *Social Text* 1: 130–48.

Jameson, Fredric (1981) *The Political Unconscious: Narrative as a Socially Symbolic Act*, Ithaca, NY: Cornell University Press.

Jenkins, Henry (1992) *Textual Poachers: Television Fans and Participatory Culture*. London: Routledge.

Jones, Carrie (2010) *Need*. London: Bloomsbury.

Jones, Joe Elwyn and Gladstone, J. Francis (1995) *The Red King's Dream: or, Lewis Carroll in Wonderland*. London: Cape.

Joughin, John J. and Malpas, Simon (eds) (2003) 'The New Aestheticism: An Introduction', *The New Aestheticism*. Manchester: Manchester University Press, 1–19.

Kaplan, Robert (2000) *The Nothing that Is: A Natural History of Zero*. London: Penguin.

Keats, Ezra Jack (1962) *The Snowy Day*. New York: Viking.

Kidd, Kenneth B. (2011) *Freud in Oz: At the Intersections of Psychoanalysis and Children's Literature*. Minneapolis: University of Minnesota Press.

Kincaid, James R. (1992) *Child-Loving: The Erotic Child and Victorian Culture*. London: Routledge.

Kipling, Rudyard (1906/8) *Puck of Pook's Hill*. London: Macmillan.

Kipling, Rudyard (1987) *The Complete Stalky & Co*. Oxford: Oxford University Press, 1st edn 1906. Online: www.gutenberg.org/files/3006/3006-h/3006-h.htm.

Kohl, Herbert (1995) *Should we Burn Babar? Essays on Children's Literature, and the Power of Stories*. New York: New Press.

Kuhn, Thomas S. (1970) *The Structure of Scientific Revolutions*, 2nd edn. Chicago: Chicago University Press.

Kutzer, M. Daphne (2000) *Empire's Children: Empire and Imperialism in Classic British Children's Books*. London: Garland.

Lacan, Jacques (1959/60) *Le séminaire, Livre VII: L'éthique de la psychanalyse*. Extract online: www.lacan.com/seminars2.htm.

Lacan, Jacques (1966/67) *Seminar XIV: The Logic of Fantasy*. Online: www.lacaninireland.com/web/wp-content/uploads/2010/06/14-Logic-of-Phantasy-Complete.pdf.

Lacan, Jacques (1973) 'The Seminar on "The Purloined Letter"', trans. Jeffrey Mehlman. *Yale French Studies* 48: 39–72. Online: www.lacan.com/purloined.htm.

Lacan, Jacques (1977a) *Écrits: A Selection*, trans. Alan Sheridan. London: Tavistock Press.

Lacan, Jacques (1977b) *The Four Fundamental Concepts of Psycho-analysis*, trans. Alan Sheridan. London: Hogarth/Institute of Psycho-analysis.

Lacan, Jacques (1988) *The Seminar of Jacques Lacan. Book II: The Ego in Freud's Theory and in the Technique of Psychoanalysis, 1954–1955*, ed. Jacques-Alain Miller, trans. Sylvana Tomaselli. Cambridge: Cambridge University Press.

Laurent, Éric (1995) 'Alienation and Separation (I) and (II)' in Richard Feldstein, Bruce Fink and Maire Jaanus (eds), *Reading Seminar XI: Lacan's Four Fundamental Concepts of Psychoanalysis*. Albany: SUNY Press, 19–38.

Leavis, F.R. (1962) *The Great Tradition*. Harmondsworth: Penguin.

Leeson, Robert (1985) *Reading and Righting: The Past, Present and Future of Fiction for the Young*. London: Collins.

Lesnik-Oberstein, Karín (1994) *Children's Literature: Criticism and the Fictional Child*. Oxford: Oxford University Press.

Lesnik-Oberstein, Karín (ed.) (1998) *Children in Culture: Approaches to Childhood*. London: Macmillan.

Lesnik-Oberstein, Karín (ed.) (2004) *Children's Literature: New Approaches*. Basingstoke: Palgrave Macmillan.

Lewis, David (2001) *Reading Contemporary Picturebooks: Picturing Text.* London: RoutledgeFalmer.

Lindgren, Astrid (1957) *Pippi Longstocking.* Oxford: Oxford University Press, 1st edn 1945.

Lindsay, Norman (1957) *The Magic Pudding....* Harmondsworth: Penguin, 1st edn 1918.

Littau, Karin (2006) *Theories of Reading: Books, Bodies and Bibliomania.* Cambridge: Polity.

Lofting, Hugh (1968) *Doctor Dolittle's Caravan.* Harmondsworth: Penguin, 1st edn 1927.

Lord, Peter and Park, Nick (2000) *Chicken Run.* Dreamworks/Pathé.

Lukács, Georg (1969) *The Historical Novel*, trans. Hannah and Stanley Mitchell. Harmondsworth: Penguin, 1st edn 1937.

Lukács, György (2001) 'Realism in the Balance' in Vincent B. Leitch (ed.) *The Norton Anthology of Theory and Criticism.* New York: Norton, 1033–1058. 1st published 1938.

Lynn, Cathy and Preston, Michael J. (eds) (1996) *The Other Print Tradition: Essays on Chapbooks, Broadsides, and Related Ephemera.* New York: Garland

Macaulay, David (1990) *Black and White.* Boston: Houghton Mifflin.

MacCabe, Colin (1974) 'Realism and the Cinema: Notes on Some Brechtian Theses', *Screen* 15 (2). Reprinted in *Theoretical Essays: Film, Linguistics, Literature.* Manchester: Manchester University Press, 1986, 33–57.

MacCabe, Colin (1978) *James Joyce and the Revolution of the Word.* Basingstoke: Macmillan.

MacCabe, Colin (ed.) (1986) *High Theory/Low Culture: Analysing Popular Television and Film.* Manchester: Manchester University Press.

MacCarthy, Fiona (1989) *Eric Gill.* London: Faber and Faber.

MacDonald, George (2008) *Phantastes: A Faerie Romance for Men and Women.* London: Paternoster, 1st edn 1858.

Marsden, John and Tan, Shaun (2008) *The Rabbits.* Sydney: Hachette, 1st edn 1998.

McCaughrean, Geraldine (2007) *Peter Pan in Scarlet*, illus. David Wyatt. Oxford: Oxford University Press.

McGillis, Roderick (2002) '"Captain Underpants is My Hero': Things Have Changed – or Have They?' *Children's Literature Association Quarterly* 27: 62–70.

McHale, Brian (2012) *Constructing Postmodernism.* London and New York: Routledge.

Mehlman, Jeffrey (1977) *Revolution and Repetition: Marx/Hugo/Balzac.* Berkeley: University of California Press.

Meirelles, Fernando and Lund, Kátia (2002) *City of God.* Miramax/Buena Vista.

Melrose, Andrew (2012) *Here Comes the Bogeyman: Exploring Contemporary Issues in Writing for Children.* London and New York: Routledge.

Meyer, Stephenie (2005) *Twilight.* New York: Little, Brown.

Miller, Alice (2002) *For Your Own Good: Hidden Cruelty in Child-Rearing and the Roots of Violence*, new edn. New York: Farrar, Straus Giroux, 1st edn 1983.

Milne, A.A. (1965) *Winnie-the-Pooh*, illus E. H. Shepard. London: Methuen, 1st edn 1926.

Modleski, Tania (1988) *Loving with a Vengeance: Mass-Produced Fantasies for Women*. London: Routledge.

Møller, Lis (2005) '"The Sandman": The Uncanny as Problem of Reading', in Steve Vine (ed.) *Literature in Psychoanalysis: A Reader*. Basingstoke: Palgrave Macmillan, 97–110,1st edn 1991.

Moore, Robert (1978) 'From Rags to Witches: Stereotypes, Distortions and Anti-humanism in Fairy Tales', *Interracial Digest* 2: 27–34.

Murdoch, Iris (1954) *Under the Net*. London: Chatto & Windus.

Myers, Mitzi (1994) 'Reading Rosamond Reading: Maria Edgeworth's "Wee-Wee Stories" Interrogate the Canon' in Elizabeth Goodenough, Mark A. Heberle and Naomi Sokoloff (eds) *Infant Tongues: The Voice of the Child in Literature*. Detroit, MI: Wayne State University Press, 57–79.

Myers, Mitzi (1995) 'De-Romanticizing the Subject: Maria Edgeworth's "The Bracelets", Mythologies of Origin, and the Daughter's Coming to Writing' in Paul R. Feldman and Teresa M. Kelley (eds) *Romantic Women Writers: Voices and Countervoices*. London: University Press of New England, 88–110.

Myers, Mitzi (1999) 'Reading Children and Homeopathic Romanticism: Paradigm Lost, Revisionary Gleam, or "Plus ça change, plus c'est la même chose"?' in James Holt McGavran (ed.) *Literature and the Child: Romantic Continuation, Postmodern Contestations*. Iowa: University of Iowa Press, 44–84.

Nelson, Claudia (1990) 'The Beast Within: *Winnie-the-Pooh* Reassessed' *Children's Literature in Education*. 24 (1): 17–22.

Nesbit, E. (1959a) *Five Children and It*. Harmondsworth: Penguin, 1st edn 1902.

Nesbit, E. (1959b) *The Story of the Amulet*. Harmondsworth: Penguin, 1st edn 1906.

Nesbit, E. (1960) *The Railway Children*. Harmondsworth: Penguin, 1st edn 1906.

Nesbit, E. (1979) *The Enchanted Castle*. Harmondsworth: Penguin, 1st edn 1907.

Neuberg, Victor E. (1977) *Popular Literature: A History and Guide, from the Beginning of Printing to the Year 1897*. Harmondsworth: Penguin.

Nicholls, Peter (1995) *Modernisms: A Literary Guide*. Basingstoke: Macmillan.

Nikolajeva, Maria (1988) *The Magic Code: The Use of Magical Patterns in Fantasy for Children*. Stockholm: Almqvist & Wiksell.

Nikolajeva, Maria (2010) *Power, Voice and Subjectivity in Literature for Young Readers*. New York and London: Routledge.

Nodelman, Perry (1985) 'The Case of Children's Fiction: or the Impossibility of Jacqueline Rose', *Children's Literature Association Quarterly* 10 (3): 98–103.

Nodelman, Perry (1988) *Words About Pictures: The Narrative Art of Children's Picture Books*. Athens: University of Georgia Press.

Nodelman, Perry (1992a) 'The Other: Orientalism, Colonialism, and Children's Literature', *Children's Literature Association Quarterly*. 17 (1): 29–35.

Nodelman, Perry (1992b) *The Pleasures of Children's Literature*. New York: Longman.

Nodelman, Perry (2008) *The Hidden Adult: Defining Children's Literature*. Baltimore, MA: Johns Hopkins University Press.

Nodelman, Perry (2010) 'Former Editor's Comments: Or, The Possibility of Growing Wiser', *Children's Literature Association Quarterly*, 35 (3): 230–42.

Nusselder, André (2013) *The Surface Effect: The Screen of Fantasy in Psycho-analysis*. London and New York: Routledge.

O'Malley, Andrew (2003) *The Making of the Modern Child: Children's Literature and Childhood in the Late Eighteenth Century*. London: Routledge.

O'Malley, Andrew (2012) *Children's Literature, Popular Culture, and* Robinson Crusoe. Basingstoke: Palgrave Macmillan.

Opie, Iona and Opie, Peter (1959) *The Lore and Language of Schoolchildren*. Oxford: Clarendon Press.

Orenstein, Catherine (2002) *Little Red Riding Hood Uncloaked: Sex, Morality and the Evolution of a Fairy Tale*. New York: Basic Books.

Orwell, George (1957) 'Boys' Weeklies', *Selected Essays*. Harmondsworth: Penguin, 175–203.

Pankenier, Sara (2006) '"in fant non sens": The Infantilist Aesthetic of the Russian Avant-Garde'. Unpublished PhD, Stanford University.

Pearce, A. Philippa (1970) *Tom's Midnight Garden*. London: Oxford University Press, 1st edn 1958.

Phillips, Adam (2000) *Promises, Promises: Essays on Literature and Psychoanalysis*. London: Faber and Faber.

Phillips, Robert (ed.) (1972) *Aspects of Alice: Lewis Carroll's Dreamchild as Seen through the Critics' Looking-glasses, 1865–1971*. London: Gollancz.

Pieńkowski, Jan (1981) *Dinner Time*. London: Gallery Five.

Pinkney, Tony (1989) 'Editor's Introduction: Modernism and Cultural Theory', in Raymond Williams (ed.) *The Politics of Modernism: Against the New Conformists*. London: Verso, 1–29.

Poe, Edgar Allen (2012) 'Berenice', *Southern Literary Messenger*, March, 1: 333–36. *The Tales of Edgar Allen Poe*. 1st published 1835. Online: www.eapoe.org/works/tales/bernicea.htm.

Pullman, Philip (n.d.) 'Achuka Interview'. Online: www.achuka.co.uk/archive/interviews/ppint.php.

Pullman, Philip (1996) 'Carnegie Medal Acceptance Speech'. Online: www.randomhouse.com/features/pullman/author/carnegie.

Pullman, Philip (2008) *His Dark Materials*. London and New York: Scholastic.

Rackin, Donald (1966) 'Alice's journey to the end of the night', *PMLA* 81: 313–26.

Radway, Janice A. (1987) *Reading the Romance: Women, Patriarchy and Popular Culture*. London: Verso.

Radway, Janice (1988) 'Reception study: Ethnography and the Problems of Dispersed Audiences and Nomadic Subjects', *Cultural Studies* 2 (3): 359–76.

Randall, Don (2000) *Kipling's Imperial Boy: Adolescence and Cultural Hybridity.* New York: Palgrave.

Reynolds, Kimberley (2002) 'Come Lads and Ladettes: Gendering Bodies and Gendering Behaviors', in John Stephens (ed.) *Ways of Being Male: Representing Masculinities in Children's Literature and Film.* London and New York: Routledge, 96–115.

Reynolds, Kimberley (2007) *Radical Children's Literature: Future Visions and Aesthetic Transformations in Juvenile Fiction.* Basingstoke: Palgrave Macmillan.

Robbins, Hollis (2005) 'A Menstrual Lesson for Girls: Maria Edgeworth's "The Purple Jar"', in Andrew Shail and Gillian Howie (eds) *Menstruation: A Cultural History.* Basingstoke: Palgrave Macmillan, 213–24.

Rose, Jacqueline (1984) *The Case of Peter Pan, or The Impossibility of Children's Fiction.* Basingstoke: Macmillan.

Royle, Nicholas (2003) *The Uncanny* Manchester: Manchester University Press.

Rudd, David (1992) *A Communication Studies Approach to Children's Literature.* Sheffield: Pavic Press.

Rudd, David (1997) 'Enid Blyton and the Paradox of Children's Literature', in Nicholas Tucker and Kimberley Reynolds (eds) *Enid Blyton: A Celebration & Reappraisal.* London: NCRCL, 17–29.

Rudd, David (2000) *Enid Blyton and the Mystery of Children's Literature.* Basingstoke: Macmillan.

Rudd, David (2004) 'Theories and Theorising: The Conditions of Possibility of Children's Literature', *International Companion Encyclopedia of Children's Literature,* ed. Peter Hunt, 2nd edn, vol. 1. London: Routledge, 29–43.

Rudd, David (2006a) 'Where It Was, There Shall Five Children Be: Staging Desire in *Five Children and It*', in Raymond E. Jones (ed.) *E. Nesbit's Psammead Books: Children's Classics at 100.* Oxford: Scarecrow Press, 135–49.

Rudd, David (2006b) 'The Blot of Peter Pan' in C. Anita Tarr and Donna R. White (eds) *J.M. Barrie's Peter Pan In and Out of Time: A Children's Classic at 100.* Oxford: Scarecrow Press, 263–78.

Rudd, David (2008a) 'An Eye for an I: Neil Gaiman's *Coraline* and Questions of Identity', *Children's Literature in Education* 39: 159–68.

Rudd, David (2008b) 'Holed and Porous but not Impossible: Children's Literature, Psychoanalysis, and Constructions of the Child', in Jenny Plastow (ed.) *The Story and the Self: Children's Literature: Some Psychoanalytical Perspectives.* Hatfield: University of Hertfordshire Press, 191–201.

Rudd, David (2009) 'Animal and Object Stories', in Matthew Grenby and Andrea Immel (eds) *The Cambridge Companion to Children's Literature.* Cambridge: Cambridge University Press, 242–57.

Rudd, David (2010a) 'Children's Literature and the Return to Rose', *Children's Literature Association Quarterly* 35 (3): 290–310.

Rudd, David (2010b) 'Humpty Dumpty and the Sense of an Unending', in Morag Styles, Louise Joy and David Whitley (eds) *Poetry and Childhood.* Stoke on Trent and Sterling, VA: Trentham Books, 111–19.

Rudd, David (ed) (2010c) *The Routledge Companion to Children's Literature.* Abingdon and New York: Routledge.

Rudd, David (2011) 'Theory', in Philip Nel and Lissa Paul (eds) *Keywords for Children's Literature.* New York and London: New York University Press, 213–19.

Rudd, David (2012a) 'Don't Gobblefunk Around With Words: Roald Dahl and Language', in Ann Alston and Catherine Butler (eds) *Roald Dahl.* Basingstoke: Palgrave Macmillan, 51–69.

Rudd, David (2012b) 'Fantasemes and Mimesemes: Unpicking the Seams of Fantasy', in Maria Lassén-Seger and Mia Österlund (eds) *Celebrating a Displaced Hedgehog: A Festschrift for Maria Nikolajeva.* Göteborg: Makadam, 85–92.

Rudd, David (2012c) 'Never, Never, Never Land: The Dangerous Appeal of the Sublime Object of Ideology', in Alfonso Muñoz Corcuera and Elisa T. Di Biase (eds) *Barrie, Hook, and Peter Pan: Studies in Contemporary Myth; Estudios sobre un mito contemporáneo.* Newcastle: Cambridge Scholars, 54–65.

Rudd, David and Pavlik, Anthony (2010) 'The (Im)Possibility of Children's Fiction: Rose Twenty-Five Years On'. *Children's Literature Association Quarterly* 35 (3): 223–29.

Rustin, Michael (1985) 'A Defence of Children's Fiction: Another Reading of Peter Pan', *Free Associations* 2: 128–48.

Ruwe, Donelle (ed.) (2005) *Culturing the Child, 1690–1914: Essays in Memory of Mitzi Myers.* Metuchen, NJ: Scarecrow Press.

Sachar, Louis (2000) *Holes.* London: Bloomsbury.

Said, Edward (1978) *Orientalism.* London: Routledge & Kegan Paul.

Said, Edward (1994) *Culture and Imperialism.* London and New York: Vintage

Sartre, Jean-Paul (1963) *Search for a Method* New York: Vintage.

Schumacher, Joel (1987) *The Lost Boys.* Warner.

Schwartz, Alvin (1989) *The Cat's Elbow, and Other Secret Languages.* Toronto: Farrar, Straus Giroux.

Scieszka, Jon and Smith, Lane (1992) *The Stinky Cheese Man and Other Fairly Stupid Tales.* New York: Viking.

Seife, Charles (2000) *Zero: The Biography of a Dangerous Idea.* London: Souvenir Press.

Sendak, Maurice (1967) *Where the Wild Things Are.* London: Bodley Head, 1st edn 1963.

Sendak, Maurice (2001) *In the Night Kitchen.* New York and London: Random House, 1st edn 1970.

Sewell, Elizabeth (1952) *The Field of Nonsense.* London: Chatto & Windus.

Siegel, Don (1971) *Dirty Harry.* Warner.

Silverstein, Shel (1976) *The Missing Piece.* New York: HarperCollins.

Sipe, Lawrence R. (1998) 'How Picturebooks Work: A Semiotically Framed Theory of Text-Picture Relationships', *Children's Literature in Education* 29 (2): 97–108.

Skriabine, Pierre (1997) 'Drive and Fantasy', *Journal of the Centre for Freudian Analysis and Research* 8/9. Online: www.jcfar.org/past_papers/Drive%20and%20Fantasy%20-%20Pierre%20Skriabine.pdf.

Sontag, Susan (1994) *Against Interpretation*. New York: Vintage.

Spielberg, Steven (1991) *Hook*. TriStar.

Spufford, Margaret (1987) *Small Books and Pleasant Histories: Popular Fiction and its Readership in Seventeenth-Century England*. London: Methuen.

Stallone, Sylvester (1979) *Rocky II*. United Artists.

Steedman, Carolyn (1995) *Strange Dislocations: Childhood and the Idea of Human Interiority, 1780–1930*. London: Virago.

Steig, William (1969) *Sylvester and the Magic Pebble*. New York: Windmill.

Stephens, John (1992) *Language and Ideology in Children's Fiction*. London: Longman.

Stephens, John (1996) 'Gender, Genre and Children's Literature', *Signal* 79: 17–30.

Stephens, John and McCallum, Robyn (1998) *Retelling Stories, Framing Culture: Traditional Story and Metanarratives in Children's Literature*. New York: Garland.

Stewart, Susan (1978) *Nonsense: Aspects of Intertextuality in Folklore and Literature*. Baltimore, MD: Johns Hopkins University Press.

Stuart, Mel (1971) *Willy Wonka and the Chocolate Factory*. Paramount.

Summerfield, Geoffrey (1984) *Fantasy and Reason: Children's Literature in the Eighteenth Century*. London: Taylor & Francis.

Sumpter, Caroline (2012) *The Victorian Press and the Fairy Tale*. Basingstoke and New York: Palgrave Macmillan.

Susina, Jan (2010) *The Place of Lewis Carroll in Children's Literature*. New York and London: Routledge.

Sutton-Smith, Brian (1995) *Children's Folklore: A Sourcebook*. New York: Garland.

Švankmajer, Jan (1988) *Alice*. Channel Four/Condor.

Swift, Jonathan (1940) *Gulliver's Travels*. London: Dent, 1st edn 1726.

Tatar, Maria (2009) *Enchanted Hunters: The Power of Stories in Childhood*. New York: W.W. Norton.

Thiong'o, Ngugi Wa (1992) 'Ambivalent Feelings about Biggles', *Guardian* 13 August.

Thomas, Ebony Elizabeth (2009) 'The Pleasures of Dreaming: How L.M. Montgomery Shaped my Lifeworlds', in Betsy Hearne and Roberta Seelinger Trites (eds) *A Narrative Compass: Stories that Guide Women's Lives*. Urbana, IL: University of Illinois Press, 80–95.

Thomas, Keith (1989) 'Children in Early Modern England', in Gillian Avery and Julia Briggs (eds) *Children and their Books: A Celebration of the Work of Iona and Peter Opie*. Oxford: Clarendon, 44–77.

Todorov, Tzvetan (1975) *The Fantastic: A Structural Approach to a Literary Genre*, trans. Richard Howard. Ithaca, NY: Cornell University Press.

Tolkien, J.R.R. (1964) 'On Fairy-Stories', *Tree and Leaf.* London: Allen & Unwin, 11–70. 1st published 1947.

Tosenberger, Catherine (2008) 'Homosexuality at the Online Hogwarts: Harry Potter Slash Fanfiction', *Children's Literature* 36: 185–207.

Townsend, John Rowe (1976) *Written for Children: An Outline of English-language Children's Literature.* Harmondsworth: Penguin.

Trease, Geoffrey (1964) *Tales Out of School.* London: Heinemann.

Trimmer, Mrs. (1798) *Fabulous Histories Designed for the Instruction of Children Respecting their Treatment of Animals*, 6th edn. London: T. Longman. 1st edn 1786. Online: http://hockliffe.dmu.ac.uk/items/0242.html.

Trites, Roberta Seelinger (2002) 'Introduction: The Uncanny in Children's Literature', *Children's Literature Association Quarterly* 26: 162.

Tucker, Nicholas (1990) 'Home Stories', in Mike Hayhoe and Stephen Parker (eds) *Reading and Response.* Milton Keynes: Open University Press, 124–131.

Turner, E.S. (1957) *Boys Will Be Boys: The Story of Sweeney Todd, Deadwood Dick, Sexton Blake, Billy Bunter, Dick Barton, et. al.*, rev. edn. London: Michael Joseph.

Turner, Ian (1969) *Cinderella Dressed in Yella: The First Attempt at a Definitive Study of Australian Children's Play Rhymes.* Melbourne: Heinemann Educational.

Usborne, David (2006) 'UN Report Uncovers Global Child Abuse', *The Independent*, 12 October. Online: www.independent.co.uk/news/world/politics/un-report-uncovers-global-child-abuse-419700.html.

Vidler, Anthony (1994) *The Architectural Uncanny: Essays in the Modern Unhomely.* Cambridge, MA: MIT Press.

Vine, Steve (2005) 'Uncanny Literature – Freud and the "Uncanny"', in Steve Vine (ed.) *Literature in Psychoanalysis: A Reader.* Basingstoke: Palgrave Macmillan, 60–67.

Vološinov, Valentin (1973) *Marxism and the Philosophy of Language*, trans. Ladislav Matejka and I.R. Titunik. Cambridge, MA: Harvard University Press.

Walkerdine, Valerie (1986) 'Video Replay: Families, Films and Fantasy', in Victor Burgin, James Donald and Cora Kaplan (eds) *Formations of Fantasy.* London: Routledge, 167–99.

Walkowitz, Judith R. (1992) *City of Dreadful Delight: Narratives of Sexual Danger in Late-Victorian London.* Chicago: University of Chicago Press

Wall, Barbara (1991) *The Narrator's Voice: The Dilemma of Children's Fiction.* Basingstoke: Macmillan.

Waller, Alison (2011) *Constructing Adolescence in Fantastic Realism.* London: Routledge.

Walsh, Sue (2002) 'Child/Animal: It's the "Real" Thing', *Yearbook of English Studies* 32. Leeds: Maney, for MHRA, 151–62.

Wannamaker, Annette (2006) 'Reading in the Gaps and Lacks: (De)Constructing Masculinity in Louis Sachar's *Holes*', *Children's Literature in Education* 37 (1): 15–33.

Watson, Victor (1992) 'The Possibilities of Children's Fiction', in Morag Styles, Eve Bearne and Victor Watson (eds) *After Alice: Exploring Children's Literature*. London: Cassell, 11–24.

Watt, Ian (1957) *The Rise of the Novel: Studies in Defoe, Richardson and Fielding*. London: Chatto & Windus.

Weber, Samuel (1973) 'The Sideshow, or: Remarks on a Canny Moment', *MLN* 88: 1102–33.

Williams, Raymond (1983) *Keywords: A Vocabulary of Culture and Society*. London: Fontana.

Wilson, Anita (1985) 'Milne's Pooh Books: The Benevolent Forest', in Perry Nodelman (ed.) *Touchstones: Reflections on the Best in Children's Literature, Vol. 1*. West Lafayette: Children's Literature Association Press, 163–72.

Winn, Marie (1983) *Children without Childhood: Growing Up Too Fast in the World of Sex and Drugs*. New York: Pantheon.

Winnicott, D.W. (1974) *Playing and Reality*. Harmondsworth: Penguin.

Wolf, Shelby Anne and Heath, Shirley Brice (1992) *The Braid of Literature: Children's Worlds of Reading*. Cambridge, MA: Harvard University Press.

Wolfreys, Julian, Robbins, Ruth, and Womack, Kenneth (2006) *Key Concepts in Literary Theory*, 2nd edn. Edinburgh: Edinburgh University Press.

Woolf, Virginia (1938) 'George Eliot', *The Common Reader*. Harmondsworth: Penguin, 161–71, 1st published 1925.

Woolf, Virginia (1966a) 'Middlebrow', *Collected Essays, Vol. 2*. London: Hogarth Press, 196–203. 1st published 1942.

Woolf, Virginia (1966b) 'Mr. Bennett and Mr. Brown', *Collected Essays, Vol. 1*. London: Hogarth Press, 319–37. 1st published 1924.

Wordsworth, William (1970) *The Prelude* ... text of 1805, 2nd edn. Oxford: Oxford University Press.

Wright, Elizabeth (1999) *Speaking Desires Can Be Dangerous: The Poetics of the Unconscious*. Cambridge: Polity.

Yeats, W. B. (1962) *Selected Poetry*, ed. A. Norman Jeffares. London: Macmillan.

Zipes, Jack (1983) *Fairy Tales and the Art of Subversion: The Classical Genre for Children and the Process of Civilization*. London: Heinemann Educational.

Zipes, Jack (ed.) (1987) *Victorian Fairy Tales: The Revolt of the Fairies and Elves*. London: Routledge.

Zipes, Jack (1992) *Breaking the Magic Spell: Radical Theories of Folk and Fairy Tales*. New York: Routledge.

Zipes, Jack (ed.) (1993) *The Trials and Tribulations of Little Red Riding Hood*. London: Routledge.

Zipes, Jack (2001) *Sticks and Stones: The Troublesome Success of Children's Literature from Slovenly Peter to Harry Potter.* New York and London: Routledge.

Zipes, Jack (2011) *The Enchanted Screen: The Unknown History of Fairy-Tale Films.* New York and London: Routledge.

Žižek, Slavoj (1989) *The Sublime Object of Ideology.* London: Verso.

Žižek, Slavoj (1992a) *Enjoy Your Symptom: Jacques Lacan in Hollywood and Out.* London and New York: Routledge.

Žižek, Slavoj (1992b) *Looking Awry: An Introduction to Lacan through Popular Culture.* Cambridge, MA: MIT Press.

Žižek, Slavoj (1994) *The Metastases of Enjoyment: Six Essays on Women and Causality.* London: Verso.

Žižek, Slavoj (2001) *On Belief.* London: Routledge.

Žižek, Slavoj (2002) *Welcome to the Desert of the Real.* New York and London: Verso.

Zornado, Joseph L. (2001) *Inventing the Child: Culture, Ideology, and the Story of Childhood.* New York: Garland.

Index